TREASON ON TRIAL
IN REVOLUTIONARY
PENNSYLVANIA

The Case of John Roberts, Miller

Roberts's gristmill at the end of the nineteenth century.

Remnant of the gristmill one hundred years later.

TREASON ON TRIAL IN REVOLUTIONARY PENNSYLVANIA

The Case of John Roberts, Miller

David W. Maxey

David W. Maxey

American Philosophical Society
Philadelphia • 2011

Transactions of the
American Philosophical Society
Held at Philadelphia
For Promoting Useful Knowledge
Volume 101, Part 2

ISBN: 978-1-60618-012-9
US ISSN: 0065-9746

Library of Congress Cataloguing-in-Publication Data

Maxey, David W. (David Walker), 1934-
  Treason on trial in revolutionary Pennsylvania : the case of John Roberts, miller / David W. Maxey.
    p. cm. — (Transactions of the American Philosophical Society held at Philadelphia for promoting useful knowledge ; volume 101, part 2)
  Includes bibliographical references and index.
  ISBN 978-1-60618-012-9
  1. Roberts, John, 1721–1778. 2. Collaborationists—Pennsylvania—Philadelphia—Biography. 3. United States—History—Revolution, 1775–1783—Collaborationists. 4. Quakers—Pennsylvania—Philadelphia—Biography. 5. Philadelphia (Pa.)—History—Revolution, 1775–1783. 6. Roberts, John, 1721–1778—Trials, litigation, etc. 7. Trials (Treason)—Pennsylvania—Philadelphia. 8. Philadelphia (Pa.)—Biography. I. Title.
  E278.R63M39 2011
  973.3'81—dc23
  [B]
                                    2011045193

For Paul and Margaret

Treason doth never prosper; what's the reason?
Why, if it prosper, none dare call it treason.

—Sir John Harington, *Epigrams*

"What's on?" he asked, in a whisper of the man he found himself next to.
"Nothing yet."
"What's coming on?"
"The Treason case."
"The quartering one, eh?"
"Ah!" returned the man, with a relish; "he'll be drawn on a hurdle to be half hanged, and then he'll be taken down and sliced before his own face, and then his inside will be taken out and burnt while he looks on, and then his head will be chopped off, and he'll be cut into quarters. That's the sentence."
"If he's found Guilty you mean to say?" Jerry added, by way of proviso.
"Oh! they'll find him guilty," said the other. "Don't you be afraid of that."

—Charles Dickens, A *Tale of Two Cities*

Contents

List of Illustrations

Cover. College Hall, where the trial took place, at the southwestern corner of Fourth and Arch Streets, in a drawing attributed to Pierre du Simitière, circa 1770.

Preface

John Roberts is a near neighbor of mine. Though he died more than two hundred and thirty years ago, the use of the present tense to describe our relationship seems a permissible liberty to take, for his troubled shade still lingers today in the Mill Creek Valley, the subject of a flourishing mythology and even of occasional sightings in and about the house where he and his numerous family lived. If reminder is ever needed of the duty to reopen his case and to focus on the long neglected record of his trial, it comes whenever I drive past the carefully preserved corner of his gristmill, located next to Old Gulph Road, barely a mile away from where I live. This vestige of a once prosperous business stands as a monument to the confusions of the early Revolutionary period that claimed my neighbor as a victim.

On November 10, 1778, six days after John Roberts and Abraham Carlisle were hanged in Philadelphia for treason, a contributor to the *Pennsylvania Packet*, identified only as "CIVIS," addressed this unanswered plea to "the Honourable the Judges of the Supreme Court [of Pennsylvania]":

> You would oblige many of the good inhabitants of this State, if you would direct an authenticated copy of the trial of the unfortunate *Carlisle* and *Roberts* to be published. As several circumstances concur to make such a publication proper at this time, it is hoped that you will have no objection to a compliance with this request.

In John Roberts's case, circumstances again concur to make that belated publication possible.

David W. Maxey
Mill Creek Valley
November 4, 2011

Acknowledgments

In the preparation of this work, I have drawn liberally on the assistance and support of experts in their fields, which I now acknowledge with deep appreciation.

I have received essential support from staff members at the David Library, the Friends Historical Library at Swarthmore College, the Historical Society of Pennsylvania, the Historical Society of Montgomery County, the Library Company of Philadelphia, the Lower Merion Historical Society, the Montgomery County Records Department, the Pennsylvania State Archives in Harrisburg, the Presbyterian Historical Society, and the Quaker Collection at Haverford College. The contributions these helpful custodians have made to ease my task are no less significant for being acknowledged here anonymously.

As I began my research, I received guidance from James Oldham of Georgetown University Law Center on eighteenth-century judges' notes and the light such records often shed on otherwise elusive court proceedings in England. He has written impressively on this subject, among many others.

James Duffin, senior archivist at the University of Pennsylvania, has been an invaluable resource in locating the properties John Roberts owned in the Mill Creek Valley. The mapping he has generally undertaken of property holdings in the environs of Philadelphia at the time of the Revolution represents a significant scholarly accomplishment.

I owe special thanks to Jude M. Pfister, Chief of Cultural Resources at the Morristown National Historical Park—first for fielding my repeated inquiries about Thomas McKean's lost trial notes and then for both locating the notes and sending me legible photocopies. For permission to publish McKean's trial notes and the notes of a Quaker observer at Roberts's trial in the consolidated perspective set forth in Appendix A, I express my sincere appreciation to the Morristown National Historical Park and the Quaker Collection at Haverford College, which hold, respectively, the original documents.

The Lower Merion Historical Society has generously assisted me in assembling from its collections several illustrations for this work. Other illustrations have come from the graphics collections at the Historical Society of Pennsylvania, the Library Company of Philadelphia, and the Historical Society of Montgomery County. The Quaker Collection at Haverford College has kindly consented to the publication of the holograph copy of John Roberts's letter to Daniel Clymer, a document that figures prominently in the text.

I am grateful for the professional assistance of Gerry Krieg of Krieg Mapping in preparing two maps for locations in Philadelphia and in Blockley and Lower Merion townships that provide the reader with necessary orientation.

On countless occasions those staffing the Computer Help Desk at my old law firm have answered my telephone calls and cheerfully extricated me from my latest word-processing blunder.

As an act of friendship, Gary Nash and Michael Kammen agreed to read my manuscript at an early stage and to make specific suggestions on how it might be improved. I am heavily indebted to both of them for the encouragement they provided. This work has also benefited from the constructive criticism of three outside readers to whom it was referred for review. If, in spite of these collective best efforts to protect me, errors of fact or interpretation remain, the fault is all mine.

Finally, my warm thanks to the American Philosophical Society for granting its imprimatur and to the Society's editor, Mary McDonald, for her help and patience—once again.

TREASON ON TRIAL IN REVOLUTIONARY PENNSYLVANIA

The Case of John Roberts, Miller

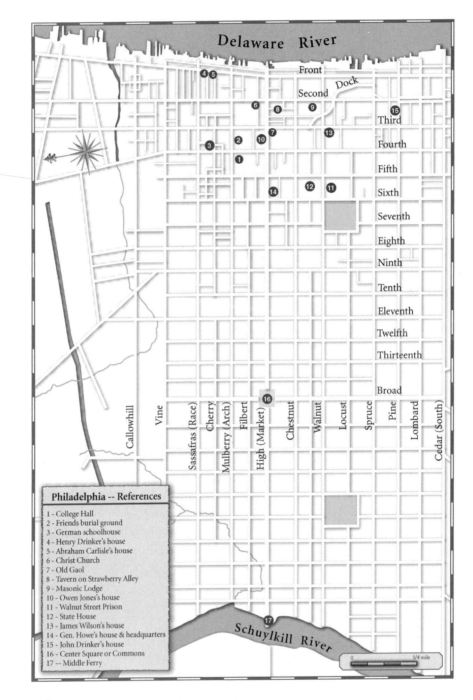

Figure I.1 Map of the City of Philadelphia circa 1778.

Introduction

John Roberts, you have been indicted, and after a very long, a very fair, & impartial trial have been convicted of High Treason. You have had all the Indulgence and advantage that the law would allow you.[1]

These were the opening words that Thomas McKean, the chief justice of the Supreme Court of Pennsylvania, used in sentencing John Roberts to death. In October 1778 Roberts stood before McKean convicted of committing treason against the fledgling government of the Commonwealth of Pennsylvania.[2] Aware of the large role he was playing in an unfolding drama and always jealously protective of his own dignity and reputation, the chief justice may have polished the text of the sentencing statement before consenting to its publication immediately after the death sentence had been carried out. Reading it now, with its invocation of angels and archangels welcoming a truly repentant sinner to the "joys of Heaven; Joys unspeakable and full of Glory," one is inclined to dismiss what McKean wrote as a grandiloquent period piece.[3]

But for the prisoner summoned to the bar of the court, it represented a devastating message. If John Roberts heard the chief justice say anything close to the text that the Philadelphia newspaper published, he could only have trembled at the prospect he faced. One by one, the judge who presided at his trial rejected the defenses Roberts's counsel had labored carefully to establish and consigned the defendant to the hangman's noose, offering no hope of reprieve. McKean concluded his monologue by extolling the Pennsylvania legislature's sense of benevolence and leniency in prescribing that "persons guilty of High Treason should be dealt with, and proceeded against as in other Capital cases." Roberts might thus look forward to a simple hanging, rather than suffering the punishment traditionally meted out to traitors in England—of being hanged, drawn, and quartered.[4]

Over the long period of two hundred and thirty years, the fairness of Roberts's trial as well as any so-called indulgence he afterward received have remained the subject of recurrent debate. On Wednesday, November 4, 1778, as noontime approached, Roberts and his fellow Quaker Abraham Carlisle, both convicted of treasonably supporting the British cause, walked haltingly behind a cart carrying two coffins to meet death by hanging on the outskirts of settled

1

Philadelphia (Figure I.1).[5] Prior to their execution, a great outpouring of sympathy occurred; hundreds, and perhaps several thousands, crossed the boundaries of politics, religion, and class to sign petitions seeking clemency for the condemned men. Few imagined that they would be denied any relief, if only in permitting a postponement until the Pennsylvania Assembly might consider the grounds urged for clemency. It seemed inconceivable that it could be otherwise, not when members of both the grand jury that had indicted Roberts and Carlisle and the petit juries that had separately convicted them petitioned for mercy, and not when Thomas McKean himself, for all his histrionic zeal in sentencing Roberts, joined the second judge present at the trials in recommending clemency.[6] That Roberts and Carlisle were summarily marched off to the gallows, on schedule, denied even the briefest stay, some commentators have attributed to vindictive Whig retaliation for nettlesome Quaker pacifism, which the Supreme Executive Council, as the executive body in Pennsylvania acting on the petitions, found it politically inexpedient to resist. Others have concluded that their execution was the justified outcome of the treason they committed, convincingly proved at their trials.[7]

But what of the chief justice's claim of great fairness in the trial of John Roberts? What do we know of the process that followed: about Roberts's arrest and arraignment, the indictment returned against him, the availability of bail, his access to competent counsel, the conduct of the trial itself, and the deliberations of the jury? Not to dismiss too quickly the sad end of Abraham Carlisle, a respected house carpenter whose trial and conviction preceded Roberts's, it is Roberts's case that has posed the more troubling issues—in part, because of his greater wealth and prominence, but also because, in the view of his contemporaries, his conviction was the harder of the two to justify. There is, however, another important factor to weigh in the continuing debate about the Roberts trial, and that is the seeming absence in his case, but not in Carlisle's, of any record that one might consult to assess the strength of the evidence against him.

In a letter dated October 21, 1778, the members of the executive council applied to Chief Justice McKean for assistance in evaluating the flood of petitions submitted on behalf of Abraham Carlisle and John Roberts. The disposition of these petitions would, the council dryly observed, be "highly interesting, not only to the criminals but also to the public," necessitating that the council obtain "as soon as possible your notes taken on the trials." The members of the council emphasized that they were "more desirous" of these notes "in the case of John Roberts" because McKean, as the presiding justice in that trial, had failed to mention "any equitable circumstances which ought to be allowed weight in their determinations in his [Roberts's] case."[8]

This distinction that the council drew between the two trials is, on the surface of its request, a puzzling one. McKean and John Evans, the other justice sitting on the bench, had submitted the petitions of the jurors in both cases to the Supreme Executive Council under the same covering message dated three days earlier. Thus, in the case of John Roberts, they begged leave "to recommend to your honors favorable acceptance [of the petition], and that you would be pleased to postpone the issuing the warrant for the execution of John Roberts until the end of the next session of the General Assembly, agreeably to the prayer of the gentlemen of the Jury above named, who were upon his trial." What was it, then, that caused the council to be particularly solicitous about the submission for Roberts?

When the petitions of the trial juries are closely examined, it becomes clearer why the council focused on Robert's case as the one of more compelling concern. Each of the petitions was addressed in the first instance to the "Judges of the Supreme Court and Courts of Oyer and Terminer, &c., for the Common Wealth of Pennsylvania," and each requested that the judges forward the petition to the Supreme Executive Council, accompanied by their own recommendation that the sentence be suspended until the General Assembly had the opportunity to act. Yet there was a marked difference in the way these two juries framed their appeals.

The members of the Carlisle jury conveyed no sign of doubt, in their petition, about the guilty verdict they had voted for, given "the whole of the Evidence before us." They based their plea for clemency on "the knowledge we have of his former blameless character, the consideration of his advanced age, and our sympathy with his distressed Family and reputable connexions." The jurymen in Roberts's case (only ten of them signing the petition as against all twelve in Carlisle's) also pleaded for compassion "to the unhappy object of this petition," but they in contrast broadly hinted that some members of the jury continued to harbor reasonable doubt about Roberts's guilt. For example, they cited as an extenuating circumstance that "the said John Roberts was under the influence of fear, when he took the imprudent step of leaving his family and coming to reside among the enemy, while they had possession of this city." Although they said that, bound by the oath they had taken, they felt in the end obligated to find him guilty, they added, in more candor and accuracy than our system of criminal justice often contemplates, that "*Juries are but fallible Men.*" If that admission standing alone did not suggest that they continued to be troubled by the verdict they had reached, what next followed in their petition surely did: "the evidence before us was of a complicated nature, and some parts of it not reconcileable [*sic*] with his general conduct, and other evidence of his good offices to many persons who were prisoners among the enemy, or had leave to come to the city on business."[9]

In successive meetings on November 2 and 3, the Supreme Executive Council took under consideration the multiple petitions it had received. Its session on November 2 would have been a turbulent one for all who participated. Roberts's wife and children appeared in person and pleaded in anguished terms that his life be spared, as Carlisle's wife and son also did for him. The minutes of that meeting record that the members of the council had read both the petitions for the prisoners and "the Notes taken by the Chief Justice on their respective trials."[10] At its second session on November 3, the council took firmer control of its agenda as it disposed of several items of routine business, including ordering the assistant quartermaster general to return four spades and four shovels previously commandeered for the state's use. The members of council in attendance at this meeting dealt almost perfunctorily with the cases of the two condemned men; neither of these misguided Quakers, the council ruled, was entitled to receive the relief prayed for. Thus, the last door having slammed shut, Roberts and Carlisle were hanged the following day.[11]

To what extent should Thomas McKean be held responsible for Roberts's death? The heavy weight of the sentence McKean pronounced, when submitted to the executive council as the court's considered judgment about Roberts's guilt (in the words of its subsequent newspaper publication, "to shew the opinion of the Court respecting his conviction"), covertly removed the support he had earlier provided in forwarding the clemency plea from Roberts's jury under the recommendation of McKean and his fellow judge that it receive the executive council's "favorable acceptance." The sentencing statement left no room for doubt about the court's view of Roberts's guilt or the consequence that should now befall him. For McKean to have sent this document, of his own initiative, to the deliberative body pondering the fate of the condemned man would have been duplicitous, to say the least.

Volatile in temperament, vain, ambitious, Thomas McKean possessed a generous assortment of human failings, but he was also sensitive to the duties of his office and the vestigial requirements of due process owed the two prisoners as they desperately sought clemency after their trials. If in our eyes he continues to bear significant responsibility for releasing his inflammatory sentencing statement, in which he proclaimed that Roberts had "but a Short time to live," we shall discover that it came to the executive council by a different route, in the ex parte submission of the lawyer who had prosecuted Roberts and Carlisle and who resisted the thought that they be granted clemency in any form.[12]

The executive council had called for the production of McKean's trial notes as the best means of gaining access to the evidence presented in the courtroom. Whether it was McKean's established practice to keep a record of the proceeding before him, or whether he agreed in advance to do so for the succession of treason trials for which he was the presiding judge, the executive council knew that he had recorded the testimony in Roberts's trial. Taken down as the trial progressed, McKean's notes should have been more neutral in content than the loaded words he employed in sentencing Roberts. The notes that judges kept during a trial were intended for their own benefit and never approached a verbatim record of trial proceedings (another century would pass before the art of shorthand progressed to the point that verbatim trial records became possible); instead, they might serve to assist the judge in instructing the jury or in disposing of post-trial motions. Subject to this caveat, judges' trial notes, when available from this period, can illuminate an otherwise opaque record—which brings us to the question of determining the value of the notes that McKean kept during Roberts's trial.[13]

McKean's notes for Abraham Carlisle's trial, as delivered to the executive council, survived and were included in the material published in 1853 in the first series of the *Pennsylvania Archives*. When it came to McKean's notes for Roberts's trial, Samuel Hazard, the editor of the *Archives*, admitted in a footnote that "we have not been able to find them [in the state's records]." The mysterious disappearance of those notes led to speculation that McKean's record had been deliberately suppressed or destroyed, on the assumption that, if the notes had been consulted, they would have disclosed how shaky the basis was for Roberts's conviction and execution. "To conceal the authentic evidences of the slender ground on which the conviction rested," wrote a mid-nineteenth-century Quaker apologist, "is probably the cause of their being thus withheld from the scrutinizing eye of the public, and from the condemnation of the proceedings by posterity."[14]

In fact, McKean's notes for the Roberts trial have not been irretrievably lost. Those notes are available today, intact and legible in the Lloyd W. Smith Collection at the Morristown National Historical Park in Morristown, New Jersey. The only unresolved mystery about this trial record is when the late Mr. Smith, a dedicated antiquarian, acquired it, and whether it came into his hands with any traceable provenance.[15] There is, in addition, a second contemporary source, equally impressive and equally neglected, that one may turn to in reconstructing the Roberts trial. It is a running compilation of the testimony of most (but not all) of the witnesses appearing at the trial, prepared by an anonymous Quaker observer. Filed away in the miscellaneous papers of the Philadelphia Meeting for Sufferings, this record also slipped out of sight during the many years that passed after Roberts was hanged.[16]

Treason on Trial in Revolutionary Pennsylvania is offered as a contribution to local history. Its aim is to cast light on Philadelphia and its environs at an early stage in the Revolution when the new government of the former colony of Pennsylvania was still struggling to take shape and enforce its decrees. Although the list of witnesses in the Roberts trial includes the names of many ordinary people who are often lost to history, whether writ big or small, major players in the Revolutionary drama also appear in the trial narrative and in the later attempts that were made to save Roberts from the gallows and then to spare his family the harshest consequences of his conviction. In this group of prominent figures are found members of the American Philosophical Society: Joseph Galloway; Thomas McKean; Joseph Reed; James Wilson; George Bryan; Philip Syng, Jr.; Benjamin Franklin; and Edward Shippen, Jr.; as well as austere Quaker noncombatants like Abel James, Henry Drinker, James Pemberton, and Nicholas Waln.[17]

John Roberts was charged with having committed treason against the Commonwealth of Pennsylvania during the passage in time from insurrection to revolution and from little more than a paper construct to a functioning, effective government, capable of providing protection to its citizenry. What defined patriotism and loyalty during that transition period remained at issue in a war that had its nasty, vindictive moments and differences that were on occasion more personal than political.[18] Not only did two opposed armies battle each other in the eastern part of that state, but any number of secondary contests occurred, not always congruent with the primary one, that further blurred perception: contests between radicals and moderates, patriots and loyalists, constitutionalists and anticonstitutionalists, merchants and mechanics, Presbyterians and Quakers, Quakers and Free Quakers, rebels and refugees, country people and city-dwellers. And none of these labels, it should be said, categorically excluded the outlier, a person who, by conviction, temperament, or momentary impulse, failed to conform.

The perspective obtained in combining the two records of Roberts's trial, each now used in its entirety for the first time, allows us to enter Philadelphia and the surrounding area while the British were in possession of the city from late September 1777 to mid-June 1778.[19] Through this double lens, we have the opportunity to witness conditions within the city and to observe how ill defined and wavering was the concept of allegiance, how neighbors' grievances escalated into partisan conflict, and how money, religion, and political ambition had the capacity to influence conduct. In the courtroom where Roberts was tried, treason itself would be put on trial — to determine what actions might constitute betrayal of the Commonwealth of Pennsylvania, a still-emerging state torn by internal conflict, sufficient to warrant the death sentence.

This study has a special concern, which is to measure the response of the Society of Friends to John Roberts's case. Quite apart from the jury verdicts rendered against them in their separate trials, he and his fellow Quaker Abraham Carlisle had violated the Quaker instruction to refrain from participating in the war. For those Friends who joined the patriot cause, disownment inevitably followed as a matter of course. How, then, would the Society treat the visible deviation of two of its members accused of supporting the British? The committee of leading Quakers appointed by the Philadelphia Meeting for Sufferings to review the proceedings against Roberts and Carlisle after they died concluded that they had become "entangled in the confusions" prevailing in those troubled times.[20] We must consider whether in this and other respects the committee, understandably sensitive to Quaker interests and exposures, came to a balanced appraisal and whether the confusion that the committee attributed to Roberts, though natural enough and experienced by many others in the Revolutionary period, represents a persuasive defense, entitling him to a long-delayed posthumous pardon.

As for the ultimate question of Roberts's guilt or innocence, a lawyer of the modern era has sought to provide context and guidance for the treason trial, conducted immediately after the British evacuation of Philadelphia when emotions were running high and according to rules of evidence and procedure peculiar to that earlier day. Gaining informed access to any eighteenth-century trial is usually a difficult task because of the absence of reliable records. In trying to decide whether Roberts was justly convicted and hanged for treason, the reader is invited to weigh all the evidence presented, both at his trial and outside it, and having done so, to return a second verdict. In the author's judgment, this is not an open-and-shut case.

On a particular charge not laid out in the formal indictment against him, Roberts should be held strictly accountable. At a crucial time, when his wife and children were subject to marauding British and American armies, he abandoned them for the comparative safety of British-occupied Philadelphia. While horror stories circulating in the closing months of 1777 do not qualify as solid intelligence, the picture of Lower Merion, Roberts's ravaged community, that Christopher Marshall, a birthright Quaker turned ardent Whig, painted from his protected vantage point in Lancaster has some claim to credibility:

> Add to this their [the British Army's] frequent excursions round about for twenty miles together, destroying and burning what they please, pillaging, plundering men and women, stealing boys above ten years old, deflowering virgins, driving into the City for their use, droves of cattle, sheep [and] hogs; poultry, butter, meal, meat, cider, furniture and clothing of all kinds, loaded upon our own horses.[21]

Roberts stayed in Philadelphia for the duration of the British occupation, almost nine months in all spent away from home and family. To speculate on his motivation and how much he deliberately calculated to put at risk in the property he had inherited or assembled and in the lives of those close to him is a problematic exercise, and yet one may turn more confidently to the historical record to document the extended trials that the members of his family suffered in consequence of his gamble, not only before his death but for many years afterward. If they were not ostracized, neither were they comfortably accepted in postwar society. Although a collective act of forgetting might have seemed advisable for all those implicated in the tragedy, neither they nor others could put aside the painful memory of what happened to John Roberts. It is a paradoxical aspect of the legacy of distress and estrangement he left them that his wife and children would be repeatedly forced, in their own best interests, to revive the record of his trial.

I

From Immigrant to Refugee

John Roberts's father and grandfather were named John Roberts. The first of them came to the province of Pennsylvania from Denbighshire, North Wales, in 1683, one of three passengers on the *Morning Star* out of Liverpool who were named John Roberts. This ancestor joined other settlers in the Welsh Tract, some forty thousand acres of land, more or less, located on the west side of the Schuylkill River, which William Penn set aside for Welsh Quakers "as a haven of rest" from the persecution they suffered in their home country. Roberts's grandfather acquired five hundred acres, principally along a tributary of the Schuylkill that would soon be named Mill Creek, in what is now Lower Merion Township (Figure 1.1), Montgomery County, a part of the Philadelphia suburbs known as the Main Line. He sold off portions of that original grant while retaining for his ownership and use two parcels of one hundred fifty and two hundred fifty acres.[1]

In 1690, at age sixty, he married at Haverford meeting Elizabeth Owen, "late of Ridley in the County of Chester," who was much younger than he. Neither of them had been married before; their marriage certificate described the bride, for all her supposed youth, as a spinster. The couple would have three children, whose births were entered in the records of the family's home meeting at Merion: Rebekah in 1691, John in 1695, and Mathew in 1698. Elizabeth Owen Roberts died in 1699.[2]

In his seventies and sensing his own end fast approaching, this first John Roberts wrestled with the problem of how to provide adequately for his young children. The will he signed on the 18th day of 12 mo 1703/04, or February 18 in the old calendar, showed the careful thinking he devoted to the matter, as well as the likely assistance of a scrivener more experienced than he would have been in drawing up such documents. He left "my now dwelling House and Plantation" to his older son and namesake, reserving, however, "one half of the use and Proffits of all the aforesd Premises towards the use and mainte-nance of my Daughter Rebekah and my Son Mathew until my aforesd Son

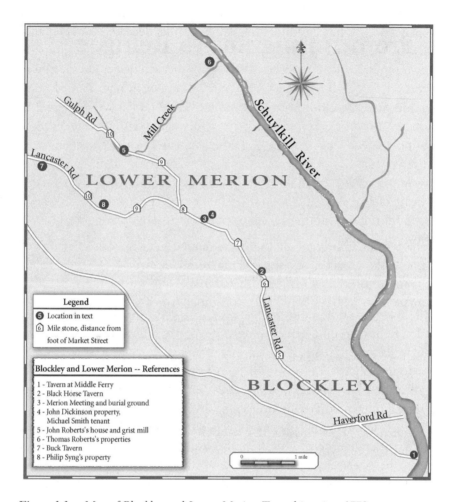

Figure 1.1 Map of Blockley and Lower Merion Townships circa 1778.

John attains the full age of one and Twenty years." As partial compensation for favoring the first son, he gave outright to his son Mathew the 150-acre parcel "lying back in the woods" and to his daughter Rebekah "my Negro girl Betty or the value thereof if my overseers see meet to Dispose of her." The three children were placed under the care of six men designated in the will, relatives and friends of Roberts, who acting as "overseers" had the duty of managing the decedent's estate and looking after his children until son John came of age.

The family patriarch died soon after signing his will, which was admitted to probate the following month in Philadelphia (Lower Merion Township remained part of Philadelphia County until Montgomery County was carved out of the latter and separately incorporated in 1784), whereupon an "Inventory of the goods Cattles and Chattels Househould Stuff ready money of John Roberts of Merion in the County of Philadelphia Miller deceased" was prepared and dated as of April 2, 1704. The decedent's appraised personal property totaled two hundred and fifty pounds. The appraisers valued in the inventory a "Negro Girl named Betty" at eight pounds, "one Negro man named Peter his wife and Sucking Child" at fifteen pounds, and four cows belonging to John Roberts also at fifteen pounds. Besides miscellaneous household goods, farm equipment, and farm animals, Roberts's assets included debts others owed him in the aggregate amount of seventy-three pounds. All in all, it was apparent that in twenty years this immigrant from Wales had securely established himself in the heart of the Welsh Tract and that adequate cash flow from various sources would not be wanting for the support of his children.[3]

The overseers kept a running account of the sums they collected and disbursed during the remaining years of the second John Roberts's minority. This account would find its way into the probate records of the estate. One of the first debit entries was payment of three pounds for John Roberts's "funerall Charges and other things had at his Sickness." Shoes would later be bought for Rebekah (nineteen shillings); the services of a midwife engaged "for Looking after ye Negro Woman" (five shillings); payment made for the board of John Roberts, the son, with John Jermain, as well as his schooling by David Evans (in all for both, two pounds, ten shillings). The biggest outlay during the administration of the overseers was one hundred sixty-five pounds, three shillings, ten and a half pence for "building a New Mill," which, when completed, generated more profit than the "Old Mill." On the credit side of the ledger, the overseers recorded rent collected from Robert Jones for the house and mill, income received from the sale of farm goods, and interest paid by the late John Roberts's several debtors.

Upon submission of the overseers' final account, Mathew Roberts's youthful signature appears at the end of the statement in what a descendant of his, more than a century later, would portray as grudging approval. Jonathan Roberts, Mathew's grandson and a prominent Pennsylvania congressman and senator in the nineteenth century, recalled the lasting bitterness over the "gaurdians [sic] charge for services & expences," which his grandfather, as ward, thought unreasonable and which caused Mathew thereafter to sever connections with his overseer relatives. A family grievance such as this can have a long afterlife, and of his distant Roberts kin, the descendants of the overreaching guardians, Jonathan Roberts wrote in 1840, "Such as we have seen of them, though respectable, have never induc'd much intercourse."[4]

The second John Roberts was a millwright, having been put out as an apprentice at age thirteen to a master in that trade. In November 1720, at age twenty-five, he married Hannah Lloyd, the daughter of his neighbors Robert and Lowry (Jones) Lloyd, reputable Welsh Quakers—endogamy proving the almost invariable rule among the early inhabitants of the Welsh Tract.[5] Not long after his marriage, an unidentified illness overtook him, and "Being weak of Body, but of a Sound and perfect memory," he executed his will on "22nd day of 2d mo called April 1721," which was probated in Philadelphia the following month. After making specific bequests to his relatives and to his still-disadvantaged brother (Mathew receiving "my Saddle and Bridle"), he left "unto my well beloved Wife my dwelling House & Plantation Together with one Grist Mill Containing by Estimation Two hundred and fifty acres of Land Towards Maintenance of her and bringing up & educating of my Child (In Case I have one) untill the Same attain to the age of Twenty one Years And afterwards the dwelling House & premises to the Sd Child or issue." In the event a child of his did not reach the age of sixteen, he divided his estate in two equal shares, one to be distributed to his two siblings and the other to his wife.

Four months after her husband's death, on 15th day of 6th mo 1721, or August 15 under the old calendar, Hannah Lloyd Roberts was delivered of a son, the third John Roberts in the family succession. Although her husband had designated her as the sole executrix of his will, he followed his father's example in naming four others (his brother among them) to serve as overseers, "to see this my Will performed." An inventory taken of his personal property, coming to one hundred eighty-one pounds, five shillings, did not differ significantly from his father's, except that this time one finds clearer evidence of the operation of both a grist and a boulting mill. What regrettably is now missing is a detailed accounting of what happened to John Roberts III over the next two decades and what supervision, if any, those appointed as overseers exercised in his upbringing and education. Yet, in contrast to his father's experience, the death of his own father did not render him an orphan.[6]

Of the years that followed, limited information exists. We know that his mother remarried, becoming the wife of William Paschall, a widower, of Whiteland, Chester County, in an exchange of vows at the Goshen meeting on November 22, 1722. Five children were born of that marriage: four daughters and one son. There is every reason to believe that Hannah Paschall's infant son by her prior marriage accompanied her to her new home in Chester County. When the meeting came to pass on the propriety of her second marriage, two members were appointed to make certain not only that the marriage was "Orderly Accomplished" but also that "what is proper to be done Concerning her Child be settled before their Marriage." Both conditions were apparently met, although the minutes of the meeting do not disclose the agreed-upon arrangements concerning her son.

Whether John Roberts remained with his mother after her second husband died in 1732 and she remarried in 1734 Peter Osborne, "Batecholour," of

Whiteland Township, by whom she is said to have had four more children, is less certain. At some point, as he approached adulthood, it seems logical to suppose that he would have taken an active role in working on and improving the property along Mill Creek that would become his outright on reaching his twenty-first birthday in 1742. Did he, growing up, sometimes feel isolated, a refugee deprived of a secure home life, forced to compete for his mother's affection, and envied by his numerous half-siblings because of the rich inheritance that awaited him? To suggest that such might have been the case is pure speculation, which nevertheless does not preclude an element of the truth. What is verifiable and worth keeping in mind for future reference is that he spent most of his early formative years in Chester County, that sprawling area in southeastern Pennsylvania that would later harbor more than its share of loyalist sympathizers.[7]

By the time John Roberts came of age, the property he inherited from his father and grandfather had been improved by the construction of at least one additional house, a barn, and a valuable gristmill. A small village had begun to emerge at this location along Mill Creek. As his father and his grandfather had done before him, John Roberts maintained membership in the Merion meeting, which, in Quaker nomenclature, was a preparative meeting coming under the umbrella jurisdiction of the Radnor Monthly Meeting. The Merion meetinghouse, of unusual cruciform design and dating from about 1695, continues to this day to be a place where Friends regularly gather for worship. With its adjoining burial ground, it lies next to a road that in Roberts's time was the route between Philadelphia and Lancaster to the west, plied by all manner of traffic and known as the Lancaster or Conestoga Road (but now in this stretch as Montgomery Avenue). It took no great effort to get from Merion meeting to Roberts's property on Mill Creek by traveling a quarter mile westward along Lancaster Road and then for the next two miles by taking Gulph Road, a narrow cart way, as it angled off to the north and descended into the Mill Creek Valley.[8]

John Roberts's membership in the Society of Friends was a pivotal fact in his personal history. If the definition of a martyr is one who suffers death because of his religion, a strong argument can be made that Roberts qualifies as a Quaker martyr. On the other hand, if undeviating adherence to Quaker tenets is also a prerequisite, he falls well short of that standard. Before the Revolution and the controversy surrounding him, he appears at all times in the records of the Radnor and Merion meetings a member in good standing, with no cloud hovering over him or any committee appointed to inquire about his conduct, a person to whom his fellow Quakers might feel safe in entrusting a variety of assignments, whether it was deciding how to apply funds received by bequest or disciplining members of meeting who had violated Quaker principles. Admittedly, the task of locating him is made more difficult by the surplus of Robertses mentioned in the minutes, for there were several families of that name in the Welsh Tract. When the minutes refer to a "John Roberts, Miller," our confidence may increase that we have located the well-to-do miller of that name living in the Mill Creek Valley. Thus, in an ironic foreshadowing of events to come, we are able to observe in March 1776 the appointment of John Roberts, the miller, as a representative of his meeting to inform two of its members that they had been disowned for renouncing "our Peaceable Profession" by taking up arms against the British.[9]

On 4th month 1st day 1743, John Roberts and Jane Downing, the daughter of Thomas and Thomazine Downing, of East Caln in Chester County, were united in marriage at the Uwchlan meeting. Their marriage represented a departure from the rule of marrying within the Welsh cohort, as the Downings, a highly respected Quaker family in Chester County (for whom the village of Downingtown would be named), came from England.[10] Twelve children of that union arrived in a steady progression: Thomas, by the end of 1743/1744; Isaac, the following year (who died at an unascertained date); Hannah, in 1748; Sarah, in 1749/1750; Jehu, in 1751; Mary, in 1754; Jane, in 1756; Thomazine, in 1758; John, in 1760 (dying in 1763); Elizabeth, in 1763; John (2), in 1765 (dying in 1769), and Ann, in 1768. Their dates of birth were duly entered in the records of the Radnor meeting, and some, but not all, of the children would remain Quakers for the rest of their lives.[11] Thomas, the eldest child who will appear recurrently in this history, gradually moved away from the Society of Friends. A bachelor until his fifties, he married outside meeting in 1796. His liberal imbibing was another sign of his having strayed from the straight and narrow Quaker path; in following his father's example of frequent tavern patronage, he ignored the meeting's admonitions against the consumption of alcoholic beverages. And yet on his death, he would join his father, his grandfather, and his great-grandfather in the burial ground at the Merion meeting.[12]

John Roberts prospered in the three decades preceding the Revolution. He enlarged and improved a comfortable house for himself and his family, and built a new stone gristmill in replacement of an older one, a paper mill, a second gristmill, and a sawmill. He acquired more real estate in the Mill Creek Valley. When properties in Lower Merion Township were assessed for the purpose of collecting the provincial tax in 1769, the property of John Roberts, "g. m. [gristmill]," consisted of 402 acres, 12 horses, 12 cattle, 3 servants, on which he paid a tax of one hundred fifty-five pounds, eight shillings, eight pence, exceeding that of any other property owner in the township.[13]

Roberts had trouble retaining in service those whom he employed. The first to run away was Emanuel Lightin, a servant of about twenty years of age, wearing "a blue thin Coat, a white double breasted Flannel jacket, with red Spots and Buttons, good leather Breeches, Yarn Stockings, strong Shoes, and half worn Fur Hat." His departure in December 1762 caused his master added vexation because he absconded with "a middle sized brown or Mouse coloured Horse." Roberts advertised his willingness to pay five pounds for Lightin's return and forty shillings for the horse. The next to leave in the spring of 1764 was William Rhoads, a servant lad of about seventeen years of age, "of a fair complexion, strait Hair, marked a little with the Small Pox"; Roberts placed an advertisement for his return, offering a reward of thirty shillings.

By far the most troublesome case was Lawrence Dunning, an Irishman, who first took off in the summer of 1767 and for whose return Roberts advertised the payment of a reward of forty shillings. When the same Lawrence Dunning, "of short black Hair, long Visage, generally walks in a Hurry," decamped in 1769, Roberts repeated the offer of forty shillings and reasonable charges to "Whoever takes up and secures said Servant, so that his Master may get him again." Back in service, Dunning pulled up stakes once more in March 1774. The picture of the ongoing tussle between the wealthy country gentleman and the unruly Irishman becomes almost endearing when Roberts, with unintended humor, described Dunning in the latest advertisement he placed as "flighty at times." On this last occasion, Roberts reduced the reward for Dunning to twenty shillings; four months later the jail keeper in Lancaster ran his own advertisement notifying Dunning's master that he was holding Dunning in custody—to be handed over on payment of the charges for his confinement.[14]

Having ample funds at his disposal, Roberts experimented in making investments beyond the boundaries of the Welsh Tract. In 1761 he formed a partnership with Thomas May, David Thomas (Senator Roberts's uncle on his mother's side), and David Davis, a nearby neighbor in the Mill Creek Valley, to manufacture bar iron on the Big Elk River in Cecil County, Maryland. The Elk Forge Company, the name of this enterprise, began by purchasing six hundred acres from William Rumsey, and then quickly doubled that holding. The partnership harvested trees for the production of needed charcoal; transported pig iron from Lancaster, Pennsylvania, to convert into bar iron; and generally saw its business flourish in those prewar years. In 1769 the executors under David Davis's will advertised for sale Davis's three-eights interest in the Elk Forge Company, which consisted, among other things, of "a large commodious stone forge, two coal houses, and carriages, a convenient large stone mill, three boulting mills, a good saw mill (plenty of water), a good dwelling house, barn, stables, and a number of houses for negroes and workmen, &c. 12 negroes, 7 of which are forgemen, about 1400 acres of land, 300 cleared."[15] In addition to this significant venture, Roberts and his sons Thomas and Jehu began, just prior to the Revolution, to obtain warrants on land located on the Pennsylvania frontier, along the West Branch of the Susquehanna River, in Northumberland County, which was part of the vast territory pried away from the Indians in the New Purchase of 1768.[16]

Though not totally a self-made man, John Roberts took pride in his possessions, and in their increase attributable to his own efforts. Senator Jonathan Roberts, the descendant of the younger brother, Mathew, who twice got short-changed in the distribution of property under the wills of John Roberts's grandfather and father, captured in a family memoir some of the pride exhibited by Senator Roberts's much older cousin—"Uncle John (as we had been us'd to call him)." He was not, Senator Roberts said, the equal "in mind" of his first cousin, referring favorably by comparison to his own father, a farmer elected to the provincial Pennsylvania Assembly in 1771 and a moderate Whig who drew back from the Revolutionary fray because of his Quaker beliefs, "but he [meaning John Roberts] had more pride and chivalry. Uncle John was a brave man, with pretty high political notions. He liv'd in a higher style than father, as his estate was larger, & more productive." In writing for his children's benefit, Senator Roberts tried to put the best face he could on their relative's sad ending:

> I remember to have seen, & had been taught, to revere, this respectable kinsman. His fate had no effect, in lowering the standing of his numerous family. Though in manner, his was a felons death; in death, he did not meet a felon's fate. He was in all points a revolutionary victim; & another turn of the wheel, might have made him a martyr to Liberty. He died in the community of friends. His offence was, having adhered too much, to the old regime, in a struggle when either side, might have been espous'd with equal honesty.[17]

When and how strongly John Roberts first demonstrated his adherence to the old regime is unclear. He was a member of a committee of forty-three men who put their names to a resolution in June 1774 protesting the act of Parliament that closed down the Port of Boston as "unconstitutional; oppressive to the inhabitants of that town; [and] dangerous to the liberties of the British Colonies." The committee was made up of a broad cross-section of "respectable" residents of the city and county of Philadelphia, many of whom, like John Dickinson and George Clymer, would support the Revolution as moderates, and a few of whom, like Anthony Morris, Edward Pennington, and Roberts, were Quakers. The Rev. Dr. William Smith, provost of the College of Philadelphia, was also a member of the committee; later thought a Tory, he saw fit to address his colleagues before they acted on the proposed resolution, exhorting them to find ways and means to restore "that harmony from which in our better days, Great Britain and her Colonies derived mutual strength and glory, and were exalted into an importance that, both in peace and war made them the envy and terror of the neighbouring nations." Such, we may reasonably suppose, were sentiments shared by Roberts, who soon veered away from an even mild expression of resistance to the Crown. Sixty years after Roberts's death, his cousin appears correct in saying that, at least for a while, in the beginning stages of the Revolution, either side might have been espoused "with equal honesty."[18]

Indeed, we must consider what defined an act of treason against the state in 1777, the year that changed everything for John Roberts. For much of that year it would have been difficult, in the war-torn Welsh Tract, to identify a functioning government capable of commanding allegiance, against which anybody might be held realistically to have committed the political crime of treason. The Pennsylvania constitution of 1776, a radical experiment in state-building, precipitated a continuing battle between two parties that refused to relent, those who supported the constitution and those who opposed it. The sometimes violent disagreement between the constitutionalists and anticonsti-tutionalists (or, if one prefers, radicals and moderates) translated into wide-spread paralysis and chaos. In a prolonged stalemate, laws the assembly passed could not be fully enforced, and government offices of essential importance remained unfilled. Not until January 28 of that year did the Pennsylvania legislature take action to revive those prior laws of the province of Pennsylvania deemed "properly adapted to the circumstances of its inhabitants" and to provide for courts at all levels staffed by judges to be "hereafter elected and appointed." As an index of the uncertainty that prevailed about the maintenance of public order, "friends of liberty," more than fifty strong, circulated in Phila-delphia for signature in late March articles that, although contemplating "a fair prospect of the restoration of order and the due establishment of civil and legal authority," pledged the signatories to support, "to the utmost of our power the civil magistrate in the execution of such wholesome laws as are or shall be enacted by the present Assembly."[19]

While judicial offices were gradually filled during 1777, only a few courts convened to address the growing backlog of cases, some of them involving serious criminal charges. For the most part, the courts that opened for business were located in counties at a safe distance from Philadelphia. In the first days of September 1777, the Court of Quarter Sessions for the County of Philadelphia, having threshold responsibility in the administration of criminal justice, succeeded in meeting at the State House, which its docket entry shows was "the first Session of the Peace held since the United British Colonies of North America were by their Representatives in Congress assembled, declared Free and Independant [sic] States." It disposed of various matters within its jurisdiction, including the appointment of constables and the approval of tavern licenses, but under the threat to the city of a British invasion, it adjourned sine die, not knowing when it might be able to resume that court's customary practice of meeting once every quarter. In this same year, the office of chief justice of Pennsylvania, critical to the functioning of the entire judicial system, remained vacant for an extended period—until Thomas McKean, accepting the appointment that Joseph Reed had previously declined, received his commission in August and took the prescribed oath of office on September 1.[20]

The absence of effective law enforcement was a concern not lost on Thomas McKean. In a 1781 case, he remarked that Pennsylvania at that earlier time was a country in a state of civil war and that "[i]n *civil wars*, every man chooses his party; but generally that side which prevails, arrogates the right of treating those who are vanquished as rebels." McKean attempted to determine when "there did antecedently exist a power competent to redress grievances, to afford protection, and generally, to execute the laws allegiance being naturally due to such a power." In answering that question, he was spared having to make any factual inquiry by concluding that the Pennsylvania Assembly had legally settled the matter when it enacted two statutes that he interpreted in conjunction with each other as effective on February 11: the statute reviving prior provincial law that also established the framework in which new judges would take office; and the statute defining treason and its punishment. His ruling, however, necessarily implied an interregnum or suspension of the duty of obedience to the Revolutionary government prior to the February cutoff date.

If continuing chaotic conditions on the ground had been taken into account, the period required to locate "a power competent to redress grievances, to afford protection, and generally, to execute the laws" would have been subject to extension. At his sentencing of Roberts a year later in 1778, McKean brushed aside the defense that Roberts had fled to the enemy in Philadelphia in October 1777 "for protection against some of your neighbors, who threatened your life, because they thought you a Tory." All Roberts needed to have done, he admonished, was to apply for and obtain protection from the "Civil Magistrate, or from the Army of your own Country," each of which, as representing a resource for Roberts to turn to, rested in the chief justice's imaginative invention.[21]

James Wilson, the preeminent expert on treason and its definition during the Constitutional Convention of 1787, posed far from rhetorical questions in lectures he gave in 1790: "[W]ho may commit treason against the United States? To this the answer is—those who owe obedience to their authority. But still another question rises before us—who are they that owe obedience to that authority? I answer—those who receive protection from it." And Wilson went so far as to suggest that the standard for determining treasonable conduct might be a subjective one, varying from case to case: "Every one has a monitor within him, which can tell whether he feels protection from the authority of the United States: if he does, to that authority he owes obedience."[22]

In the trial of Abraham Carlisle that preceded Roberts's, William Lewis, serving as Wilson's co-counsel in defending Carlisle, took the even bolder step of arguing on behalf of their client that all bets were off once Philadelphia was occupied by the British in September 1777: "It is allowable for a conquered city to join the Conquerors. People in Philadelphia were not undr the protection of the laws." That was a startling proposition to advance, especially in close proximity to the recently ended British occupation of Philadelphia in June 1778. Such reasoning would seemingly have excused even the most flagrant Tory misconduct. Although Lewis cited no authority in support, he could have turned to Thomas Hobbes, who, in justifying a shift in obedience at the time of the English Civil War, contended that the tie of allegiance was only as strong as the power in place that provided protection. "When it is that a man hath the liberty to submit," wrote Hobbes in an about-face for the exponent of obedience to sovereign authority, "it is when the means of his life is within the Guards and Garrisons of the enemy."[23] Had he chosen to, Lewis might have taken an even bolder step and referred to the opening recital in Pennsylvania's brave new constitution that stated that "the inhabitants of this commonwealth have, in consideration of protection only, heretofore acknowledged allegiance to the king of Great Britain," which could only be read to mean that protection was the indispensable price paid for allegiance.[24]

In the year 1777, John Roberts would have felt the weight of harassment more than protection from the government of Pennsylvania. With radicals in control, the Pennsylvania Assembly enacted legislation in March calling for compulsory military service for all white males between the ages of eighteen and fifty-three, and those who refused to serve because of religious scruples were assessed substantial fines. Reciting that "from sordid and mercenary motives sundry persons have or yet may be induced to withhold their allegiance from the commonwealth of Pennsylvania as a free and independent state," the assembly strengthened the bite of the militia law in June 1777 when it provided for a test oath, equally offensive to conscientious Quakers, requiring all white male inhabitants of the Commonwealth above the age of eighteen to swear or affirm allegiance to Pennsylvania as an independent state and to promise to expose any traitorous conspiracies against that state or the United States of which they had knowledge. Nonjurors were made subject to serious legal disabilities and to forfeiture of any arms in their possession. Although Roberts himself was past the age for militia service, his sons Thomas and Jehu were very much in the eligible class. All three of them ran risks in declining to take the oath that the legislature prescribed. Those risks were increased by legislation enacted at about the time Roberts left for occupied Philadelphia that provided for the summary arrest and imprisonment, "without bail or mainprise," of any who refused to take the prescribed oath or affirmation.[25]

As the summer of 1777 waned, a British fleet appeared in the Chesapeake Bay. Rumors circulated about the intentions of the British, which became clearer after forces under the command of General William Howe disembarked at the head of the Chesapeake and began moving toward Philadelphia over a route that would take them through the Welsh Tract. (By coincidence the British landed at a spot in northern Maryland very close to the Elk Forge in which Roberts had invested.) In view of the imminent arrival of the British army, Roberts might well have anticipated the collapse of the insurgency and a marked change for the better in his fortunes. The war had already exacted a heavy toll in his calculations. The new government's enforcement measures in support of the militia were a constant worry, and finding grain to grind and a market in which to sell flour at a profit was no longer the easy task of the prewar years. For a person of wealth in John Roberts's exposed position, the prudent course would have been to lie low and let events determine the outcome, but for this prideful, striving Quaker, impulsive by nature, such restraint was asking too much of him.[26]

What he elected to do in these circumstances ran counter to every lesson caution and his religious beliefs taught. A birthright Quaker, called to defend the testimony against war (more frequently in modern usage, the peace testimony) and to maintain neutrality in the Revolutionary conflict, the owner of valuable property that required his daily care and supervision, the husband and father of numerous children, some of still tender age, and the resident of a community vulnerable to the skirmishes and foraging of two armies in frequent close engagement, Roberts became a refugee for real, abruptly leaving home and family and moving to British-occupied Philadelphia. He took this step at some point during the period when the British were prevailing in the Battles of Brandywine, Paoli, and Germantown. Owen Jones, a witness friendly to Roberts at his trial and his summer neighbor in Lower Merion, testified that Roberts came to Philadelphia "about the 12th of October," just after the Battle of Germantown, and about two weeks after the British had taken possession of the city. For the next four months, Owen Jones said, Roberts boarded as a guest at the house of Jones and his wife in Philadelphia, on the north side of Market Street, between Third and Fourth Streets.[27]

How he arrived at that decision, fraught with such grave consequences for both him and his family, the court and jury would learn from Michael Groves, a witness hostile to Roberts at his trial. Groves told of an astonishing confession Roberts made in April 1778 to a large group, many of whose members were well along in their cups, at a tavern near the Middle Ferry, a crossing of the Schuylkill River located at Philadelphia's western extremity. Though Groves and his testimony were subject to challenge, the jury, in finding Roberts guilty, evidently gave credence to what he said. Chief Justice McKean clearly did;

in later sentencing Roberts, he referred to this confession as a basis for imposing the death penalty.

According to Groves, during the course of "conversing on public affairs," Roberts confided in the raucous gathering at the tavern how, in mid-September, at about the time of the Battle of Brandywine, he reacted with immediate concern to the news that the Whigs had arrested and detained as crypto-Tories leading members of the Philadelphia Yearly Meeting, including Israel Pemberton, Henry Drinker, and Miers Fisher. While their patriot captors debated where to send them for secure, long-term detention, these weighty Quakers were confined at the Masonic Lodge in Philadelphia. Roberts hurried into the city for the purpose of determining from those arrested "if they would condescend not to go" and commission him to procure their freedom.[28]

Failing to receive encouragement from his fellow Quakers who naturally shrank from any thought of bloodshed, Roberts went home, saddled a fresh horse, and set off for the British lines in Chester County, which was no casual jaunt, even for someone familiar with the terrain like Roberts, when elements of two battered armies remained scattered about the countryside. After he arrived in the British camp, he approached with the help of a friend—this is Groves still testifying—Joseph Galloway, by then an avowed Tory and soon to be appointed General Howe's superintendent of police in occupied Philadelphia. His objective, Roberts explained to Galloway, was to persuade General Howe to send "a party of Light horse" to intercept on the road out of Philadelphia the exiled Quakers who that night (probably September 12) were scheduled to be at Pottsgrove. When Galloway took this proposal to Howe, Howe flatly refused. Howe told Galloway that, in the wake of Brandywine, "the horse were very much fatigued, not fit," and that he was unwilling to run the risk of losing prime troops in such a far-out scheme.

While waiting for Howe's answer, Roberts hovered in the background, "for fear of being seen as there was a terror in his mind." Yet, once he heard of Howe's rejection, he volunteered to lead the rescue mission "at the risque of his life" if the general would but give him twenty-five horses. Rebuffed a second time, Roberts turned down Galloway's invitation to stay with the army, and instead made his way back home to ponder his next step. Some weeks later, after the British had taken possession of the city, he reached a decision and left for Philadelphia as a refugee.[29]

Another witness, Edward Stroud, followed Groves and corroborated, practically word for word, what the latter had testified to. Stroud's only new contribution as a witness was referring, in a flight of creative hearsay, to a snatch of conversation Roberts had with his wife before setting off to find the British in Chester County. To her question where he was going, Roberts replied laconically, "to take a ride."[30]

Were it not for Roberts's temperament and proclivity to talk, this so-called confession that these two witnesses, testifying in unison, recounted would seem inherently suspect. It would have been foolhardy and implausible for Roberts to blurt out incriminating information, more than six months after the fact and apropos of nothing in particular, in a crowded barroom and in the midst of what a defense witness accurately termed "mixed company."[31] Furthermore, there is no documentary evidence of Roberts's intimate connection with any of the Quakers dispatched to Winchester, Virginia, such that would have prompted him to consider forcibly freeing them from the patriots' grasp. Miers Fisher, a lawyer and an influential member of that group who would have known about any rescue scheme had it been proposed, testified at Roberts's trial that he never heard of Roberts's having made "an application to the Friends at the [Masonic] Lodge for permission to apply for Light horse to rescue them."[32]

When, however, it came time, after the deaths of Roberts and Carlisle, for the Philadelphia Yearly Meeting to review the evidence against the convicted men and to assess its strength, the committee charged with making that determination concluded that Roberts acted in the impetuous manner revealed in the confession at the Middle Ferry tavern:

> In the 9th mo 1777, several friends and others of their fellow citizens being unjustly apprehended and imprisoned, and afterwards sent to banishment without an examination or hearing; Suffering his mind to be too much moved by this arbitrary violation of Civil and Religious liberty, he [Roberts] hastened away without previously consulting with them, to give intelligence thereof to the General of the British Army on the march towards this City, in hope to frustrate the intention of sending them into exile, which proceeding of his when it became known gave sensible pain and concern to friends.[33]

And well it might have given sensible pain to Friends. As Chief Justice McKean remarked in sentencing Roberts, "offering to put yourself at the head of a troop of horse of the Enemy, and to effect their rescue at the risque [sic] of your life, was a strange piece of Conduct, in one who pretended that he was consciously scrupulous in bearing Arms in any case." Much better would it have been in McKean's view had Roberts "fallen under like indulgent restraint and been sent also to Virginia" with those whom he was so rashly trying to rescue.[34]

About Roberts's presence among British troops in another setting, whether he was a reluctant recruit or not, witnesses both for and against him at his trial were in substantial agreement. His involvement with the enemy on that later occasion wound up being the critical charge against him. The district outside the city limits in which Roberts and his family lived became a kind of no-man's land during the British occupation; neither army, British or American, had complete control of the area, and skirmishes between them routinely occurred there. On the morning of December 11, 1777, Lord Cornwallis led troops and light horse across the Schuylkill to Lower Merion, first engaging American forces in number at the Black Horse Tavern and then moving westward to forage aggressively as the Americans fell back. Roberts was seen riding on horseback with the British, forced against his will, he would later contend, to serve as their guide. Although this limited military probe of Lord Cornwallis and his troops does not figure prominently in accounts of the Revolution, the indiscriminate plundering and destruction of private property that the British engaged in would survive in the memory of the region's outraged inhabitants. At Roberts's trial his lawyers sought to neutralize their client's apparent service to the enemy by lining up witnesses to testify that he repeatedly interceded to spare some of his neighbors the worst of the pillaging.[35]

But one neighbor may have been a target too tempting for Roberts, as a guide for the British, to resist. Michael Smith and his family lived next to the Merion meeting, a little more than two miles from Roberts and his family. In retrospect, it seems safe to say that, were it not for the trouble he had with Michael Smith and his wife, John Roberts would not have been tried for treason. Almost from the time the two men first met bad blood flowed between them, but at this distance we can't be sure exactly why. Both of them were hotheaded, and for all we know, their animosity may have originated in harsh words they exchanged over some minor matter, possibly in a barroom encounter. More substantial issues could also have separated them. Smith was a patriot, probably of German background, and a hardscrabble tenant farmer, whereas Roberts was a wealthy miller, the descendant of a first settler, and the owner of a large plantation who would have invoked his Quaker principles in opposing the war that Smith outspokenly supported. Whatever the root cause or causes of the friction between them, their relationship became even more strained during the late summer of 1777 as the British forces landed in Maryland and began moving menacingly northward toward the Welsh Tract and Philadelphia.

Michael and Mary Smith were among the first to testify for the prosecution at Roberts's trial. Mary Smith's testimony will be considered at greater length in the chapter to follow. In beginning his testimony, Michael Smith volunteered that he had known John Roberts "for about four years, & that to his [Smith's] sorrow." Smith said that, on the day in late September when the British were about to enter Philadelphia, he rode down Lancaster Road to the five-mile stone, close enough to see "a terrible smoke" rising from Philadelphia. On his way back, he met Roberts near the Black Horse Tavern (Figure 1.2), where, in a shouting match, they almost came to blows. Roberts accused Smith of being an "Old Rebel" and threatened to have Smith hanged because he

Figure 1.2 Black Horse Tavern, located at the gateway to Lower Merion Township, prior to its demolition in 1911. Roberts and Michael Smith had an angry confrontation near the Black Horse Tavern in late September 1777.

Reproduced by permission of The Historical Society of Montgomery County.

had ordered his son to shoot Roberts for not paying "the Three pounds fine" levied on Quakers who refused to join the militia. In his testimony against Roberts, Smith quickly denied (maybe a little too quickly) that he had ever given such an order to his son. Other than providing a splash of local color, what Michael Smith recounted, however, did not implicate Roberts in treasonable activity. It was his wife's testimony that would do that.[36]

Roberts remained in Philadelphia through the entire British occupation. When Elizabeth Drinker and the wives of three other Virginia exiles set out in the early spring of 1778 on a trip to Lancaster to petition the Supreme Executive Council for release of their husbands, their first stop on the night of April 5 was at "John Roberts Millers, about ten miles from home," where Elizabeth Drinker recorded in her diary they were "kindly entertain'd by the Woman of House and her Daughters, the Owener [*sic*] being at this time a Refugee in Town." It was also during that month of April that witnesses from both sides at his trial placed John Roberts among numerous drinking companions at the tavern near the Middle Ferry.[37]

The Pennsylvania Assembly resorted to strong measures to combat loyalist sentiment and to land hard on those who had actively assisted the British during the long winter of 1777–1778. In March 1778, the assembly passed in its session in Lancaster a conditional bill of attainder, naming thirteen prominent individuals who had allegedly collaborated with the British. Under the statute, they were required to surrender on or before April 21 and to stand trial for treason; if they failed to surrender by that date, they were automatically attainted for high treason and thereafter deprived of any legal remedy or recourse. The penalties for treason, stiffened in successive acts of the legislature, were the forfeiture of all property to the Commonwealth, the loss of the right to inherit or to provide for one's heirs, and, on capture, death by hanging. On May 8 the Supreme Executive Council expanded the list of suspected traitors by naming by proclamation fifty-seven additional persons, all of whom were likewise required to submit before June 25 or suffer attainder and its consequences. John Roberts and Abraham Carlisle were included in this second list.[38]

The action the assembly took diverged from the guidance that Congress simultaneously attempted to give the state legislatures, but guidance that the legislatures by and large chose to ignore. On April 23, 1778, Congress adopted a resolution that encouraged a broad granting of pardons to those who had aided the enemy and yet, "now wishing to be received and reunited to their country, . . . may be deterred by fear of punishment." On the face of this resolution, Roberts could have taken heart. There was no equivocating about the scope of Congress's recommendation to pardon those who "have levied war against any of these states," or, not to put too fine a point on it, those who had committed treason:

> Resolved, That it be recommended to the legislatures of the several states to pass laws, or to the executive authority of each State, if invested with sufficient power, to issue proclamations, offering pardon, with such limitations and restrictions as the several states shall think expedient, to such of their inhabitants or subjects, who have levied war against any of these states, or who have adhered to, aided or abetted the enemy, and who shall surrender themselves to any civil or military officer of these states, and shall return to the State to which they may belong, before the 10th day of June next: and it is recommended to the good and faithful citizens of these states to receive such returning penitents with compassion and mercy, and to forgive and bury in oblivion their past failings and transgressions.

Lord Richard Howe's secretary, once he learned of the British decision to evacuate Philadelphia, thought that only one step remained to seal the victory of the colonies: "I told him [Lord Howe] that the Congress, if they knew their Business, had only one measure more to take, which is, to publish a Genl. Amnesty, and they drive us from this Continent forever."[39] It is intriguing to imagine what might have happened if the state legislatures had followed the recommendation of Congress, seconded by Lord Howe's secretary, and granted a blanket amnesty, but the temper of the times would not permit any such indulgence. Governor William Livingston of New Jersey, while regarding it as his duty to submit the resolution of Congress to the New Jersey legislature, criticized it as "both unequal and impolitic," revealing that Congress was "less acquainted with the particular circumstances and internal police of some of the States than those who have had more favourable opportunities for that purpose."[40]

Pennsylvania clearly refused to accept Congress's message of conciliation, much less welcome back "returning penitents with compassion and mercy." Roberts and Carlisle faced a Hobson's choice: they could either pack up and leave town with the British, who, by the middle of May, were getting ready to evacuate Philadelphia, in which case the property each of them owned would be forfeited to the Commonwealth and their families rendered destitute, or turn themselves in, swear allegiance to the patriot cause, and take their chances with the rough justice awaiting them.

During the course of a 1779 parliamentary inquiry, Joseph Galloway, who had no choice but to depart with the British, answered the charge that he had given less than satisfactory advice to his friends and allies when the British army was preparing to leave. "There was not a person," he maintained, "who had taken an active part, to my knowledge, but what I advised to come away with the British army." That was true for Abraham Carlisle, whom he "positively advised to leave the city, because I knew he would not be safe" since Carlisle had conspicuously served during the British occupation as a guard at the city gates, issuing or withholding passes to those seeking to cross the picket lines. Roberts's case was, however, a different matter. He had not consulted Galloway, who, in his testimony before parliament, said that Roberts "had a very large family, and a large estate, and many friends more confidential than myself, with whom he advised, and whose advice he followed." But not the advice, it would appear, he received from his cousin Senator Jonathan Roberts's father, who, the senator recalled, "thought that his return within the power of the Whigs, was unwise."[41]

Whatever misgivings they should have had, both Carlisle and Roberts chose to stay. On June 19, the day after the British completed pulling out of Philadelphia, Roberts came before Zebulon Potts, a justice of the peace, to affirm his allegiance to the Commonwealth and otherwise to comply with the terms of the Supreme Executive Council's May 8 proclamation. To ensure his appearance "at the first Court to be held for said County [Philadelphia] to answer all such Matters & things as Shall be then and there objected to him," he gave his own recognizance in the amount of one thousand pounds and provided the additional security of bonds posted by Thomas Livezey and Joseph Mather, each in the amount of five hundred pounds. Potts thereupon issued an order commanding "all Sheriffs, Constables &c not to detain or keep in custody the said John Roberts on any Account, Cause, Action Matter or thing relative to the above-mention proscription [of the Supreme Executive Council]."[42]

The liberty Roberts gained would be of short duration. A month later James Young, another justice of the peace, issued a warrant for the arrest of "John Roberts, miller, now or late of the Township of Lower Merion," on the strength of a sworn statement made by "Michael Smith, yeoman, and Mary his wife, of said Township," charging Roberts "with High Treason, by aiding and assisting the Enemies of this State and of the United States of America and joining their armies at Philadelphia in the month of December last." The Smiths, it was clear, had not forgotten the impact of the sudden incursion of Cornwallis and his troops, nor the presence of John Roberts as their guide.[43]

Taken into custody on August 10, Roberts applied for bail to Chief Justice McKean. In a letter he had sent two months before to a newly appointed colleague on the Supreme Court, McKean had expressed a liberal view about granting bail to those named in the attainder bill and in the subsequent proclamations of the council, especially "if the Evidence amounts to no more than common fame, or public notoriety, that the party named in the proclamation had left his usual place of abode and gone into the city of Philadelphia, without some proof of an Overt-Act." McKean even went so far as to anticipate that the Commonwealth might grant a general pardon to these alleged traitors, "excepting your cruel fellows & some men of property, whose estates really ought to be confiscated." He thought that to respond favorably to the entreaties of "relatives & friends of the culprits for mercy will create respect to the Rulers, and their granting it on every reasonable occasion will reconcile & endear men to the Government." Events would prove him wrong in that rosy view.[44]

The growing clamorous hostility, not only to those who had openly assisted the British but also to those suspected of doing so, was too strong to ignore. This newspaper warning in mid-July certainly amounted to more than a mere hint of what might lie ahead:

> A HINT to the TRAITORS and those TORIES who have taken an active part with the enemy, during their stay in this city. You are desired, before it is too late, to lower your heads, and *not stare down your betters* with *angry faces.* For you may be assured the day of trial is close at hand when you shall be called upon, to answer for your *impertinence* to the Whigs, and your *treachery* to this country.

Two days later in the same newspaper the drumbeat increased when "Astrea de Coelis" declaimed, "Now their friends have forsaken them, they are offering up a death-bed repentance; flying to the magistrate with a tender of their allegiance and fidelity, like Joab (a traitor of old) to the altar for safety; but why should not the fate of Joab be theirs? Even the ark of the Lord should be no sanctuary for crimes so heinous."[45]

The next month the targets of these fiery patriots were more plainly in sight. The Philadelphia Meeting for Sufferings addressed a petition and remonstrance to the Pennsylvania Assembly dated 5th day 8th mo, 1778, over the signature of Nicholas Waln, as clerk. In protesting the punitive measures enforced against Quakers who were but following the dictates of their religious belief, the Meeting for Sufferings harked back to the heritage of "our first worthy Proprietary William Penn" and his commitment to religious and civil liberty "so that Pennsylvania hath since been considered an asylum for men of tender consciences." Immediately upon its publication in the newspaper, this appeal ignited a firestorm of indignation. In the *Pennsylvania Packet*, "Philadelphiensis" thundered, "Was piloting the enemy for the specific purpose of shewing them where the Americans were, that they might kill them, consistent with your 'peaceable principles'?"[46]

It was in this angry and vengeful environment that Roberts, seeking bail, appeared before Thomas McKean at a hearing held on August 20. One of the lawyers who represented him at that hearing was Elias Boudinot, a member of Congress from New Jersey and a staunch patriot. But impeccable credentials didn't shield Boudinot from an attack in the press for acting on behalf of "an infamous tory, now confined in the gaol of this county on a charge of high treason." The writer gave the knife a further twist by posing this question: "How far is it consistent with the dignity of Congress for a Delegate representing one of the Thirteen United states, actually attending his duty in congress, to appear as Attorney or Council in favour of notorious disaffected persons?" Since this assault on Boudinot appeared a week after the bail hearing for Roberts, who was by the newspaper report still confined in jail, it seems safe to conclude that, notwithstanding the liberal sentiments McKean had expressed to his fellow judge, he had denied Roberts's application for bail.[47]

That fall term of the Court of Oyer and Terminer and General Gaol Delivery for Philadelphia County began on September 21, with the justices of the supreme court acting as trial judges. A parade of prisoners charged with treason came before the court—John Roberts among them. On that opening day a grand jury of eighteen "good and Lawful men" of the county of Philadelphia returned a presentment, or indictment, against Roberts in archaic language that showed how old forms had been adapted (and somewhat incongruously) to meet new exigencies. Accused of being as of January 1, 1778, "and at divers days and times as well before as after," a "false Traitor," and a person "not having the fear of God before his eyes, but being moved and seduced by Instigation of the Devil," he was further charged with participating in "a public and cruel war against the Commonwealth [and] then and there committing and perpetrating a miserable and cruel Slaughter of and amongst the faithful and Leige [*sic*] subjects and inhabitants thereof." In more specific terms, the indictment alleged that he had joined the invading army "under the command of General Sir William Howe"; that he had served "the same army as a Guide and by enlisting and procuring and persuading others to enlist"; and that he had given and sent intelligence to these same malign enemies of the Commonwealth.[48]

John Roberts was formally arraigned on that same day. After hearing read the charges against him, he entered a plea of not guilty, or, as noted in the court records, "non culpabilis & de hoc ponit se super patriam"—"not guilty, and from here puts himself upon the country," the ancient formula for requesting a jury trial by one's peers. By the simultaneous entry of "Similiter," the attorney general acknowledged and joined in the issue and request for a jury trial. Once those formalities were completed, the prisoner was remanded to the custody of the sheriff—to await his day in court.[49]

II

The Prosecution

During the weeks preceding the Declaration of Independence, the Continental Congress became concerned about colonists who remained loyal to the Crown. In a spirit quite different from the conciliatory approach it would recommend to the states two years later, it called on the legislatures of the "several United Colonies" to prescribe appropriate punishment for those who, "adhering to the king of Great Britain," gave aid and comfort to the enemies of any such colony. Probably because, in adopting this resolution, Congress had accepted the report of its Committee on Spies (of which James Wilson was a member), it cast its net wide enough to haul in as potential traitors subject to punishment "all persons passing through, visiting, or making a temporary stay in any of said colonies."[1]

On September 5, 1776, the Pennsylvania convention meeting to frame a new constitution for that state promulgated an ordinance defining treasonable activities by its inhabitants and the punishment that those found guilty would suffer. The ordinance was general in much of its language and relatively mild in the penalties it provided: Convicted traitors were subject to forfeiture of all their real and personal estate and to imprisonment for a term not exceeding the duration of the war; those who knew of and concealed the commission of treason by others, or assisted a traitor, got off even more lightly for the crime of misprision of treason.[2] The situation changed dramatically at the beginning of the following year. With a new constitution precariously in place, Pennsylvania moved to shore up its governmental system by organizing its courts and reviving so much of the preexisting statutory and common law that did not directly conflict with the principles of the Revolution. As part of its responsibility to counter treason, the Pennsylvania Assembly enacted a much tougher statute defining and punishing it.

By way of preface, the framers of the legislation sought to answer the question that James Wilson (see Figure 2.1) later propounded in his law lectures about who owed a duty of allegiance: "all and every person and persons (excepting prisoners of war)," the statute specified, "now inhabiting, residing or sojourning within the limits of the state of Pennsylvania, or that shall voluntarily come into the same hereafter to inhabit, reside or sojourn." If a person indicted for treason was found guilty "by the evidence of two sufficient witnesses," the legislature prescribed as punishment the death penalty and the forfeiture to the Commonwealth of all the convicted person's property, "except such parts thereof as the judges of the court wherein such conviction may be shall order and appropriate to the support of such traitor's children or wife and children (if any)." It was under this statute that Carlisle and Roberts would be tried.

The statute laid out seven separate grounds for finding that treason had been committed against Pennsylvania or the United States of America by aiding or assisting any of their enemies "at open war":

> by taking a commission or commission from the enemy; by joining their armies; by enlisting or procuring or persuading others to enlist for that purpose; by furnishing such enemies with arms or ammunition, provision or any other article or articles for their aid or comfort; by carrying on a traitorous correspondence; by forming a combination, plot or conspiracy to betray Pennsylvania or the United States of America; or by giving or sending any intelligence to the enemies for that purpose.[3]

In the indictment brought against him, the Commonwealth had charged John Roberts with certain acts of treason that came within these statutory specifications. A jury of his peers would now determine whether the prosecution had assembled sufficient evidence to convict and hang him.

John Roberts's trial began on Wednesday, September 30, and ended two days later, when, after reportedly twenty-four hours of protracted deliberation, the jury returned a verdict of guilty. Abraham Carlisle's fate was sealed more quickly; according to the *Pennsylvania Evening Post* of September 26, "[h]is trial began yesterday forenoon at ten, and continued until past five this morning."[4]

During the 1778 fall term of court in Philadelphia, a string of treason trials proceeded one after another, with scarcely a pause in between, and often with juries empanelled of overlapping composition. The trials were held in the great hall on the second floor of the College of Philadelphia's main building, located at the southwest corner of Fourth and Arch Streets (see cover drawing). Constructed in the 1740s as a combined charity school and place of public worship in response to the evangelical fervor that George Whitefield's preaching stirred up, and converted in the 1750s for use by the nascent College of Philadelphia, this facility provided the only suitable space in the city for such proceedings. Holding court in College Hall may have been a last-minute decision entailing improvisation, for the minutes of the trustees are silent about any approval sought for this arrangement. In fact, from June 1777 to September 25, 1778, the trustees of the college did not meet, "on Account of the State of Public Affairs." The State House, where, under more settled conditions, the trials would have taken place, had been left in shambles as a result of the extraordinary wear and tear it sustained during the recently ended British occupation.[5]

At the northern end of this makeshift courtroom Chief Justice McKean (Figure 2.1) and Justice John Evans sat behind the bench on a raised platform that provided the elevation befitting their high judicial rank while they presided over the trials. Though responsible in his capacity as attorney general for representing the Commonwealth or Respublica, Jonathan Dickinson Sergeant withdrew during Roberts's trial because of illness, and Joseph Reed, his combative and politically ambitious colleague, who would soon become president of the Supreme Executive Council, took the laboring oar in presenting the prosecution's case (Figure 2.1). Reed had been retained in August as special counsel to assist Sergeant in these capital cases for the annual fee of two thousand pounds. If the barbed criticism at the time of Roberts's bail hearing had scared off Elias Boudinot, the defendant was nevertheless able to call on outstanding legal talent to represent him in the persons of two experienced lawyers, both signers of the Declaration of Independence, James Wilson and George Ross, and an up-and-coming member of the bar, William Lewis.[6]

The first item of business was empanelling a jury. Roberts's lawyers were entitled to receive, not less than one day before the trial, a copy of the whole indictment against him (but not the names of the witnesses the prosecution intended to call) and a list of all the prospective jurors or veniremen summoned by the sheriff to try the cases coming before the court in the weeks ahead.[7] It is not known exactly what the qualifications for jury service were, how the sheriff, James Claypoole, went about the task of assembling prospective jurors, or what were the names of all the veniremen whom Claypoole assembled for this session of court. Nor can we do other than speculate on what objectively determinable facts—like age, ethnic and religious identification, wealth, occupation—actually figured in the thinking of counsel for Roberts in winnowing down the list of prospective jurors to the panel of twelve finally selected to serve as Roberts's jury.

In a recent illuminating study, Carlton F. W. Larson has undertaken a comprehensive analysis of the twenty-three treason trials prosecuted in Philadelphia between September 1778 and April 1779, demonstrating, among his other valuable findings, that the same jurors repeatedly served in these cases. Larson's thesis is that defense counsel, through the use of peremptory challenges, deliberately maneuvered to achieve serial service, which, he believes, accounts for the high number of acquittals eventually obtained.[8] Although in the longer perspective serial service may have produced or contributed to such a result, in part because it ensured that the memory of what befell Carlisle and Roberts would not be lost in subsequent jury deliberations, the trend toward acquittals

Figure 2.1 Portraits of *Thomas McKean* (1734–1817), at top, who, as chief justice, presided at Roberts's trial; *Joseph Reed* (1741–1785), at lower left, counsel for the prosecution; and *James Wilson* (1742–1798), at lower right, principal counsel representing Roberts.

Reproduced by permission of The Historical Society of Pennsylvania.

had yet to develop as a reliable phenomenon at the time Roberts's counsel picked a jury in his case. They had for their immediate guidance the guilty verdict returned by the jury in Carlisle's case and a verdict of acquittal by a jury in perhaps the only case that intervened between Carlisle's trial and Roberts's. One might assume, therefore, the defense's automatic use of the challenge to eliminate any prospective juror who had previously voted to convict Carlisle, and yet two Carlisle jurors were permitted to join the ten others chosen to decide Roberts's fate.

Under established practice, the prisoner had the right to challenge without cause as many as thirty-five prospective jurors from the array of veniremen.[9] In the margin of the notes he was taking, the chief justice kept meticulous count of the peremptory challenges the prisoner's counsel thus exercised. When later sentencing Roberts, McKean found peculiar comfort in the fact that, having challenged only thirty-three names, Roberts had virtually given his blessing to the jury that had convicted him. "The jury who have found you guilty," McKean congratulated Roberts, "were such as may be justly said you yourself approved of, for although the law gives you the liberty to challenge thirty-five, you have challenged but thirty-three so you allowed the rest to be an indifferent Jury to pass between the State and you upon your life and death."[10]

The chief justice relied on his ear in recording at the head of his trial notes "Nomina Juratorum," or the names of the jurors finally selected. They were, as he noted, both "sworn and affirmed," which meant that one or more of them would have declined on religious grounds to being sworn as a juror, choosing instead to affirm the obligation to serve. Those who expressed that scruple were not necessarily, however, members in good standing of the Society of Friends, or, for that matter, predisposed toward the accused. No conscientious Quaker would have agreed to serve on a jury whose verdict might result in the death of a fellow Quaker, even a misguided one.[11]

The Philadelphia Monthly Meeting wasted no time in disciplining Cadwalader Dickinson, a shoemaker and its maverick member who served on Carlisle's jury (and also, by Carlton Larson's count, on the jury in fourteen other treason trials to follow), "for the support of Measures inconsistent with our Religious principles, in the prosecution of which he joined with others in condemning a Member of our Society to Death." It was not in Dickinson's nature meekly to accept this reprimand. The members of the meeting appointed to confer with him reported that he "still continued in a Disposition to Vindicate his Conduct," and they recommended his disownment.[12]

By the time in 1779 that these treason trials were over Dickinson had emerged as someone closely identified with the government. That's how Samuel Rowland Fisher, imprisoned for his stubborn attachment to Quaker principles, regarded Dickinson after the latter, admitted as a visitor to the Old Gaol, tried unsuccessfully to draw Fisher out in conversation; Fisher facetiously referred to him as "a very active Statesman of the present times." Dickinson joined the Society of Free Quakers, the breakaway group of Quakers who supported the Revolution and were ready to take up arms, if need be, in its cause. During the ensuing politico-religious disagreement, the Free Quakers published in 1782 a memorial and remonstrance in which they complained, among other things, about the harsh and inconsistent treatment of Cadwalader Dickinson, disowned for his service on the Carlisle jury while the two convicted traitors, who had violated the testimony against war, were not. What's more, the Free Quakers contended that Dickinson had been "requested to serve on that duty by a relation of one of those men," which, if true, may provide a further clue about the process followed in constituting a jury.[13]

For a brief moment, Cadwalader Dickinson appears to have taken a seat in the jury box in Roberts's case, only to have the chief justice strike his name from the list, no doubt because of the exercise of one of the defense's peremptory challenges. The name of John Campbell, who would later serve on four juries, was similarly stricken from the chief justice's list. In spite of the availability of two remaining challenges, both John Drinker and Isaac Powell, who had served on the Carlisle jury, survived the cut. Isaac Powell, a joiner by trade and a Baptist by religion, would serve on seventeen juries in all, strongly implying that defense counsel had early developed confidence in his judgment and maybe even in his partiality for their clients.[14] The presence of the second holdover from the Carlisle jury represents a still more intriguing choice.

The Drinker name had a powerful resonance in Quaker circles. During the Revolution, the Drinker family seemed, from top to bottom, impeccably Quaker, and as such, a persistent thorn in the patriot side. Henry Drinker, a wealthy merchant and the husband of Elizabeth Drinker, the famous diarist, was one of the Virginia exiles, while his slightly older brother, John Drinker, also a merchant and Quaker paragon, maintained an infuriating flow of pious lectures chastising the Whigs. Soon to be selected clerk of the Philadelphia Yearly Meeting as an added sign of the esteem in which he was held, this John Drinker was obviously not the John Drinker who served on the Carlisle and Roberts juries.

There was, however, a black sheep among the Drinkers, another John Drinker, the uncle of the aforesaid Henry and John Drinker. A bricklayer and house carpenter, he constructed a complex of buildings on the north side of Pine Street between Second and Third, known as "Drinker Court," which remains intact today. At about the age of sixty-two, this John Drinker, with little else to distract him, is the most likely candidate for having set the astonishing record of jury service in twenty of the twenty-three treason cases.

The Philadelphia Monthly Meeting did not move to sanction him as it so promptly did Cadwalader Dickinson, for the simple reason that "John Drinker the Elder of this City, Bricklayer," had been read out of meeting six years previously—"for want of watchfulness," having "drawn aside from that purity of Life which he professed, and made appearance of, and [having] associated with disreputable & dissolute company to the great scandal of himself, and grief of his Friends." His disownment was necessary "for the clearing of Truth & our Religious Society from the reproach occasioned by his declension." Paradoxically John Drinker's censure may have recommended him as a juror in Roberts's case, sympathetic to someone who had also deviated from that path of unswerving rectitude that Quakers were exhorted to follow.[15]

How confident could Roberts's lawyers be that, through the judicious use of challenges, they had weeded from the jury finally chosen angry radicals who looked on all Quakers, especially wealthy ones, as partisans in camouflage, hiding behind religious principle when in reality they supported the Crown? Unfortunately, with the exception of Cadwalader Dickinson and John Campbell, the two whose names McKean had to strike from his list, we have no record of those suspect veniremen whom the defense challenged in this and other treason trials. One thing, though, is clear: as the person critically interested in the outcome, Roberts would have participated in his counsel's close scrutiny of the jury list and supplied information and advice about particular candidates, many of whom he should have known at least by reputation. What lawyers refer to as the *voir dire*—a preliminary examination of prospective jurors—has never approached scientific exactitude in eliminating bias, but neither was it then, any more than now, an entirely hit-or-miss process. If Roberts and his lawyers lacked the predictability that accumulated experience with jury panels in subsequent trials may have provided, they should nevertheless have been able to make informed judgments about most of the names on the jury list. A 1773 civil proceeding tried in the Pennsylvania Provincial Supreme Court illustrates the care taken in selecting a jury and in attempting to weed out dubious candidates. In that suit, the defendant carefully annotated, one by one, the full list of forty-eight veniremen whom the sheriff of Berks County had summoned for jury duty, identifying for his counsel such factors as age, religion, wealth, temperament, and sobriety, which he thought might be relevant in choosing the jury. With his life at stake, Roberts had an even greater incentive to assist his counsel by providing such guidance.[16]

It was, of course, impossible for the defense to pick a sanitized jury, free of any political bias. Risks had to be taken, and the extent to which counsel for Roberts were prepared to take such risks may be seen in the selection of two jurors, both of whom were strongly committed to the patriot cause. From the 1760s onward, William Adcock offered for sale a wide variety of dry goods at his shop located at Second and Market Streets; after the Revolution, he seems to have specialized in the sale of carpets and carpeting. He early aligned himself with the radical Whigs, becoming a founding member and then president of the Committee of Privates, formed in September 1775 to promote aggressively the interests of rank-and-file militiamen. Although Roberts and his lawyers might have taken some comfort in his belonging to the Christ Church congregation, Adcock didn't hesitate to put distance between himself and those of his fellow congregants who, torn by conflicting pressures, clung to the hope of reconciliation with the mother country. Four months after serving as a juror in his fifth and last treason trial, he received a dual commission as justice of the peace and judge of the Philadelphia Orphans Court, in continuation of the prior practice of staffing the lower rungs of the judicial ladder with men considered deserving of recognition but lacking in any legal training. Adcock died in 1817 at the age of eighty-six and was buried with the Masonic honors due a Grand Master in the Christ Church burial ground at Fifth and Arch Streets.[17]

Less is known about David Pancoast, a Quaker who relocated to Virginia after the Revolution. Originally from Burlington, New Jersey, a builder by trade, he came to Philadelphia in about 1760, where his marriage is recorded in the minutes of the Philadelphia Monthly Meeting. In the opening months of the war, Pennsylvania employed him in assembling gun carriages; he later joined the militia as a "Fighting Quaker," rose to the rank of captain, and mustered out in the spring of 1778. These activities were, needless to say, incompatible with Quaker beliefs and led to his disownment.[18]

In July 1778, a month after the British evacuated Philadelphia, a group of one hundred and eighty-three men, styling themselves the Patriotic Association, published a manifesto aimed at tracking down Tories then scurrying for cover. Not everyone in the Patriotic Association was a radical, but among the subscribers were notably three who were: Joseph Reed (see Figure 2.1, p. 34), whose name appeared at the head of the list, Thomas Paine, and Charles Willson Peale. William Adcock, David Pancoast, and Cadwalader Dickinson were also enrolled in this vigilante group whose members went on record collectively pledging themselves, "in the furtherance of public justice," to disclose any facts or circumstances that might bring to trial "sundry persons notoriously disaffected to the American cause, and others of suspicious characters, presuming upon the indulgence and lenity of their virtuous and forbearing countrymen." Of particular moment, the members of the Patriotic Association undertook to provide support for "all other faithful inhabitants of this State, who may be restrained by any undue influence from making such discoveries against any oppression or insult." It seems more than mere coincidence that Michael Smith and his wife swore out a warrant for John Roberts's arrest two

Figure 2.2 German Schoolhouse, just east of Fourth Street on the north side of Cherry Street, in a photograph by Frederick DeBourg Richards, circa 1865. The Patriotic Association met in the schoolhouse to plot strategy for the treason trials, which were taking place a half block away in College Hall. As restored, the schoolhouse is today used for commercial purposes.

Reproduced by permission of The Library Company of Philadelphia.

days after the *Pennsylvania Packet* published this call to arms from so many respected members of the community.[19]

During the rest of the summer, the Patriotic Association continued to meet and recruit new members. Its roll book, somewhat cryptic in its entries, records the names of two hundred and sixty-two men who eventually signed the articles of association. During the month of September, notices in the newspaper repeatedly summoned members of the Association to meet at the German schoolhouse (Figure 2.2) on Cherry Alley, between Third and Fourth Streets, a half block north of College Hall—where court was in session. On September 26, the day Carlisle's jury returned a guilty verdict and four days before

Roberts's trial began, this notice appeared: "The Members of the Patriotic ASSOCIATION are requested to meet this evening at the Schoolhouse in Cherry alley, where business of great importance will be laid before them. It is hoped none will be absent." On September 29, on the eve of Roberts's trial, a similar notice urged members to assemble at six o'clock that evening. How many actually attended these meetings late in September cannot be determined from the roll book, but one must assume that those who did attend—to consider "business of great importance"—were unlikely to have been neutrally disposed toward the accused in the pending treason trials. In the newspaper calling for the meeting on September 26, the editor preliminarily set the tone and the agenda for strengthening the resolve of witnesses testifying against those on trial for treason: "The amazing industry with which the Tories have propagated a report of the intention of the enemy to return to this city, however improbable, may be accounted for by the near approach of the supreme court: If they can intimidate evidences from appearing at the court to lay open the conduct of the traitors, they will answer a great purpose."[20]

It should have been unnecessary for defense counsel to use peremptory challenges to disqualify members of the Patriotic Association from jury service; the publicly announced objectives of the Association would have rendered them, at least in more composed circumstances, subject to challenge for cause. Yet Roberts's lawyers appeared willing to underwrite the risk that Adcock and Pancoast, rather than having prejudged their client, would serve "indifferently," as the quaint legal lexicon of the day expressed it. By reference to the list of jurors that the chief justice was keeping at the head of his trial notes, Adcock and Pancoast were, in sequence, the first and third to be seated in the jury box.[21]

The jury having been chosen, the trial could begin in earnest, but not according to the rules of engagement that govern in a criminal trial today. For one thing, the eighteenth-century trial moved along at a much brisker rate, probably because the right of the accused to legal representation was a relatively new development and lawyers were still feeling their way in mounting an effective defense. To be sure, the former colonies had progressed beyond England in granting defendants charged with serious crimes the right to retain trial counsel. Of the anomalies of criminal trial practice in mid-eighteenth-century England, Blackstone lamented:

> [I]t is a settled rule at common law, that no counsel shall be allowed [to] a prisoner upon his trial, upon the general issue, in any capital crime, unless some point of law shall arise proper to be debated. A rule, which seems to be not all of a piece with the rest of the humane treatment of prisoners by the English law. For upon what face of reason can that assistance be denied to save the life of a man, which is yet allowed him in prosecutions of even petty trespass?

Even in England, however, the rule against permitting counsel to act for defendants in capital cases had been undergoing an almost sub-rosa change, for, as Blackstone acknowledged, "the judges themselves are so sensible to this defect that they seldom scruple to allow a prisoner counsel to stand by him at the bar, and instruct him what questions to ask, or even to ask questions for him, with respect to matters of fact." The enlarged role of counsel in felony trials was no doubt attributable in part to the explicit protection provided in the Treason Trials Act of 1696, which notably allowed a person accused of treason "to make his full Defense, by Counsel learned in the law."[22]

For another thing, and as a corollary to the still evolving role of lawyers in criminal proceedings, testimony flowed more or less freely, without the delays caused by adhering strictly to the question-and-answer format or by the interruptions occurring when counsel objected on technical grounds to what opposition witnesses were on the verge of saying. Relevance was at best an attenuated concept, and not until the end of the eighteenth century did lawyers succeed in challenging as suspect evidence under the hearsay rule statements that witnesses quoted others making outside the courtroom. In some respects, the eighteenth-century trial, though gradually reshaped by significant change, continued to partake of a battle of sworn witnesses in which the power of the oath could often overcome the inherent weakness or implausibility of the testimonial narrative.[23]

The seven witnesses who came forward to testify against Roberts were ordinary people. None of them as they took the stand would have bowled over judge or jury. They were small-time farmers from Roberts's general neighborhood or persons whose occupations the trial record does not disclose but who, though self-sufficient by all appearances, held no position of particular note. The two witnesses who gave the most damaging testimony attributed Roberts's ill will toward them to the fact that they had sons serving in the Pennsylvania militia. Three witnesses were drinking companions of Roberts, and two of them partners with him in a fishing company on the Schuylkill River whose business, it was intimated, might have led to personal differences. Were these three acquaintances of several years' standing simply doing their patriotic duty in testifying against him, or did they have ulterior, less noble reasons for attempting to bring him down? Two witnesses were women forced to defend home turf in the absence of men folk. The five men who testified would have felt newly empowered under the Pennsylvania constitution of 1776, which broadened the franchise and, in its Declaration of Rights, significantly enlarged the protections granted ordinary people.[24]

Mary Smith was the first witness called by the prosecution. The persistent hostility of the Smiths, husband and wife, would prove to be Roberts's undoing. Whatever the exact nature of the first clash they had with him, and no matter who initially was at fault, they were now determined not to let their prosperous neighbor off the hook. The Smiths were farmers and tenants of John Dickinson, who in 1774 acquired a sizable tract of 236 acres next to the Merion meeting and on both sides of Lancaster Road. The land the Smiths farmed was two and a half miles from Roberts's property on Mill Creek, and that much closer to Philadelphia. When Michael Smith testified, he acknowledged that he had known the prisoner for about four years, which would make their first encounter coincide with Dickinson's purchase.[25]

Once sworn as a witness, there was no stopping Mary Smith, who proceeded seemingly unchecked by lawyer or judge in the highly charged emotional account she gave. She had two quite different stories to tell. The first related to the foraging expedition that the British troops under the command of Lord Cornwallis embarked on during the early morning of December 11, 1777. She testified that she saw John Roberts in their company and that, in spite of her pleas for help, he refused to come to her aid. A horn was blown, whereupon she said that troops rushed forward and "tore off her cloaths" (the chief justice delicately clarified the record of the Quaker note-taker by adding "except her under-petticoat"). The nub of her complaint against Roberts appears to have been that he failed to provide the protection she must have subsequently learned he gave to others in the neighborhood, or, as she testified, he "could as well have prevented their being plundered, as the other neighbours." Although her testimony to this point did no more than establish his passive presence alongside the British troops, it was enough to constitute evidence of an overt act committed by Roberts in joining the enemy army, one of the charges specifically set forth in the indictment.[26]

Continuing her testimony, Mary Smith described how she next went to Philadelphia for a dual purpose: to obtain, if she could, the release of one of her sons who, three days later in December, had been captured and locked up in the Walnut Street Prison (the "New Jail"); and, second, to present for payment the certificate that a British commissary officer had given for cattle the troops had seized from the Smiths during the raid. While in the city she twice sought out John Roberts for help, but he remained unwilling to intercede, telling her, so she testified, that, unless her husband and her other son would leave General Washington's army and take the oath of allegiance to the Crown, she had no hope of succeeding. Not accepting that as a final answer, Mary Smith "got a petition wrote to Genl Howe" to submit for her son's release. When she presented her petition in person to the British commanding general, Roberts was lurking in the vicinity, and she implied that some communication occurred between Roberts and Howe that resulted the following day in Howe's unexpectedly rejecting her request.

Near the conclusion of her testimony, the trial notes indicate that her credibility was tested in cross-examination. In reply, she embellished the story of John Roberts's refusal to assist in obtaining her son's release, this time testifying that he told her that "thirty thousand Russians would come & kill us all, and therefore her husband, & sons had better come, & deliver themselves up." She was asked whether it wasn't true that John Roberts had carried out a mission inconsistent with the callous picture she had painted of him, by delivering, presumably at her request, "hard money" to her son while he was in prison. She was also asked what clothing John Roberts wore on the occasions she had seen him, and how she was able to recognize a personage of the rank of General Howe—what decorations he wore and whether he "was pitted with the small pox." Though Mary Smith stuck to her guns, her recorded answers to this cross-examination were not totally convincing.[27]

The next witness the Commonwealth called led to a lawyers' clash about admissibility. Some initial disclosure or offer of proof must have preceded John Ellis's appearance on the witness stand, alerting Roberts's counsel to the gist of the testimony Ellis would give. One count in the indictment against Roberts paralleled language in Pennsylvania's recently enacted statute defining treason; the indictment charged him with "procuring and persuading others to enlist" in the "army under the command of Gen'l Sir William Howe." Ross and Wilson jumped in with legal authority to block Ellis from testifying. The language in the treason statute, they protested, required more than idle conversation and a hypothetical enlistment. In James Wilson's submission to the court, it did not pass the essential evidentiary requirement merely to show an effort to persuade if that effort in fact failed, or, as Wilson was quoted arguing to the court, "where no actual inlisting there can be no persuasion to inlist."

Joseph Reed came armed in reply with his own authority, a volume that counsel for the Commonwealth and Roberts would each in turn have occasion to cite to bolster their positions. It was an influential treatise on the criminal law of England, first published in 1762 and authored by Sir Michael Foster, one of the judges of the King's Bench holding commission in 1746 to try Jacobite rebels for treason, many of whom were convicted and sentenced to death. Foster's work consisted of two parts: a report of law cases, and a legal textbook that dealt at length with the crime of high treason. No law library being close to the courtroom in College Hall, lawyers and judges, of necessity, shared the volumes referred to in argument. One can imagine Reed handing Foster's treatise up to McKean and his fellow judge while directing their attention to those pages in Foster that should allow Ellis's testimony. "Loose words," Foster wrote, could not of themselves constitute treason, nor represent an overt act necessary to prove treason, but they might be accepted as evidence "quo animo," that is, of an intent to commit treason as to which an overt act would have been independently established.

McKean needed no more. The abbreviated official report of the trial appearing in the first volume of Dallas's reports, which covers only the legal issues that arose, has the chief justice acceding to Wilson's proposition that treason couldn't be founded on an unsuccessful attempt at recruitment. He nevertheless accepted Foster's authority almost word for word, stating that Ellis's testimony, though not directly probative of treason, should be allowed to show "quo animo," or the motive the prisoner might have had in joining the British army. Mary Smith had thus laid the necessary groundwork for this ruling by testifying to an overt act of treason that Roberts committed in acting first as a guide and then as a consultant to the British.[28]

Today, during such an exchange on a contested evidentiary matter, the jury would be excused from the courtroom so as not to hear in the course of argument the substance of testimony that the court might decide to exclude. Almost certainly the jury listened to this give-and-take about Roberts's having persuaded others to serve in the British army.[29] With the benefit of the introduction they got, John Ellis's testimony, once they heard it, could have struck the members of the jury as tepid and anticlimactic. Ellis began by setting the scene on Strawberry Alley in Philadelphia, in a tavern that both McKean and the Quaker note-taker heard him identify as "Moyers." Strawberry Alley exists today as Strawberry Street, running between Market and Chestnut a few steps west of Second Street. At that time "nearly every dwelling upon the Market street end of the passage was either a tavern or a lodging house," and "Moyers" was probably "Myers" for Benjamin Myers was then the proprietor of the long-established Bull's Head, the chief public house in Strawberry Alley, which in the early days of the Revolution had the reputation of being a Tory establishment.[30]

It is not inconceivable that this John Ellis, who had known the defendant "very well" for five or six years but who happened by chance, in his telling, to enter a Philadelphia tavern during the British occupation, would later that year curry favor with the Whigs back in power by acting as a levying officer and seizing property from Quakers who declined to pay fines for militia service. The John Ellis who testified at the trial said that Roberts pitched a soft-sell message in the Strawberry Alley barroom to various hangers-on, "some of them," in Ellis's description, "very full of liquor." As an assist to Captain James, the British recruiting officer, Ellis quoted Roberts saying, "[I]t is a fine corps Lads, if you have a mind to inlist." A Lieutenant Vernon then turned to Ellis, remarking that he seemed like a stranger sitting by himself and that, if he would enlist, Vernon guaranteed that he would be "quartermaster to the Troop," a proposal that Ellis testified Roberts seconded by saying that "it is a very good offer, if you have a mind to engage, I don't know how you could better yourself." Whether those lined up at the bar were "full of liquor" or not, nobody stepped forward as a volunteer, and Ellis, by his own admission, having "no intention to engage," left.[31]

The trial notes are silent on who Captain James and Lieutenant Vernon were, other than recruiting officers for the British. In the tight community of Philadelphia during the Revolution, the court and the jury did not need background information concerning these two notorious Tories. Jacob James was an innkeeper in Goshen Township, Chester County, who joined the British as a guide the day after the Battle of Brandywine and headed a troop of cavalry for the British known as the Chester County Light Dragoons. Rumored to have been active in kidnapping prominent Whigs during the British occupation of Philadelphia, James joined other loyalist émigrés taking refuge in Canada after the war. Lieutenant Vernon was probably Nathaniel Vernon, Jr., the son of a former sheriff of Chester County of the same name. Both father and son were branded traitors; the younger Vernon served under James in the Chester County Light Dragoons and continued on in British service until the surrender at Yorktown. Both Vernons also settled in Canada after the war. Given their Chester County connections, neither of the two men wearing British uniforms in the tavern in Strawberry Alley would have been a stranger to John Roberts; on the contrary, there is every likelihood that either Jacob James or the elder Vernon was instrumental in persuading him to leave Lower Merion and go to British-occupied Philadelphia that winter.[32]

Ann Davis, the third witness for the prosecution, testified that she knew John Roberts well and that, when in early April she was detained on suspicion in leaving Philadelphia and taken before a Tory magistrate, she sought Roberts's support as a character witness in her application for bail. That was a mistake on her part, for Roberts proceeded to tell the examining magistrate, one Potts, that her whole family, including "even the Mother," was a bunch of "Rebels" who had made off with cattle. She and her sister had both been arrested but were subsequently released on bail thanks to a James Harris. She conceded in apparent cross-examination that Roberts was not present when the British had plundered clothes from her family, abusive treatment that led to the unfortunate trip to Philadelphia.[33]

Michael Smith took the stand briefly to confirm the long-standing animosity between himself and the accused. Pressed at the end of his testimony, he admitted that, unlike his wife, "he never saw the prisoner with the British Army."[34]

Andrew Fisher, a farmer living in Blockley, two miles closer to the city than the farm Michael Smith worked, testified next. Erased as a separate township in the municipal consolidation of 1854, Blockley encompassed at its high-water mark a sizable area west of the Schuylkill River and north to the Lower Merion Township line. It was from their departure point at the Middle Ferry and thence northward along the Lancaster Road that Cornwallis and his troops marched on the foraging expedition of December 11, 1777, landing hard in their first progress on Blockley's inhabitants.

One morning during the previous fall, Fisher told the jury that he saw Roberts on horseback with the British army moving toward Gulph Mill and Roberts's house. He couldn't be precise about the month, but he knew it was in the morning, between seven and eight o'clock. In the chief justice's notes, he testified about the losses he suffered at the hands of the British: "5 cows, 9 sheep, £ 9 hard money, £ 50 Congress-money & some linen." A soldier threatened him with a gun, saying that he and his sons were rebels. Subsequently, four or five weeks later, Fisher was imprisoned in the "Old Jail" in Philadelphia, where a Frederick Vernor was in charge and where Roberts came "to look for Friends." In these jailhouse encounters, "he was very often at Mr Roberts to help him out," but the only reply he got was that his release depended on persuading his two sons to leave the Rebel army and turn themselves in. After seven months in jail, he was exchanged for a prisoner held by the Americans.[35]

When Michael Groves and Edward Stroud approached the witness stand, the defense made a second attempt to block potentially damaging testimony. Groves, as a turnkey in the Walnut Street Jail, and Stroud, as a city constable, were presumably both newly installed (or reinstalled) in those positions and beholden to the powers that be. Each of them had also been in Whig employ as a paid express rider at the end of 1776—Stroud going in November "to Lancaster, York & Carlisle to order the Militia to march to this City [Philadelphia]," and Groves in December "to call the Militia, & hasten their March to join General Washington."[36]

The issue was the admissibility of what purported to be Roberts's incriminating confession given in the presence of Groves and Stroud. James Wilson cited ancient English authority to the effect that no man should be convicted of treason except by the testimony of two witnesses to an overt act or by his confession freely given in open court, an evidentiary standard that Wilson would later be responsible for incorporating in the definition of treason in the United States Constitution (article 3, section 3). As far as confessions were concerned, he contended that the Pennsylvania Assembly in the recently enacted treason statute had abolished confessions of every kind and quality as the basis for a treason conviction.

This time it was the defense that relied on Sir Michael Foster and his treatise. Foster recognized, albeit hesitantly, the necessity of barring out-of-court confessions "made to persons having no authority to examine" as being "the weakest and most suspicious of all evidence." He enumerated a series of problems posed by such confessions that Roberts's counsel clearly had to worry about in the testimony of Groves and Stroud:

> Proof may be too easily procured, words are often mis-reported, whether
> through ignorance, inattention, or malice, it mattereth not to the defendant,
> he is equally affected in either case; and they are extremely liable to mis-
> construction: and withal, this evidence is not, in the ordinary course of things,
> to be disproved by that sort of evidence, by which the proof of plain facts may
> be and often is confronted.

Undeterred by Foster's cautionary advice, Reed countered, as recorded in
McKean's notes, that "A dozen judges have settled this Point—Confessions
may be given in evidence to corroborate other proofs of overt acts by two
witnesses," and without counting judicial heads precisely, language may also
be found in Foster supporting Reed in his rejoinder.[37]

The defense won another Pyrrhic victory. McKean agreed with Wilson that
proving a confession in the manner proposed was contrary to the statute, but
he ruled that the otherwise inadmissible confession might supply corroborative
evidence of the independently established overt act of Roberts's joining the
enemy army. Once again, after having listened to these arguments, pro and
con, the jury may have been disappointed in hearing the testimony that
followed from Groves and Stroud about Roberts's statements at the Middle
Ferry tavern. It also bears noting that what Groves and Stroud have Roberts
spilling forth about his attempt to procure the rescue of his fellow Quakers
by enlisting General Howe in the mission does not line up with the more
nebulous (and sinister) confession attributed to him in the report of the case
published twelve years later. In Dallas's 1790 version, the substance of Roberts's
confession that the defense resisted disclosing was to the effect "that he was
going to the Head of the Elk, in order to communicate some information to
Mr. Galloway, who had, at that time, gone over to the enemy."[38]

With a mobility that might have raised a question about where the witness's
own loyalty lay, Groves told of floating freely between the city and the outlying
districts during the British occupation. He frequently saw Roberts "examining
people in the market [in Philadelphia]" and yet remained on friendly enough
terms with the prisoner to testify of his own knowledge that the latter repeatedly
expressed support for the British cause. But, on cross-examination, he admitted
that he never saw the prisoner in arms or marching with the enemy. Nor, he
said, did he ever have any dispute with Roberts—a possibility that counsel
may have explored in cross-examination since he and others were partners with
Roberts in a fishing company that maintained a "sein[e]" on the Schuylkill.[39]

Chief Justice McKean devoted barely any space in his notes to Edward
Stroud's testimony; in any event, it was far short of what the Quaker note-
taker set forth. His terse entry, "Says the very same with Michael Groves," was
accurate enough as borne out in the longer Quaker account. Stroud was also
a member of the fishing company partnership, but, like Groves before him,
he denied that he had any quarrel or difference with Roberts relating to that

business. Anticipating that Joseph Pritchard would soon follow as a witness for the defense, Stroud volunteered a picture of Pritchard as being present but "so much intoxicated as not to be able to stand straight."[40]

In two respects, however, McKean's notes improved on the Quaker record. The chief justice made the notation beside Stroud's name that Stroud, alone among the witnesses the prosecution called, elected to affirm the truth of what he would testify to, suggesting that this witness may have retained a residual Quaker hesitancy about oath-taking. Second, the chief justice recorded that Stroud began by saying that he had known the prisoner for twenty years, a longer period of acquaintance than any of the prior witnesses claimed, which leads one to wonder what the relationship might have been between the two of them, presumably close to the same age, that ended in this hostile testimony.[41]

Strouds are absent from Lower Merion at that time, although, in the 1750s, two Edward Strouds, father and son, members of the Gwynedd Monthly Meeting, may be located in Whitemarsh Township across the Schuylkill River. An Edward Stroud appears in the first Philadelphia city directory of 1785 on Catharine Street, but not in subsequent directories or in the 1790 census. Nor is there any sign in Philadelphia of an Edward Stroud having a Quaker connection.[42]

What we know about the person of that name who testified against Roberts would be hard to square with Quaker principles. In the warrant for commitment issued against Roberts on July 27, 1778, at the instigation of Michael Smith and his wife, prospective witnesses were named and summoned on their recognizance to give evidence at his trial, subject to the penalty payment in each instance of fifty pounds for failing to do so. "Edward Stroud City Constable" was among those thus identified. As a matter of fact, he held the position of constable in September of the prior year when he personally served a summons on that resolute Quaker Samuel Rowland Fisher, requiring Fisher to come before a magistrate and answer for the expenditure of a sum necessary to find a substitute to serve in the militia for Fisher. Stroud appears in the detailed Quaker accounting of losses sustained by members of the Philadelphia Monthly Meeting as a levying constable who seized personal property of Friends, in the months of August and September 1778, for noncompliance with the requirements of the Revolutionary government. Take as one such example the seizure on August 5 by Stroud and John Alexander of the following property belonging to Samuel Coates for failure to pay a substitute fine of £29.17.6: a mahogany pier table; a window chair; a pair of andirons, tongs, and a shovel; and a looking glass.[43]

The Edward Stroud who half-heartedly echoed the testimony of Michael Groves may have repented his doing so. Although the existence of more than one Edward Stroud in Philadelphia cannot be ruled out, an Edward Stroud did join in a petition requesting that the Supreme Executive Council grant a reprieve to Carlisle and Roberts and take "such further Measures as may, agreeable to the Constitution be necessary to obtain Pardon to the said Prisoners." If this was the same Edward Stroud of the trial, he had come to the judgment, late in the day, not just that Roberts's life should be spared, but that he should be pardoned.[44]

The prosecution rested its case after Stroud testified. It would have been understandable had Roberts's lawyers felt encouraged both by what they had heard and by what they had not heard in the courtroom. For someone who had left his home and family to take refuge in Philadelphia during all nine months of the British occupation of the city, with time on his hands and ample opportunity to be seen in the wrong company, only seven witnesses had come forward to implicate Roberts in questionable conduct. In contrast, eleven witnesses appeared for the prosecution in Abraham Carlisle's trial concluded just a few days before, unequivocally identifying him as a guard issuing passes during the British occupation. Carlisle's defense also suffered from the introduction of a paper written by Joseph Galloway, certifying that Carlisle was "a person appointed by the Commander in Chief to superintend one of the Passes." No such commission was proved for Roberts.[45]

Over objection, John Ellis had been permitted to testify about a tavern conversation in which he reported that Roberts had meekly seconded a recruiting effort by a British officer that yielded no volunteers among the inebriated. Over renewed objection, Groves and Stroud had been permitted to testify about another tavern conversation in which Roberts allegedly poured out at length to a large group the convoluted tale of setting off more than six months earlier to persuade General Howe to dispatch light horse, under Roberts's own implausible command, in an attempt to rescue exiled Quaker pacifists, by force of arms if necessary.

George Ross confidently argued at the conclusion of the Commonwealth's evidence that such futile efforts did not provide a basis for finding his client guilty of treason, punishable by death: "Being barely seen in Philadelphia or with the British army is not treason, he [Roberts] ought to have been concerned in some act of hostility."[46]

III

The Defense

Despite the argued thinness of the case against him, Roberts remained in serious danger because of the testimony of Mary Smith. Overwrought though she may have been on the witness stand, Mary Smith put Roberts squarely in the saddle during the British foraging expedition in December when he refused, she said, to respond to her cry for aid. Andrew Fisher also saw Roberts on horseback with the British at that time. There were thus two witnesses who had testified to the overt act of Roberts's having apparently joined the enemy in a hostile operation against his countrymen. Mary Smith, Andrew Fisher, and Ann Davis sounded another theme, and that was Roberts's intervening to their prejudice when they sought relief from the authorities in occupied Philadelphia. Mary Smith and Andrew Fisher both said that he conditioned any assistance he might give on the willingness of other members of their families to abandon the American cause and turn themselves in to the British. The cumulative effect of this testimony could not be left unrebutted.

Counsel representing Roberts had some difficult decisions to make in constructing an effective defense for their client. The key in their effort to save him was to cast doubt on an essential element of a criminal offense, which is the intent to commit the crime charged. The indictment alleged such an intent when it set forth in archaic language that Roberts acted "with all his might intending the Peace and tranquility of this Commonwealth of Pennsylvania to disturb," and further "in pursuance and execution of such his wicked & traiterous [sic] intentions and purposes."[1] During the prosecution's case Chief Justice McKean admitted dubious evidence against Roberts, ostensibly not for its inherent factual value of proving that he had sought to recruit soldiers for the British or that he had dashed off to enlist General Howe in a harebrained scheme to rescue the Virginia-bound Quaker exiles, but rather to establish, in the term borrowed from Foster's treatise, "quo animo," with what intent or motive Roberts had acted. Now it was the defense's turn to pursue that very question and to convince the jury that Roberts lacked any settled, consistent intent to commit treason. Although it was indisputable that he had accompanied the British when they moved aggressively against the residents of Blockley and Lower Merion in December of the previous year, it remained open to the defense to prove that he had been forced to do so against his will and under the threat of bodily harm.

In attacking the character and credibility of the Smiths and Andrew Fisher, the prosecution's star witnesses whose testimony was so damaging to Roberts, his lawyers had to ask themselves whether that tactic might backfire by alienating members of the jury who looked upon them as people of modest means, true patriots steadfastly committed to supporting the Revolution, whose sons had taken up arms in the American cause. Nor could they neglect considering the character and liabilities of the witnesses who were prepared to testify on Roberts's behalf. Would the jurors be inclined to credit what they said, or would they dismiss their testimony as coming from those who, it was well known, had ties to the British?

There was another aspect to the issue of intent in developing a defense that did not find precise definition in the law books. It lay in an attempt to show how Roberts's conduct during all of this period was confused and vacillating, the opposite of what one would expect of a convinced traitor. As often as not, Roberts befriended patriots in need of help, or provided a safe overnight stop at his house for American officers operating in the no-man's land of Lower Merion when the British occupied Philadelphia. The hope had to be that the jurors would personally identify with Roberts's shifts and hesitancies. After all, in Revolutionary Pennsylvania, the "King's friends" were not a rigidly demarcated class apart. As a student of the loyalist phenomenon has written, "One of the prime features of Pennsylvania Loyalism (and chief reason for its feebleness) is its equivocal, neutral, and, it must be argued, sometimes subtle nature. A striking number of Pennsylvanians did not know which way to turn."[2]

When it later came time to sentence Roberts, McKean discarded all pretense of the impartiality of the presiding judge, but even so he felt compelled to take notice of this particular defense—and a weakness at the heart of it. "It is true, and I mention it with pleasure that your interest with the Commander in Chief of the British Army was frequently employ'd in acts of humanity, charity, and benevolence. This must afford you some comfort, and your friends some consolation; but a good General should have done the same thing to a vanquish'd Army, and they can by no means compensate for Treason."[3] It will become apparent during this phase of the trial how Roberts's benevolence was a double-edged sword that only someone having influence with the British command might wield.

One option Roberts's counsel could not pursue. Even if John Roberts's own testimony would have helped his case, Messrs. Wilson, Ross, and Lewis were prevented under a long-standing exclusionary rule from calling him as a witness, or, by extension of that rule, anybody related to him, like his wife or children.

We need not explore here the historical basis for excluding the testimony of an interested party, a prohibition that gave way as the means available to prosecution and defense in the conduct of a criminal case became more evenly balanced. It will be sufficient to observe that the rule, often eroded in practice, remained in effect in England until finally abolished by parliament in 1898, and in Pennsylvania until the enactment of a statute in 1885 eliminated the last vestige of it. The tension between two contradictory rules of evidence, one excluding the defendant's testimony in court and the other admitting hearsay testimony about what he supposedly said out of court, was glaringly apparent when Michael Groves and Edward Stroud collaborated in their story of Roberts's confession at the Middle Ferry tavern.[4]

Wilson and his colleagues recruited twenty-seven witnesses to testify on Roberts's behalf, far outdistancing in number the witnesses who had appeared for the prosecution. It was a mixed lot consisting of several neighbors of Roberts who qualified as ordinary people, officers in the American army, two lawyers, tradesmen, a retired silversmith, an innkeeper, a printer, four women, and a judicious sprinkling of Quakers, some of whom the defense had no choice but to call so as to contradict the prosecution's witnesses on vital points. Unlike the witnesses called by the prosecution, the jury and the two judges presiding at the trial would have had no trouble in recognizing many of these witnesses when they took the stand.

The first witness for the defense was Daniel Clymer, the cousin of the more famous George Clymer, but a patriot and person of prestige in his own right. Chief Justice McKean, in his notes, carefully added "Esquire" after Clymer's name in recognition of his standing as a member of the bar. He graduated in 1766 from the College of New Jersey, read law, and entered into a successful legal career that would be temporarily suspended during the Revolution when he moved through the officer ranks of the militia to become, as Colonel Clymer, deputy commissary general of prisoners in 1777. Careful and calculating by nature, he did not enjoy an untainted record among Quakers who had dealings with him. The part he played in Roberts's tragedy is a complicated one in which his motives remain obscure.[5]

Forced to leave hastily as the British approached Philadelphia in September 1777, Clymer ran a newspaper advertisement after the British left the city to recover a list of articles missing from his house on Market Street; the items ranged from an eight-day clock made by Owen Biddle to four beds and nine family pictures. He offered a reward to any person or persons who voluntarily came forward with the missing articles, but he also warned in lawyer's language that anybody found in possession of the unreturned property would be dealt with sternly as a pillager.[6]

The Quaker observer at the trial failed to record Clymer's testimony in the summary he was preparing. The failure to do so could have been because

Clymer's appearance as the first witness called by the defense came as a last-minute surprise. His testimony, when given, seemed strangely out of sequence in view of the priority concern of Roberts's lawyers to neutralize the testimony of Mary Smith and Andrew Fisher. Yet he did introduce a completely new element in the proceeding that threw light on Roberts's confused state of mind during the closing months of 1777.

On January 2, 1778, at Valley Forge George Washington gave Clymer, as the American army's commissary general of prisoners, written "permission to pass to Philadelphia with twelve head of Cattle, Thirty two Barrels of Flour, and a parcel of Baggage for the use of American prisoners there."[7] The American prisoners of war, ill treated and starving, were detained in the Walnut Street prison (the "New Gaol"), where they were worse off than the troops at Valley Forge. Clymer said that Roberts, seeing him at the prison, asked to speak to Clymer alone. Initially concerned that their conversation might be overheard by Mr. Ferguson—the British commissary of prisoners and the husband of the hapless Elizabeth Graeme Ferguson—they were able to withdraw and confer in private. Roberts told Clymer that he regretted having stayed in Philadelphia but that "he was afraid to return home on acct of some of his neighbours." In admitting that he had served as a guide conducting Lord Cornwallis to the Gulph Mill the month before, he nevertheless insisted that he was forced to do so. If he had had his own way, he told Clymer that he would have remained strictly neutral.[8]

What Clymer next related came totally out of the blue. As Congress and other governmental officials were scrambling to leave Philadelphia at the end of September a year earlier, the journals of the Continental Congress, containing highly confidential information, came close to being seized by the enemy. Roberts confided in this prison interview that he had been asked to take possession of the journals and to transport them to his plantation where they were buried for safekeeping. He requested Clymer to inform George Washington of this secret operation lest the journals now fall into British hands. Upon his return to Valley Forge, Clymer told Washington about the buried journals, and as a consequence, they were safely retrieved from Roberts's property. If McKean heard correctly, "some things belonging to ws.," meaning Clymer, were also recovered from Roberts's property, which leads one to ask how they got there in the first place. The crucial point the defense wanted to establish through Clymer was that, only three weeks earlier during the foraging expedition, Roberts had refrained from telling the British about the location of the journals and that he therefore had continued to safeguard material of value to the Americans. Before Clymer stepped down as a witness, he acknowledged the welcome Roberts and his wife extended to American officers who were able to stay safely overnight at his house, without fear of disclosure to the British forces in the immediate neighborhood.[9]

Clymer's testimony about the buried journals differs in some respects from another account of their recovery provided by James Lovell, a distracted member of Congress from Massachusetts. Lovell would eventually be forced to admit that he had entrusted the journals, at the very last moment in September, to a neighbor of Roberts, the papermaker Frederick Bicking. For an extended period thereafter, Lovell proceeded to forget what he had done, or had failed to do. On December 31, 1777, he finally got up his courage to send a letter to Washington at Valley Forge in which he struggled to explain how Bicking, "an honest timorous Man," had turned to Roberts, "a Tory," to transport the journals and the type used to print them to a hiding place that Bicking designated. Would it not now be prudent, Lovell sheepishly inquired of Washington, to dispatch "some active Pennsylvania officer, who, being acquainted with the Spot of Ground mentioned, will take a proper speedy method of gaining the Journals & forward them to Lancaster or York"? Washington wrote in reply to Lovell on January 9, informing him that the journals, but not the type, had been found "without difficulty" by "a Gentleman well acquainted with the ground and the Inhabitants in the vicinity" and forwarded to York under close escort. Whether recovery of the journals was accomplished in response to Lovell's tardy communication or as a result of Clymer's prompt delivery of Roberts's message, and whether the journals were secreted on Roberts's plantation or Bicking's, are questions that matter less than Roberts's sense of discretion and his apparent desire not to jeopardize the American cause.[10]

Five witnesses followed Clymer in rapid order, all of whom resided in the Welsh Tract. If Clymer's testimony seemed out of sequence in the logical development of the case for the defense, Isaac Warner, John Zell, Jesse Thomas, David Zell, and Jacob Jones were all called for a particular and essential purpose. All five of them, of Quaker origin, declined to swear to the truthfulness of what they would testify. Once they qualified as affirming witnesses, they each had the same message to deliver: Michael Smith and his wife were a troublesome pair, of notoriously bad character, whose testimony should not be believed.

John and David Zell were doubtless related, probably as father and son. Thanks to a newspaper advertisement John Zell ran, it is possible to locate his property in Lower Merion near the Black Horse Tavern on the Lancaster Road, midway between the Smiths and Andrew Fisher. Based again on newspaper advertisements, we know that he had bad luck in losing two runaway servants: one a Scottish girl named Martha M'Loud, "about 18 years of age, a likely well set person, of a fair complexion" who was last seen wearing "good clothes, of British manufacture"; and the second, the less regrettable loss of "a Dutch woman who spoke broken English," described in unflattering detail as "middle sized, round faced, yellow complexion, thick lips, round shoulders, brown hair, intermixed with white, and bald on the top of her head, a small short thumb on her right hand, large lumps on her big toe joints, much addicted to lying." David Zell, who served in the American army during the Revolution in the same battalion as Michael Smith, Jr., appears to have enjoyed the special distinction of having married his wife on July 4, 1776, in Philadelphia. John Zell died in 1796, and was buried in the graveyard of the Merion meeting, where David Zell followed him thirty years later.[11]

Jesse Thomas was a blacksmith, slightly more prosperous than the Zells to judge by entries in the tax assessor's book for 1780. Jacob Jones was a wealthy farmer who, when he died at the ripe old age of ninety-seven in 1810, generously endowed in his will a school for the education of as many poor and orphan children as possible; his academy would be the precursor of common or public schools in Lower Merion. Colonel Isaac Warner was a member of a well-known first family that had settled in Blockley Township, and an officer in the American army whom his fellow Quakers disowned for serving in the military. As the first of these five to take the witness stand, he added heightened color to the portrait painted of Michael Smith when McKean records him as saying that "Michael Smith lived near him this winter [and was] a warm, hot-tempered, rash man."[12]

These witnesses were close neighbors. They had made common cause together during the turbulent summer of 1777. Three dozen inhabitants of Lower Merion and Blockley Townships petitioned Thomas Wharton, Jr., president of the Supreme Executive Council, to come to their rescue and order the removal of the battalion from the State of Georgia under the command of Colonel John White. The troops, encamped in that area, showed, in the words of the petition, an "aversion for all Law, Divine or Human" by their "Robbing the Neighborhood of everything they could lay their hands on." When protests were lodged, "they, with the most unparalleled impudence, would threaten the lives of the Complainants or their Houses with fire." The petitioners were especially concerned that the marauding troops might deprive them of their principal crop, Indian Corn, which was "drawing to a State of maturity." Those who signed the petition included the two Zells, Jacob Jones, Jesse Thomas, and a John Roberts. That a broad segment of the population, not just Quakers, had suffered from the presence of the Georgia troops is borne out by the added name of Michael Smith, who affixed his mark to the petition. Four months later the tables would be turned, at least for Michael Smith and his family, who were victims of pillaging by the British army.[13]

The defense gambled that the next witness it called, Joseph Pritchard, might undermine the testimony of Groves and Stroud. A little more than a year later Pritchard occupied a cell in the Old Gaol where Roberts and Carlisle had been imprisoned. A jury had found him guilty of misprision of treason "for having been employed by the Brittish [sic] when in this City to attend at the Middle ferry on Schuylkill to inspect all persons going in and out of the City & was also charged with having since used words derogatory of the present Rulers." Such was the report of his cellmate then and for most of the next two years, Samuel Rowland Fisher. Through Fisher one may take measure of Pritchard's temperament and attitude toward the "present Rulers." At his trial in "what they call the Supreme Court," Fisher contemptuously wrote, he was excoriated by McKean on several counts, including having served as a "Spy for the Quakers." Later visited by George Duffield, a Presbyterian minister, who conveyed a message from Joseph Reed, then president of the executive council (and also a Presbyterian), that he would be released only if he consented to go "within the Enemie's [sic] Lines (meaning New York)," Pritchard shot back that "he thought he already was within his Enemy's Lines." In relying on Pritchard, Roberts's lawyers were clearly taking a risk of his saying too much or antagonizing the court.[14]

Pritchard may also have had Quaker antecedents, for he, too, chose to affirm rather than to swear at the commencement of his testimony. He didn't dispute the testimony of Groves and Stroud that John Roberts was present at a large gathering in a tavern near the Schuylkill in the spring of that year. The tavern, possibly known as the Old Fish, was owned by Joseph Ogden, who prior to the Revolution controlled traffic back and forth at the Middle Ferry under a lease granted by the proprietors. Located north of Market Street on the west side of the river, Ogden's tavern would have stood approximately where the central railroad station in Philadelphia is today. In 1787 a newspaper advertisement offered for rent a "neat stone House, situate on the west side of the Schuylkill, adjoining the Middle-ferry," licensed as a tavern, with interested parties directed to: "Mr. *Joseph Ogden*, at the Middle ferry."[15]

According to Pritchard, on an evening either in April or as late as the beginning of May, a group of about fifteen people assembled in the barroom following a day when Roberts and nine others having an interest with him in the "Seine" or fishing company had been out on the Schuylkill fishing. This was the first time, Pritchard testified, that the fishing company had met since a difference had arisen some six weeks earlier between Roberts, on the one hand, and Stroud and Groves, on the other, "respecting their Seine & fishery." As for Roberts's supposedly confiding to the barroom audience the abortive attempt he made to rescue the banished Friends on their way to exile in Virginia, Pritchard had no recollection of any such disclosure, which, in "mixed company," he thought Roberts would have been too prudent to make. By "mixed company," Pritchard must certainly have meant to include Groves and Pritchard, both of whom, as we have seen, had been in patriot service at one time or another. In concluding his testimony, Pritchard labeled the general character of Stroud and Groves as bad and "deficient in veracity."

The chief justice for one was far from persuaded; he inserted in the notes he was taking that both Stroud and Groves had previously described Pritchard as being "very much in liquor." If he intended the notation as a reminder to himself when it came time to charge the jury, McKean would nevertheless have realized that, whatever his own opinion might be about a witness's truth-telling, it was up to the jury to resolve issues of credibility.[16]

Of the numerous witnesses called by the defense, more than a few acted as proxies for the prisoner in reporting on conversations he had with them which he was not permitted to confirm by his own testimony. Eight witnesses who had served in the American army in one rank or another were of particular value in this respect. They testified that Roberts had made his house available as a secure overnight stop for American officers; that he voiced his regret to them about leaving home and entering Philadelphia; that he tried to shake loose from the hold of the British, especially during the fateful foraging expedition of December 11; and that he intervened in attempts to alleviate the distress of many who were victimized by the British forces. In the post-trial petition ten of the jurors submitted requesting clemency for Roberts, they highlighted the contradictory character of the evidence they heard, some parts of which were not reconcilable "with his general conduct." How else to explain, for example, that a person accused of betraying his country would offer his house as a safe haven for officers serving in its army?[17]

Colonel Thomas Proctor was one of the army witnesses whom the defense called, but largely for the sake of appearance. Of combustible temper, a carpenter by trade who had immigrated to Pennsylvania from Ireland, Proctor took the initiative in organizing an artillery company as early as 1775. By all accounts, he fought bravely in the Battles of Brandywine and Germantown. In 1780 he stood trial before a court martial on multiple charges of fraud; among other allegations, he was accused of "mustering men in his regiment as soldiers, who were not actually doing the duty of soldiers, and returning them on command, whilst doing the duty of servants, in his and other families in the city of Philadelphia." In spite of his acquittal and the statement of his commander-in-chief that this was another instance "where personal pique has given birth to prosecutions as unjust as they are indelicate and improper," he may still have been smarting from this experience when he resigned his army commission a year later—reportedly because of serious differences he had with Joseph Reed, the prosecutor in Roberts's trial who became the president of the Supreme Executive Council. For a three-year period in the 1780s, Proctor served as the high sheriff of Philadelphia.

The little he contributed on the witness stand in Roberts's trial was to testify that, when accompanying Daniel Clymer under a flag of truce in early January, he stopped at the house of John Roberts, whom he didn't know personally and who, he understood, was then away in Philadelphia. While Proctor stayed the first night in Governor Penn's house on the outskirts of the city, he spent the second night at Roberts's where, he was assured, he would be in no danger. Evidently the word had circulated among officers in the American army that Roberts's house provided a safe lodging for them.[18]

In a cameo appearance that followed, Miers Fisher dismissed out-of-hand any possibility that Roberts had proposed to the Quakers confined in the Masonic Lodge, of whom Fisher was one, that they might be rescued by force, if necessary, on their way to exile in Virginia. He never knew or heard of such an idea until Roberts appeared before McKean on his request for bail, at which time the Commonwealth presumably outlined the principal elements in its case against him. As a respected lawyer, Miers Fisher deserved better treatment in the courtroom than McKean now accorded him. When a delegate to the First Continental Congress meeting in Philadelphia in 1774, John Adams was more appreciative of Fisher as a lawyer and his host. Adams recorded in his diary that he had been invited to dinner at the house of Miers Fisher, "a young Quaker and a lawyer. We saw his library, which is clever. But this plain Friend, and his plain, though pretty wife, with her thees and her thous, had provided us the most costly entertainment." Included in that lavish dinner party was "a large collection of lawyers," who held forth on the practice of the law in the different provinces and the limits of parliamentary jurisdiction; among the guests taking part in the conversation were Thomas McKean and Joseph Reed.[19]

John Chaloner was a merchant on the rise before the Revolution and a prosperous one afterward. Six months after the Roberts trial, he publicly aligned himself with eighty-one other members of the Republican Society like James Wilson, George Ross, and Robert Morris, who announced in the press their opposition to the Pennsylvania constitution of 1776 as trading one tyrannical system of government for another. Earlier Chaloner had the unenviable double assignment as the American army's assistant commissary for purchases to find scarce supplies for the troops at Valley Forge and to provision the soldiers captured by the British and imprisoned in Philadelphia. Chaloner testified that he had stayed at Roberts's house more than once, and on one occasion with "Colo Bodenot and several other Officers," the same Colonel Boudinot who would come under fire for representing Roberts at his hearing in August. He had gone under a flag to Philadelphia in the middle of January to deliver supplies to the American prisoners, much as Clymer had done a week or so before. On his way back he met Roberts at the Middle Ferry (he may have known Roberts in the past, for the recognition seemed immediate), whereupon Roberts quizzed him on whether Chaloner thought he might be permitted to return home. Chaloner poured cold water on the idea, telling Roberts that it was widely believed that he had served as a guide to the British army. Roberts maintained that he did so only under duress and that he had come to the city in the first place "because his brother millers had been taken up, & confined without a hearing, & Some of his illdisposed neighbours had threatened to take him up also."[20]

McKean's trial notes and the Quaker record are in conflict on the final part of Chaloner's testimony, demonstrating that two people listening to the same witness may hear different things. McKean has Chaloner saying that, on the day the British army crossed the Schuylkill, Chaloner and Mr. Lawrence, the Judge Advocate General, were given lodging that night at Robert's house, as well as hay for their horses. With the British on the rampage in that neighborhood, it would have been a strange and hazardous time for two American officers to find themselves adrift in Lower Merion. The Quaker version has Chaloner testifying that this hospitality was provided "on the day our Army crossed the Schuylkil [sic] to meet the Enemy near the White horse." The signal event on December 11 was the British crossing of the Schuylkill that resulted in an initial engagement on the Lancaster Road at the Black Horse, not the White Horse, Tavern, and yet it could have been McKean who misunderstood if Chaloner was referring to an earlier crossing of the Schuylkill by the American army in September of that year when the White Horse Tavern in Chester County became a destination and when Roberts in person would have welcomed Chaloner and Lawrence and declined payment for the hay their horses were fed.[21]

The defense next turned to Susanna Jones, the wife of Owen Jones (Figure 3.1), the elder, to lend substance to what, if convincingly established, might have amounted to a valid legal excuse—that Roberts had been forced against his will to serve as a guide. It was in their house on Market Street that Roberts stayed the previous winter during most of the British occupation. She recalled that, twice in the early hours of December 11 (she stumbled over the date), Roberts had been summoned out of bed to accompany Lord Cornwallis and his raiding party, and that, after first protesting, he relented when "a numb[e]r of Light horse were drawn up before the door." Upon his return from the foraging expedition, he told Mrs. Jones that, kept under strict guard "as soon as he got on the Bridge," he had witnessed scenes of devastation and distress "more than his nature could bear," which he nevertheless did his best to alleviate when he could.

Susanna Jones also sought to help the defense by stating that Roberts had come to the city and taken refuge with her husband and herself "for fear of loss of life from some malicious neighbours, & particularly Mich Smith & wife." Mary Smith had frequently, she testified, relied on Roberts to deliver

Figure 3.1 Silhouette of Owen Jones, Sr. (1711–1793), as cut by Joseph Sansom. For four months during the British occupation of Philadelphia, Roberts lingered as a guest in the house of Owen Jones and his wife on the north side of High (Market) Street between Third and Fourth Streets. Jones had been the provincial treasurer of Pennsylvania before the Revolution.

Reproduced by permission of The Historical Society of Pennsylvania.

money and such things as linen and a great coat to her son in prison, confident that he would carry out the assignment. (When asked during her own testimony whether Roberts had acted in that way for the benefit of her son, Mary Smith had avoided answering the question.)

Owen Jones seconded what his wife said. So often did Roberts assist people employed in the American service that "he was lookt upon [by the British] as an Offender, & troublesom in doing more than he ought to do." Because semantic niceties mattered, Jones contradicted the suggestion, probably by the prosecution in questioning him, that Roberts referred to American soldiers as "Rebels"; Jones never heard him call the contestants in the struggle other than the "American & British Armies."[22]

More witnesses came forward to attest to Roberts's kindness and assistance both during the December 11 raid and generally while he was in Philadelphia. One of them was Philip Syng, Jr., the famous silversmith and a friend of Benjamin Franklin. Syng had moved from Philadelphia to Lower Merion before the Revolution began, acquiring as Roberts's neighbor a forty-acre property and a former tavern on the Lancaster Road in what is now the town of Ardmore. Syng told the jury that "at the time Lord Cornwallis was up the Country John Roberts prevail'd on his Lordship to place a gaurd [in a similar spelling lapse, McKean wrote "centinel"] at his Gate" to ensure that his property was not plundered.[23]

The problem with testimony like this from Syng and from others who similarly chimed in to praise Roberts as protector was that it put him in a position of being able to influence the conduct of the British and even of Lord Cornwallis himself. Consider, for example, the net value to Roberts's defense of John Smith (no relation to Michael Smith), one of several residents of the Welsh Tract who, having served in the militia, were taken prisoners by the British during the raid that began on December 11. He found himself under the same guard as John Roberts, whom, he said, Lord Cornwallis prevented from visiting his family nearby. Smith's testimony permits us to track the movement of the British troops, giving a sense of how deeply the enemy penetrated into this outlying area, ranging well beyond the Mill Creek Valley. If Smith is correct, Roberts would have stayed with the foraging party at least over night, returning to Philadelphia the next day, December 12. (Owen Jones in his testimony may be read as saying that Roberts returned the same day he left.) While together under guard, Roberts repeated to Smith the now-familiar refrain of how the British had pulled him out of bed in the dead of night.

Obviously sympathetic to Roberts, Smith said that Roberts went to Lord Cornwallis and asked for release of prisoners the British had captured whom Roberts identified as peaceable neighbors of his, never connected with the Rebel army. It would have strained credulity for the jury to imagine a mere guide, literally dragooned into service, succeeding in such an application to the commanding officer. John Smith may, however, have been of greater assistance to the defense in contradicting Mary Smith's account of Roberts's having failed to answer her call for help. Chief Justice McKean eliminated from his trial notes John Smith's testimony, of more than incidental value, that, while he was riding alongside Roberts when the British went by "Michael Smith's lane end," they did not stop and that, far from hearing Mary Smith's cries for help, he saw no sign of her or any member of her family. For good measure, John Smith threw in as a closing remark that Michael Smith was "a malicious and spiteful man."[24]

Andrew Murray testified that he had been taken as a prisoner "when the Enemy march'd up the Lancaster Road" and that he was put under the same guard as John Roberts and John Smith. He confirmed Roberts's statement, made to both Smith and Murray, that he had been forced to act as a guide. Roberts also applied three or four times to Cornwallis to procure Murray's release, in spite of the fact that he knew Murray belonged to the Continental army.[25]

The testimony of the next witness for Roberts, Robert Shewell ("Sewell" in McKean's spelling), whether recorded by the Quaker note-taker or by McKean, was of marginal value to the defense. McKean omits from his notes any reference to a Roberts daughter, who, if the Quaker note-taker is relied on, seems to have accompanied her father when he delivered to Shewell on December 29 of the prior year a letter from Captain Hopkins of Colonel Moylan's Light Dragoons. What was then said that might have had any bearing on Roberts's guilt or innocence is open to guesswork. There was in fact a Captain David (not "Stephen" as McKean wrongly inserted) Hopkins of Colonel Stephen Moylan's Light Dragoons stationed at Valley Forge, whom Shewell apparently identified as "a sincere friend" and somebody who "might be trusted," but by whom and for what purpose, we are left to guess. Roberts interjected in the brief conversation with Shewell, as the chief justice recorded it, that he was "forced to go with the army," which represented one more attempt, in the litany of protests attributed to Roberts, to bolster the defense of coercion.[26]

If we have the witness correctly identified, Shewell's reputation was not without its recognizable blemishes. One of several children of Robert and Elizabeth Barton Shewell, Robert Shewell, Jr., became a ship captain who, as the Revolution progressed, sailed close to the prevailing wind. Like Roberts, Shewell stayed in Philadelphia during the British occupation, but as the British were getting ready to leave, he betook himself to Valley Forge to obtain permission for his vessel the *Charming Nancy* to leave Philadelphia with a cargo of contraband, or so it was later alleged. He obtained a pass for the schooner from Benedict Arnold, who, having afterward acquired a share in the cargo, was called to account for his dealings with Shewell and Shewell's shady partners. Acquitted in a 1779 court-martial proceeding of most of the charges brought against him, Arnold nevertheless received a reprimand from Washington for issuing the permit to the *Charming Nancy*, which Washington found "peculiarly reprehensible." While Arnold had already advanced in his plans to betray his country, the commander-in-chief's reprimand because of this affair did nothing but strengthen his resolve.[27]

As the trial moved on, the attention of both the Quaker note-taker and the chief justice began to falter. McKean's patience seems to have worn thin after hearing repetitive testimony from the defense, a reaction it would have been unlike him to conceal in court. In his trial notes, he contented himself with notations like "Nothing to the purpose," or "Ditto," placed beside the names of witnesses. Though less inclined to dismiss what was said, whoever had the responsibility of recording the proceeding for Quaker purposes inexplicably omitted the final three witnesses entirely.

What some of the remaining witnesses were driving at is not always clear, even when more fully reported in the Quaker record. To verify the prisoner's good reputation and good works the defense continued to call a succession of Roberts's neighbors and friends. Though neither a close neighbor nor even an acquaintance of Roberts, it is a pity that William Young was not allowed to testify at greater length. Young, "a man of most 70 years of age" who owned property in Blockley about three miles west of the Schuylkill on the Haverford Road, said in his brief appearance on the stand that he, his son-in-law, and grandsons had been taken prisoner by "Refugees" (meaning loyalists serving in the British army) and succeeded in getting out on parole only through Roberts's compassionate intervention.

Young was much more informative in the clemency petition that he and the other members of his family submitted for Roberts three weeks after the trial. In picturesque language he recounted the two raids that he and his family were victims of. The second one occurred at the end of March when "the Most Hellish Refugees, called Galloways Volunteers" plundered his house and property of everything, with "not a single creature [left] on the place except Dogs & Cats." Galloway had Young marked, in spite of his age, "as one of the most active Rebels in America, a very Dangerous person, who constantly did Inspire & encourage the People to go in their Rebellion, &c, and so did sent him to the old Goal [sic]." Even after his release from jail, Young was forced to stay in the city for the rest of the British occupation. His plea for clemency, joined in by the other members of his family, seemed entirely genuine in its handcrafted simplicity: "As then the said Jo. Roberts has don[e] so much goods to many Prisoners, has thereby even saved the life of several; your Petitioners can also prove, if Required, that he has strongly protested against these wicked Refugees & their wicked actions, and therefore was at last not much any more esteemed as a friend to the king & kings

Government, Neither at Head Quarter nor by Galloway." But handcraftsmanship didn't rule out craftiness, for Young included in his petition a specific reference to the April resolution of Congress recommending the broad granting of pardons: "What a pleasure must it be to every Reasonable man to Read that Resolve of our Honourable Congress, in Recommending to the United States that we wanted Inhabitants in our county, & not to destroy them."[28]

One of these remaining witnesses had an improbable name, which the chief justice put down as "Bostean Ale" and the Quaker reporter as "Sebastian Hall." The witness was, in fact, Sebastian Ale, a resident of Blockley, called to impeach the credibility, again depending on the reporter, of either Andrew Fisher or Michael Smith. McKean has him testifying to a conversation he had with Andrew Fisher in which Fisher told him that, if Roberts would give him a cow, he would not swear against him. In the Quaker version, it is Michael Smith who sought a "good cow," and yet Smith's implacable hostility toward John Roberts makes it very unlikely that he would have been cowed into silence.[29]

Near the end of the list of witnesses for the defense was Robert Aitken, a prominent bookseller and printer who befriended Thomas Paine shortly after Paine's arrival in Philadelphia by hiring him in 1775 as editor of a newly launched publication *The Pennsylvania Magazine; or, American Monthly Museum*. Among his tasks as printer, Aitken had held the commission to print the journals of the Continental Congress. His testimony at the trial dovetailed with that of Daniel Clymer; he told the jury that, at the hurried departure of the Americans from Philadelphia as the British approached the city, Roberts "took care of the Proceedings of the Congress and other things, books, & printing types," while assuring Aitken that "he would be true to his trust," which Aitken believed he had been. Through Aitken we are able to obtain a piece of incidental information that, having little direct bearing on the charges against Roberts, adds to the portrait emerging of a person of divided sympathies, subject to considerable confusion in what he did. Aitken volunteered that Roberts "came to justify himself to the Whig-club—Pelatiah Webster, Walter Shee, &c." That statement of Aitken's, more in the nature of an afterthought, regrettably leaves unanswered tantalizing questions about the Whig Club, including when and where Roberts made his case before its members and what he said in attempted justification of the twists and turns his course had taken.[30]

The last two witnesses for the defense were Mary Miller and Jacob Beary (probably Beery), whom the chief justice alone recorded as testifying. It is not clear what counsel for Roberts, or Roberts himself, hoped to achieve in calling them as witnesses at the end of the trial. With a mere snippet of testimony given for each of them (Mary Miller, for example: "She saw P. at home that day of the battle of Brandywine abt. Sunset—or the evening after"), it appears that the objective may have been to supply Roberts with an alibi by establishing his presence near home at the time of the Battle of Brandywine. Neither of them, however, in the few words that McKean took down, excluded the possibility that Roberts had ridden out to propose to General Howe rescuing the exiled Quakers. Would it not have been the wiser course to forgo their testimony entirely, rather than to require the jury to return, at this climactic moment in the trial, to the strange initiative attributed to Roberts, the subject of his much disputed confession at the Middle Ferry tavern?

A Jacob Beery did live in Haverford Township, Chester County, within relatively easy riding distance of the Brandywine battlefield. Though not possessed of an uncommon name, Mary Miller was probably the widowed proprietress of the Buck Tavern, a popular watering place located on the Chester County line, about two miles southwest of Roberts's property on the Mill Creek. If the trial witness of that name was this Mary Miller, she might indeed have seen Roberts turn up one day, to be followed by General Washington and his troops the next. After Brandywine, the American army had retired to Germantown, but soon moved back across the Schuylkill, passing through Lower Merion on its way westward. Washington's aides issued dispatches from the "Camp at the Buck Tavern on Lancaster Road" on September 14, and at three o'clock in the afternoon of September 15, Washington sent a report from that same location to John Hancock, president of Congress, on various aspects of the fallout from the Brandywine engagement.[31]

The very last person to testify was Llewellyn Young, someone whom the prosecution appears to have called as a rebuttal witness. In all likelihood he commanded as a captain the first company in the same battalion of militia in which Isaac Warner, who had briefly testified for Roberts, served as a colonel. A small farmer in Lower Merion Township, whose property holdings were assessed at a value comparable to that given Michael Smith's, Young testified that he was captured in the days just before the British occupied Philadelphia. While confined in jail, he had a run-in with Roberts, who upbraided him as "a busy meddling fellow," for Young previously had the assignment of collecting fines levied on Quakers who refused to serve in the army. In Young's account of the tense exchange between them, Roberts angrily told Young that a hundred rebels were walking the streets of Philadelphia, whom a tender-hearted General Howe ought to have thrown in prison to keep Young company.[32]

Before the case was submitted to the jury, George Ross, one of the defense lawyers, argued that he and his two colleagues had successfully "got over every charge of treason," but subject to a vulnerability he was forced to concede that remained in the testimony of Michael and Mary Smith and Andrew Fisher, "the only witnesses," Ross said, "to prove the overt act of joining the

Army." As to the reliability of their testimony, while Roberts's lawyers had opened multiple lines of attack, nothing could alter the fact, established by both prosecution and defense witnesses, that Roberts had been seen accompanying the British army during the punitive foraging raid it conducted the previous December in his home territory. William Lewis tried to navigate around that serious exposure in his final argument by returning to the defense contention that Roberts had participated in the December raid only out of fear for his safety, and in making that argument he turned once more to Sir Michael Foster's treatise, which regrettably gave him very little support in the specific reference he made to it. Joseph Reed summed up by saying that Roberts's leaving home and coming into Philadelphia when he did clearly confirmed an intent to side with the British. "Coming from the Country into Philadia, whilst in possession of the enemy, is very different thing," McKean has Reed making the effective point, "from being surprized [sic], or dwelling in Phila. & not having it in their power to remove when the Enemy arrived."[33]

Neither the Quaker record nor McKean's trial notes contain any part of the charge McKean delivered to the members of the jury before they retired to begin their deliberations. In that era it was permissible for a judge to comment on the evidence and its probative value, in an attempt to guide, if not direct, the jury to its verdict. As the eighteenth century drew to a close, judges began limiting their instructions to matters of law, giving the jury the sole responsibility of resolving all factual issues and indeed granting it latitude even as to applicable law.[34]

The few examples that we have of McKean's instructions leave uncertain how far as trial judge he might have gone in trying to influence the jury verdict. His instructions from that period, studded with legal authority, are often difficult to follow. *Respublica v. Chapman*, a 1781 treason trial, illustrates the problem. According to the official reporter, McKean delivered "a learned and circumstantial charge to the jury" on what lawyers and judges refer to as a "nice question" (meaning one not readily disposed of). As judge he had to determine when, in the tumultuous time immediately following the Declaration of Independence, the defendant became, if he ever did, a subject of the Commonwealth of Pennsylvania, sufficient to be convicted of the crime of betraying it. McKean's long-winded exposition seemed tantamount to directing a verdict in favor of the defendant, who had elected to join the British at the very end of 1776 but prior to the time when, in the chief justice's analysis, Pennsylvania had achieved solid enough governmental status to protect its citizens. After laboring to understand what direction McKean was providing in this diffuse charge, the jury had the good sense to return a verdict of acquittal.[35]

In *Respublica v. McCarty*, the chief justice revisited his rulings in the Roberts case three years before. Once more in a treason trial, the court confronted the issue of the admissibility of a confession. This time the confession the accused allegedly made occurred at his arraignment, or as McKean saw it, in open court, thus satisfying the traditional requirement for admitting a confession of treasonable conduct. In a further reprise of the Roberts case, McKean was called on to weigh the strength of McCarty's contention that he had acted out of fear by enlisting "in a corps belonging to the enemy" only after his imprisonment. The instruction that McKean gave the jury on the defense of coerced service in the army of the enemy could not have been substantially different from the one he delivered to the Roberts jury on the same subject. Of McCarty's attempt to rely on the defense, McKean told the jury: "He [McCarty] remained with the *British* troops for ten or eleven months, during which he might easily have accomplished his escape, and it must be remembered, that in the eye of the law, nothing will excuse the act of joining an enemy, but the fear of immediate death." Yet the court's authoritative direction on the law did not prevent the jury from proceeding to acquit McCarty.[36]

When charging the Roberts jury, McKean may, in fact, have left the door open to acquittal. He may even have invited the jurors to consider Roberts's state of mind and the many good works it was testified he performed for others regardless of party affiliation, as bearing on his intent to commit treason.[37] In their petition requesting the judges presiding at the trial to support the plea for clemency on behalf of John Roberts, ten jurors appealed to the sense of "humanity" that the court manifested "in the charge you gave us on the trial." After a number of treason trials had taken place in the autumn of 1778, resulting in a string of acquittals, Joseph Reed confided to George Bryan, then the acting president of the Supreme Executive Council, soon to yield the position to Reed as the duly elected president, that "[t]he Court begin to think their Charges give too much Countenance to Acquittals," which was Reed's opinion, he said, "from the Beginning."[38] Although McKean may have lacked the ideal temperament for a judge, it would be unfair to characterize him as a hanging one. He recognized that the life of an accused depended on the jury's determination of guilt or innocence and that, insofar as any instruction he gave might seem to bind them, "the Jury may, unquestionably, on this, as on every other, point of evidence, believe one part, and disregard another."[39]

In the delicate balancing act between judge and jury, we see McKean at work again toward the end of the century in a murder case in which he expressed a view that the jury adopted in returning a guilty verdict. The issue was whether the defendant who had taken an axe to strike down a Negro by the name of David during the course of a riotous Easter Monday wedding celebration had done so with the requisite premeditation to sustain a charge of first-degree murder, or whether he might be convicted instead of a lesser degree of homicide if it were found that he acted in the heat of sudden passion.

McKean had no doubt that Mulatto Bob, having time to cool off, was guilty of deliberate and premeditated murder. Yet he left the matter to the jury with these words, a variant of which the Roberts jury might also have heard:

> Tenderness and mercy are amiable qualities of the mind; but if they are exercised and indulged beyond the control of reason, and the limits of justice, for the sake of individuals, the peace, order, and happiness of society, will inevitably be impaired and endangered. As far as respects the prisoner, I lament the tendency of these observations, but as far as respects the public, I have felt it a sacred duty to submit them to your consideration.[40]

Elizabeth Drinker's immediate reaction to the guilty verdict was one of both astonishment and dismay. She recorded in her diary that, based on the evidence presented, Friends who attended the court did not expect it. In the same vein, the Quaker Thomas Franklin wrote to Elias Boudinot on October 4: "the people who attended thought No Evidence produced wd. Authorize ye Jury to bring him in Gilty." That Carlisle and Roberts were nonetheless convicted was all the more puzzling to Hamilton because of "ye Judges favorable Charge to ye Jury."[41]

IV

Inclemency

Counsel for John Roberts moved the court to set aside the guilty verdict and grant a new trial on the ground that "the evidence given respecting his declarations, or confessions, was altogether illegal, and ought not to have been allowed." Though the court heard argument from both sides, McKean had already crossed that bridge; the terse docket entry indicates that the request for a new trial was "quashed upon argument." On October 17, the defendant stood at the bar of the court and was asked whether he had anything finally to say before being sentenced. The ritual notation entered in the formal record — the defendant "nothing further saith unless as he before had said" — could be read as implying that, contrary to his enforced silence, Roberts had spoken on his own behalf during the trial. McKean then proceeded to deliver the sentence that doomed Roberts, not only because of the punishment of death so sternly pronounced but also because of the fatal effect the sentencing statement would have when submitted to the Supreme Executive Council during its final deliberations on granting clemency as purporting "to shew the opinion of the Court respecting [Roberts's] conviction."[1]

Losing not a moment after the jury returned its verdict, two appraisers acting for the authorities descended on Roberts's property in the Mill Creek Valley to make a detailed inventory of his moveable possessions. Under the attainder statute and the subsequent proclamation of the Supreme Executive Council, all his property, both real and personal, was subject to forfeiture to the Commonwealth. To the consternation of Jane Roberts and her daughters in residence, the appraisers went systematically from room to room in the main house, starting on the first floor and moving upward until they got to garret space and then shifting to the adjoining kitchen wing. They have left an itemized trail that today provides the opportunity to put objects back in particular spaces and to make educated guesses about who occupied which rooms. Take, for example, the southwest room on the first floor. Based on the inventory of its contents, it seems safe to conclude that it was John Roberts's own, as the appraisers recorded the following articles in it: a desk and bookcase; coins and paper money coming to seven pounds, three shillings, seven pence; a dressing table and bedstead; a map of the city and liberties of Philadelphia; fishing hooks and fishing tackle; an inkstand; a bullet mould; and forty-four bound books and several pamphlets.[2]

The appraisers moved outside the house to inspect the cellar, the shed, the garden area, the ash house, the stable, the cooper shop, the barn, the merchant or gristmill, the lumber mill, and the springhouse. In the cellar, they found an iron-bound hogshead full of "Cyder," valued at five pounds, and one barrel two-thirds full of Rye whiskey, valued at twenty pounds, more evidence of the owner's propensity, at variance with Quaker precepts, to imbibe. In keeping with the use of such structures then and now, the shed held a grand miscellany of things, from iron pots and kettles to a copper boiler, buckets, casks, iron dogs, frying pans, churns, pails, and jars. The four beehives in the garden were valued at two pounds.

But it was the other outbuildings, and not the house itself, that contained the most valuable personal property: in the stable, a "bright bay gelding," valued at fifty pounds, a "waggon," valued at sixty pounds, and ten tons of hay in the loft, worth ninety pounds; in the cooper shop, 15,000 staves and heading, valued at one hundred pounds; in the barn, more quantities of hay and wheat, another wagon, an apple mill and trough, three full hogsheads of cider, and a range of miscellaneous farm material and equipment. By the inventory of their contents, the gristmill and lumber house did not seem at that time to be in active operation. The springhouse was home to a sow "and 10 pigs after her," at a value of fifteen pounds, another large sow "and 8 shotes," at a value of twenty pounds, and "1 dark red cow," at a value of eighteen pounds. The absence in the inventory of all but these few farm animals corroborates that Roberts had lost much of his farm stock to foraging armies, or as a Quaker report pinpointed the culprits, "by parties of the army Commanded by George Washington commonly called the American Army."[3]

James Haslet and George Miller, the two appraisers, certified that these various possessions of John Roberts had a total value of 4,378 pounds, six shillings, seven pence. Surprisingly, more than two-thirds of that sum was attributable to an accumulation found in the barn of "A quantity of iron supposed to be 40 tons," which the appraisers valued at 3,000 pounds. That stockpile represented a major investment in a scarce commodity needed during the war years to produce cannons, musket barrels, and bullets. How to account for its presence? One possible explanation is that the Elk Forge, which Roberts and his partners had established to manufacture bar iron, was using the barn as a warehouse for storage purposes. Another explanation for this "quantity of iron" is that it belonged to Jonathan Robeson, Roberts's neighbor and a blacksmith who, as a witness for the defense at trial, obliquely referred to "50 tons of barr Iron." In any event, there is no record of what happened to the inventoried bar iron, which disappeared sometime after the appraisers inspected the property.[4]

It would not have taken long for the prisoner in Philadelphia to learn of the appraisers' unwelcome visit, nor to calculate in his turn the significance to him and his family of the assignment they carried out with such alacrity. Roberts had returned to the same jail where he had been imprisoned since his arrest in July, wrongly identified by some as the Walnut Street prison, whose construction had barely been completed by the start of the Revolution. Located on the south side of Walnut Street between Fifth and Sixth Streets, the New Jail, as the Walnut Street prison was familiarly known, had been built to alleviate the severe overcrowding in the old prison facility; during the Revolution it would be used exclusively to house captured soldiers — in rotation, first British, then American, and again, after the evacuation of Philadelphia in June 1778, British soldiers. The Old Gaol, going back to fifty years before and located at the southwest corner of Third and Market Streets, got a new lease on life as being the only place available in which to detain those charged with crimes against the Commonwealth (Figure 4.1). It is due to Samuel Rowland Fisher, a cantankerous Quaker, and the journal he kept from 1779 to 1781 while he was a prisoner in the Old Gaol, that we know that Roberts spent his prison time there. In February 1780, Fisher recorded in his journal that he and Joseph Pritchard were "busily employed in making walking sticks of some Hickory wood we had purchased of Jehu, the Son [of] John Roberts, that was hanged by the present Rulers, after some time of Imprisonment in this Goal [sic]." For both prison authorities and inmates, the Old Gaol was seriously deficient: escaping from it took no great ingenuity, but for those who didn't escape, it was an overcrowded, rat-infested ordeal.[5]

Roberts realized he had limited time in which to devise a strategy that offered him any hope. As Dr. Johnson famously remarked, "Depend upon it, Sir, when a man knows he is to be hanged in a fortnight, it concentrates his mind wonderfully."[6] He needed to enlist help on the outside in formulating a plan and then working to carry it out. On October 8, he sent a letter to "My good Friend," Daniel Clymer, the first witness who appeared at the trial on his behalf (Figure 4.2). The letter is the only surviving example we have of Roberts's writing. If he himself wrote it — and there is no reason to doubt that he did — his hand seems remarkably steady as he composes a message of vital importance. It is a small matter of spelling precision, perhaps credited to careful Quaker schooling, that at the very beginning he records his current address as the Philadelphia "gaol"; Chief Justice McKean and others routinely invert the vowel sequence, making jail for those confined there a "goal." The hallmarks of Quaker authorship are, however, conspicuously absent in the rest of the letter, such as the numerical labeling of the day of the week and the

STONE PRISON S.W.COR 3ª & MARKET ST.

1723

FROM OLD DRAWING IN PHILAD. LIBRARY

Figure 4.1 Old Gaol, at the southwest corner of High (Market) and Third Streets, in a drawing purporting to show it as of its construction in the 1720s. Roberts was imprisoned in the Old Gaol during his trial and while awaiting execution.

Reproduced by permission of The Historical Society of Pennsylvania.

month of the year, the use of the familiar second person style of address, and any sign of prayerful regret for having strayed, involuntarily or not, from the testimony of peace (unless one finds that sign in his alluding to "Natural Infirmities" as a cause for his present distress).

Roberts wasted no time in getting to the point. His "present unhappy Situation," in having been tried and convicted of high treason "notwithstanding every Step has been taken to prevent that Calamity," led him to call on Clymer for assistance. He felt satisfied, he wrote, that "in your power I shall not be disappointed":

> Some few measures properly taken and supported may yet rescue me from Destruction, and as your influence in the City may be of great advantage to me I must take the liberty of praying in the most earnest manner that you would indulge me with a Sight of you as soon as possible and every Expence attending your Journey shall be gratefully repaid you. I know well that your

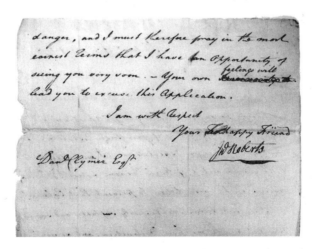

Figure 4.2 Letter Roberts sent from prison to Daniel Clymer, urgently requesting Clymer's help after the trial.

Humanity will lead you to take any steps toward affording Assistance to an unfortunate Man, borne down by popular prejudice and his own Natural Infirmities to the lowest Degree. In cases where Life is concerned all delays are attended with danger, and I must therefore pray in the most earnest Terms that I have the opportunity of seeing you very soon. Your own feelings will lead you to excuse this Application.

I am with respect,
Your unhappy Friend,

Whether Daniel Clymer ever responded to this letter, either in the interview between them that Roberts sought or by a message Clymer sent in reply, is not known. What is known is that Clymer received the letter, although it took a hundred and seventy-five years for the letter to come to light confirming Clymer's receipt of it. The letter remained in a box of Clymer family correspondence until inherited by Mrs. Natalie Clymer, a telephone operator for the *Main Line Times*, a weekly newspaper published in the locality where Roberts once lived. In 1955 Mrs. Clymer offered to sell the family papers to an antiquarian collector who, on examining the material, discovered Roberts's plea for help and told Mrs. Clymer that the communication should be of interest to the readers of the newspaper for which she worked. A week later the *Main Line Times* published the text of the letter, accompanied by a long article on John Roberts and his conviction for treason that was a mix of historical fact and popular mythology. Thereafter the letter migrated into the possession of the public library in the village of Gladwyne near John Roberts's house, where it stayed until its rediscovery about ten years ago, at which point the Gladwyne library's board of trustees voted to give the letter to the Quaker Collection at Haverford College for safekeeping.[7]

Would Roberts have turned to Clymer for help had he known that the day before Roberts's trial began Clymer joined the Patriotic Association and pledged, in signing its articles, to bring suspected traitors to justice? More than hypocrisy, it would have been a serious breach of professional ethics for Clymer, a lawyer but also a recently initiated member of the Patriotic Association, to consent to visit Roberts in prison, pretending to be sympathetic to his plight.[8] But if Clymer couldn't properly respond to this request, the need to organize a concerted effort to save Roberts remained urgent, and all the more so because his trial counsel were continually engaged in court representing others charged with treason. The many petitions for clemency eventually submitted on the prisoner's behalf were not spontaneously generated. It took the coordinating skills of undisclosed allies to prepare and then to circulate the petitions for signature among a diverse group of people, scattered over a broad area.

A critical issue Roberts had to grapple with was whether he should submit a petition in his own name to the Supreme Executive Council, and if so,

76

what he ought to say in it. Compelled by the rules of evidence to remain silent during his trial, could he now clarify or supplement the record to his advantage? For instance, the trial testimony left far from clear what moved him abruptly to leave his home and family for British-occupied Philadelphia. Of even greater significance was the question of how he happened to be in the company of Cornwallis's troops, ostensibly serving as a guide, during the foraging expedition of the previous December. If his life was to be spared, the impression that he willingly went along for the ride had to be faced and, if possible, convincingly refuted.

The first entry in the minutes of the executive council on November 2 may be read as establishing that Roberts did make a personal plea for mercy. The minutes refer to "[t]he petition of John Roberts," distinguishing that document from the petition received from "the wife of John Roberts, his Children & relatives." However, like the missing trial notes of Chief Justice McKean, no petition from John Roberts appears in the papers relating to the trial that the Commonwealth of Pennsylvania published in the nineteenth century; nor can any petition from him be found in the Pennsylvania State Archives today.[9]

Something resembling such a petition appears in a history of Chester County published in 1881, not an entirely illogical place in which to find it. Roberts's wife, Jane Downing Roberts, came from a respected Chester County Quaker family, and in the last years of her life, she returned to Chester County with her son Jehu. In addition, a Roberts daughter married George Thomas, of West Whiteland Township, reinforcing the family connection with Chester County.[10] The authors of the history, J. Smith Futhey and Gilbert Cope, made no attempt to conceal their bias in favor of Roberts, which may account for their being given access to "a paper written by him during his imprisonment in Philadelphia." As directed toward issues left open at his trial, the document they quote bears all the marks of authenticity.

The narrative begins by establishing the precise date of Roberts's arrival in Philadelphia. He arrived there on October 10, 1777, after "having been frequently threatened by malicious Persons in my Neighbourhood, both as to my Person, Family and Property, — without any Design whatever to aid or arise [sic] the enemy or to injure my Country, the person or property of any Individual in it." Five days later, militia under the command of General James Potter showed up at his plantation, threatened his family, shot at one of his sons while taking the other prisoner, and departed with "5 Horses, 21 head Horned Cattle and 38 sheep," a haul that would explain why the appraisers a year afterward found so few livestock at the Roberts property. This raid by the American soldiers, "joined with the most pressing solicitations of my Family, who thought my Life in Danger, deterred me from returning home as I intended." Here emerges, with more detail than at his trial, the outline of a defense based on threat of bodily harm, weak though Chief Justice McKean might still have characterized it.

Roberts turned his attention to the call in the middle of the night to join the marauding party led by Lord Cornwallis. Jacob James, the Tory from Chester County in the employ of the British who was on familiar terms with Roberts, attempted to rouse him from bed at three o'clock in the morning on December 11 with the prospect of his seeing his family "as the army were going over to Schuylkill into that neighborhood." Roberts's equivocal reply was that "it was time enough for me at daylight" to decide what to do, whereupon he went back to bed, only to receive an hour later a second, peremptory summons from James, who informed him that Cornwallis was waiting "at the Bridge, and if I would not go a Guard would be sent and compel me to go." Not until he got to the bridge did it dawn on him, Roberts wrote, why he had been summoned: "I then began to think that I was intended for a Guide and went & begged the Gen'l that he would not take me along for his Guide, as it would be attended with the most disagreeable and fatal consequences for me." That statement, if he made it, would prove to be painfully prophetic.

After Cornwallis refused to release him, Roberts urged the British commander "to use his authority to prevent his army from plundering the Inhabitants upon the march," which Cornwallis pledged to do, but as Roberts soon recognized, his lordship's assurance was honored more in the breach than in the observance. At the end of the day, when the army was about to encamp for the night, and not having been able to see his family, Roberts received permission to return to Philadelphia. The next day, December 12, as he saw the British returning to the city with prisoners and booty, "I made it my Business by every means in my power to have them set at Liberty, their property restored or satisfied for"; the trouble he went to elicited from the British officers "threats and abusive treatment" that should have convinced all those present "in what Light I was viewed by the B. army." Roberts supplied the names of several prisoners whose discharge he obtained, and concluded this post-trial defense by stating that he had to remain in Philadelphia as long as he did, until the British evacuation had been completed, because he had stood surety to the occupying forces for an American prisoner who had apparently violated his parole and escaped. Thomas Franklin, a Quaker who acted as an intermediary in Philadelphia for imprisoned American soldiers, verified that last claim of Roberts. While the British were still in possession of the city, Franklin twice wrote to the commissary of prisoners at the American camp about Roberts's having given his bond as security for John Egolf, whose forced return to Philadelphia, "if he can be found," Franklin thought would serve "as a good example to others."[11]

If this petition, assuming that's what it was, is the best case John Roberts could make for himself, it raises more questions than it disposes of. In this account, he avoids any mention of the quixotic mission to rescue the Quaker exiles on the road out of Philadelphia, which was the subject of the confession Groves and Stroud testified he made at the Middle Ferry tavern, even though the two Chester County historians, tapping their own sources a hundred years later, state as a fact that he undertook this "dangerous expedient" over the objection of George Thomas, who, the night before, sought to impress on his father-in-law the risks he was running. Nor does Roberts identify in this paper who among his neighbors caused him such concern that on October 10, in wartime conditions, he suddenly abandoned home and family. Was Michael Smith his chief tormentor?

There is, of course, an alternative explanation for his leaving home and going to Philadelphia, which is that, on the heels of successive American defeats at Brandywine, Paoli, and Germantown, Roberts thought it time to side with the winner. If not because of his known defection to the British, why five days later did American soldiers under General Potter go out of their way to try to track him down, and then, failing to find him, pick a fight with his two sons? And how adamantly in this paper do we see him resisting service as Cornwallis's guide when, from Jacob James's first attempt to haul him out of bed, there could have been little mistaking what his role would be in accompanying the British forces across the Schuylkill on the morning of December 11?

Those who prepared and circulated the clemency petitions were responsible for producing an extraordinary demonstration of sympathy on behalf of Carlisle and Roberts, even if we discount the estimate that as many as seven thousand people petitioned the executive council to show mercy to the condemned men. With knowledge that both of them faced death, Jasper Yeates wrote to a family friend on October 11, "The City is in the greatest Ferment. Most good Men wish for an Act of Oblivion," by which Yeates meant an amnesty or pardon.[12] In the petitions that were later published in the *Pennsylvania Archives*, some names stand out in bold relief, as much because of their omission as because of their appearance. A cautious man of property like Samuel Powel, who with his wife stayed in Philadelphia during the British occupation of the city and whose attachment to the Revolutionary cause might have been thought at that stage ambiguous, overcame his caution and signed a petition. So did the old and very wealthy Quaker merchant Reese Meredith; the Catholic merchant partners and brothers-in-law George Meade and Thomas Fitzsimmons; Dr. Thomas Cadwalader and his son John, a general in the American army; Thomas McKean, Sr., the uncle of the chief justice and a resident of Chester County, who affixed his mark to a petition; and a number of the witnesses who testified at Roberts's trial, including, unless there were another of the same name, Edward Stroud. Quakers signed but not as a separately identifiable group; the petition submitted, "with the most piercing grief," by the numerous relatives of John Roberts necessarily included a host of Quakers in both the Roberts and the Downing families.[13]

That radical firebrands like James Cannon, Timothy Matlack, Daniel Roberdeau, Thomas Paine, David Rittenhouse, Charles Willson Peale, and James Claypoole didn't sign (although Owen Biddle, arguably a member of that group, did) is not surprising. The conspicuous absence of high Quakers like Henry Drinker, Abel James, the Pembertons, the Parrishes, and Nicholas Waln is less easy to explain. They had been at the forefront of defending in mild but nonetheless provocative language the Quaker commitment to disengagement in the armed conflict and the refusal to lend any tangible support to the American cause.

For Abraham Carlisle and John Roberts it was their deep misfortune that, as their trials approached in the summer of 1778, the Philadelphia Meeting for Sufferings infuriated the radical element in the population by publishing an appeal to the Pennsylvania General Assembly about laws that the assembly had passed in recent times having "a tendency to oppress tender consciences." Such legislation, the appeal stated, could not be reconciled with the "liberal foundation" of the province and the First Proprietor's insistence that religious liberty be preserved inviolate. Long smoldering issues about the failure to defend the province in the past against Indian attacks flamed up again. If Quakers refused to contribute revenue to support the war through the payment of taxes, or pay fines in lieu of military service, or confirm their loyalty under the test laws, then one critic lectured, "It may be worth your serious consideration to determine whether you are members of any *civil* society," entitled to the protection of the laws or to plead for the redress of grievances, and another fulminated that "your religion [is] nothing more than a political and commercial system."[14]

The Quaker elite could not have failed to realize that the principled positions their religious society was taking put at greater risk the lives of two of their members who had become prime targets for retributive justice. The charge of hypocrisy, directed against Quakers, would be enlarged and exploited if Quaker leaders, like those who had returned from exile in Virginia, participated in an organized campaign to save Roberts and Carlisle, found guilty of a breach of the very code that scrupulous Friends, "of tender consciences," proclaimed morally binding on the meeting and its members. Moreover, any semblance of justifying or excusing what the prisoners were accused of doing in helping the British wage war could only add to the widespread conviction that these Quakers were undercover allies of the Crown. Thus, high Quakers lay low, confining themselves, for the most part, to behind-the-scenes encouragement of their imprisoned coreligionists. The visits that representatives of the meeting made to Roberts and Carlisle in jail were sessions of induced penitence and piety that may now strike us as less than completely comforting. Two days before the date set for execution, John Pemberton, John Parrish, Samuel Smith, and Henry Drinker went to see the prisoners. They carried a sobering message for the condemned men: a member of the executive council, when asked that morning, had ruled out any hope of reprieve. The delegation urged the prisoners to turn their thoughts toward an acknowledgment of how they had deviated "from what our Christian profession calls for."[15]

In the countdown to execution, Daniel Clymer and fifteen others submitted on October 29 a petition that smacked more of a lawyer's cold logic than an impassioned plea that lives be spared on humane grounds. From the opening words of the petition, the subscribers denied Roberts and Carlisle the slightest glimmer of doubt concerning the verdict and sentence against them: "Sensible as your Memorialists are, that the unfortunate John Roberts and Abraham Carlisle, most justly merit the Sentence which the Law has lately pronounced against them, and of the fairness of their Trials." The purpose of punishment was, according to the petition, "not so much to give pain to the Offender as to deter others from acting on similar occasions," and because, "from the present happy Prospect of public Affairs, (of which we beg leave to congratulate you)," it appeared highly probable that "the British Enemy will never again visit this State," hanging the defendants would serve no deterrent purpose. This petition fell short of the influence and assistance to an "unfortunate man" that Roberts had hoped to obtain from Daniel Clymer, who had discovered a convenient way to satisfy his conscience at no risk to himself.[16]

A strange last-minute attempt to save John Roberts came from an unexpected quarter. At the very emotional meeting of the Supreme Executive Council on November 2, when the families of both condemned men begged for mercy, Samuel Wallis, of Muncy, located in Northumberland County (later, as to that part, Lycoming County), stepped forward to provide testimony reflecting "on the Credit in which John Roberts was at Gen'l Howe's Head Quarters." Even though, at that advanced stage, the executive council had concluded to carry out the death sentence on schedule, as Henry Drinker and others had confirmed to Roberts and Carlisle in their visit of that same day, the members of the council, for the sake of form only, ordered Wallis to go before a justice of the peace and affirm in writing the truthfulness of what he was prepared to say. Wallis complied by appearing the next day before Plunkett Fleeson, an upholsterer by trade but also a magistrate, to complete a formal but useless deposition that would become still another item in the growing official record later published in the *Pennsylvania Archives*.[17]

Looking back, one may debate, as in the pages of this study, whether John Roberts was guilty of treason, or in any event guilty enough to justify his execution. Yet, there can be no such debate about Samuel Wallis: he was a traitor to the American cause, and had the extent of his treasonable activities been known during his lifetime, he would have deserved to die. More than a century and a half would pass before Carl Van Doren in his *Secret History of the American Revolution* unmasked Wallis as a paid messenger in the negotiations between Benedict Arnold at West Point and the British in New York. By mining the papers of General Sir Henry Clinton, then recently acquired by the Clements Library at the University of Michigan, Van Doren was able to look behind code names and trace Wallis's trail of treachery in Arnold's negotiations with the British.[18]

When Wallis attempted to intervene at the last moment on behalf of Roberts, he already was deeply implicated in playing a dangerous double role, pretending to be a patriot member of the militia on the Pennsylvania frontier while in fact working for the British. A master at covering his tracks when engaged in questionable undertakings, Wallis had acted as the undisclosed agent in speculative land transactions for Quakers of the wealth and respectability of Abel James and Henry Drinker; in spite of violating almost every article of the Quaker code of conduct, he succeeded in maintaining his membership in the Society of Friends, perhaps by relying on these weighty connections.

By 1778 Wallis had a long-established working relationship with Henry Drinker, a relationship that would continue until Wallis's death twenty years later. Prior to the Revolution, Wallis had also retained James Wilson to represent him in contentious land litigation that the Pennsylvania proprietors had brought against Wallis. Although either Drinker or Wilson might have sought to persuade Wallis to step forward and testify on behalf of Roberts, there is no evidence that either of them did. Never easy to pin down as to his exact location, Wallis had probably retreated at about the time of Roberts's trial to Philadelphia from Muncy, some one hundred and fifty miles away on the West Branch of the Susquehanna River. Letters he sent permit us to place him at this remote frontier outpost as late as August of 1778, but conditions in Muncy became so unsettled and dangerous because of repeated Indian raids that he would have risked his family's safety by staying there any longer.[19]

Even if the executive council had been disposed seriously to consider it, the testimony Wallis at last gave, whether of his own volition or under pressure to do so, did nothing to help Roberts in extremis. Quite the contrary, not only did it have the potential to hurt Roberts but it also opened up awkward questions about Wallis and his proximity to the British in occupied Philadelphia, creating exactly the kind of exposure that Wallis was usually at great pains to avoid. In the deposition he completed before Plunkett Fleeson, Wallis started by identifying himself as "one of the people called Quakers," and by affirming rather than swearing to the truth of what he was about to say. During the previous April, while the British were still in possession of the city, Wallis just "happened to overhear a conversation between Joseph Galloway, late of this City, Esquire, and Colonel Balfour of the British Army, then one of the Aid de Camps of General Howe." Though not stated in the deposition, Wallis had known Galloway for many years; both of them came from Maryland Quaker background, and Wallis had employed Galloway as counsel in legal proceedings in which Wallis was repeatedly involved. Although it is not difficult to believe that, as a result of his familiarity with Galloway, Wallis could have stationed himself close enough to overhear this conversation, one must ask what it says about Wallis's credentials as the patriot he professed to be that he had the opportunity to eavesdrop on Howe's superintendent of police when Galloway was confidentially advising a senior British officer. And one must also ask what possible value he thought could attach to his reporting on the substance of an overheard conversation that, by any realistic assessment, hurt Roberts more than it helped him. Wallis produced the following hearsay-laden narrative of the exchange between Galloway and Balfour:

> that intelligence had been received of a party of American Troops being somewhere over the Schuylkill, and that it was intended to send a party of British in pursuit of them, and that he, Balfour, was desirous of being informed of some person who being acquainted with that part of the Country, might assist the party going out as a Guide or Conductor; whereupon the said Galloway mentioned John Roberts, as a proper person; on which Balfour shrugged up his shoulders and said, he believed John Roberts was a good kind of man, but that he, Balfour, thought he was not to be depended upon.

In sum, four months after the foraging expedition to Lower Merion Township, in which Roberts claimed he was a coerced guide, we find Galloway recommending him for the same kind of an assignment. Balfour, in reply, did not question Roberts's commitment to serve the British, only his competence and dependability. From the privileged vantage point he had, Wallis therefore came to the conclusion that "John Roberts was a person in whom the enemy had no confidence." The words that Wallis attributed to Balfour in his appraisal of Roberts were more nuanced and correspond to the view of him we have through others' eyes: "a good kind of man but not to be depended upon."[20]

No explanation immediately rings true for Wallis's uncharacteristic disclosure of his activities at a critical time in the Revolution and of his ability to move in and out of the city freely during the British occupation of Philadelphia. Like the petition Daniel Clymer brought himself to sign at the eleventh hour, his arrival on the scene at the beginning of November could not have affected the outcome of Roberts's ordeal, already agreed upon by the members of the executive council. One explanation is that he and Roberts may have identified themselves during the occupation of Philadelphia as being in the employ of the British and that, under pressure from Roberts or somebody acting for him, Wallis felt he had no choice but to come forward and recount a story that, though seldom the case for him, was largely true.[21]

Because money considerations always figured prominently in his reckoning, another factor may have contributed to Wallis's making this late and lame effort to assist Roberts. Roberts and his two sons, Thomas and Jehu, are recorded in 1774 and 1775 as the holders of warrants on substantial acreage in the vicinity of Wallis's own large holdings in Northumberland County. On the eve of the Revolution, it would appear that Roberts, as a man of considerable means, sought investment opportunities beyond those in the Mill Creek Valley. Through a network of religious and business associates, he may have learned of Wallis as a resourceful agent facilitating promising investments on the frontier. However it happened, he and his sons would have been unable to take up the warrants in Muncy, Wallis's closely guarded preserve, without the latter's knowledge and cooperation. This prior business connection might therefore have played a part in Wallis's decision to appear before the executive council and give the testimony he did.[22]

The several clemency petitions submitted on behalf of Roberts and Carlisle varied in their particular prayers for relief. Though all of the petitions were directed to the Supreme Executive Council, there was manifest uncertainty about the extent of authority the executive council could properly exercise. A petition signed by citizens of the State of Pennsylvania requested that a reprieve be granted, "and such further Measures be taken by the Council as may, agreeable to the Constitution be necessary to obtain a Pardon to the said Prisoners." The members of the grand jury who had indicted Roberts and Carlisle limited themselves in their petition to recommending the prisoners "as suitable objects of mercy." Five ministers of the gospel in the city of Philadelphia petitioned that the lives of the condemned men, "who are now advanced in years, may be spared, & such measures of mercy and forgiveness extended to them as may be thought consistent with the public safety." The many relatives of John Roberts pleaded that "you will show mercy to the unfortunate prisoner, by granting him his life, & thereby afford consolation to an already but too much distressed and disconsolate family." Another petition submitted by "sundry persons" living in the city of Philadelphia asked that Roberts be granted "the clemency of the Government."[23]

A petition from residents of Philadelphia County (which included Lower Merion Township, where Roberts's property was located) and Chester County envisioned a two-step process whereby the Supreme Executive Council would first suspend the execution of the sentence while at the same time referring the case to the "Legislative Body of the State," accompanied by the council's recommendation for clemency, and then the General Assembly would act to grant John Roberts "the benefit of a full, free, & general Pardon." The scheme of relief spelled out in this petition appears to be the handiwork of a skilled lawyer familiar with the legal terrain. In a memoir of the Potts family published a century later, the author wrote that a draft of the document, retained in her family papers, was in Joseph Galloway's handwriting, proving that the loyalists who fled Philadelphia had "tried every means in their power to save the lives of the tools they had led into this dangerous business." The draft does track word for word the petition actually signed and submitted on behalf of Roberts. If Galloway, as that skilled lawyer, prepared the petition and sent it from New York to Philadelphia, he would have acted in some haste since his departure for England in October 1778 was imminent.[24]

This was not the only petition that followed the two-step approach. The bleak petition that Daniel Clymer and others signed ended with a similar request: "All that we ask on this occasion are the lives of Messrs Roberts and Carlisle, by respiting their Sentence till the close of the next session of Assembly." In the same vein, the justices of the Supreme Court in forwarding the clemency petitions from the members of the grand jury and the petit juries were careful to ask only that the executive council "postpone the issuing [of] the warrant for the execution of John Roberts until the end of the next session of the General Assembly."[25]

The possibility that the executive council might evade the difficult task before it by granting a stay of execution until the General Assembly could act in some manner on the clemency petitions prompted an indignant protest from one "Rectifier." In a letter dated October 26 and published five days later in the *Pennsylvania Packet*, Rectifier took the sound historical position that the power to pardon inherently rested in the executive authority, and not in the legislature. In relation to this extraordinary power to suspend or dispense, he made some telling points:

> Can it be, I asked myself, that the body which enacts the laws today, may, when they please, stop the ordinary execution of those laws, and annul them in particular cases? Will this not be rendering all law uncertain, and making the laws binding on some men, or classes of men, as they may have chance to have interest or influence? Shall a large Assembly, properly calculated and appointed to general business, discuss the causes of individuals, and descend to apply their general rules or laws, or suspend them in particular cases?[26]

The framers of the Pennsylvania constitution of 1776 had erected a barrier to a clear-cut executive pardon in treason cases. Distrustful of a single chief executive, they created a plural one; and on issues of great moment, they placed in the unicameral legislative body the power to constrain the executive authority. Thus, under section 20 of the constitution, the Supreme Executive Council was given the "power to grant pardons and remit fines, in all cases whatsoever, except in cases of impeachment; and in cases of treason and murder, shall have the power to grant reprieves, but not to pardon, until the end of the next sessions of assembly." Yet what was the effect of this limitation? Did it mean that the Supreme Executive Council simply lacked the ability to pardon in cases of treason and murder—that power being lodged in the assembly—or that its power to pardon was suspended during a reprieve it granted and until the assembly concluded its next sessions either in taking action or in not doing so?[27]

James Wilson, in his law lectures of 1790–1792, saw the power to pardon as a power "to insult the laws," which Blackstone and others had concluded was "incommunicable to the democratic species of government." Wilson nevertheless held that providing for the exercise of such discretionary power was essential in every state, however organized, even to rescue condemned criminals. He may have had a particular example in mind when he wrote: "When the cry of the nation arises in their favour; when the judges themselves, descending from their seats, and laying aside the formidable sword of justice, come to supplicate in behalf of the person, whom they have been obliged to condemn; in such a situation, clemency is a virtue; it becomes a duty."

In giving his approval to the pardoning power, Wilson placed its exercise with the chief magistrate, either the president of the United States or the governor of a state. When, however, he canvassed the constitutions of the several states in 1790, he recognized that this was not a unanimous view. New York, for example, provided in its constitution that in cases of treason or murder the governor had the power only to suspend the execution of the sentence while referring the application for a pardon to the legislature, whereupon the legislative body had the ability to pardon, or direct the execution of the criminal, or grant a further reprieve. Such may have been the intended but awkwardly expressed allocation of responsibility between the executive and legislative branches provided in the Pennsylvania constitution of 1776.[28]

Rectifier criticized the petition prepared for Abraham Carlisle because he saw as defective the prayer for relief that requested the executive council to postpone carrying out the prisoner's sentence until the assembly might finally determine either to grant or to deny clemency. Little wonder, then, that, lacking any settled understanding or precedent to guide them, those drafting the petitions for Roberts and Carlisle hesitated over what relief specifically to request, and from what body to request it. The petitions seeking only a stay of execution from the executive council until the assembly might take action would appear to have been closer to the spirit of the constitutional requirements for obtaining pardon in treason cases.

Given the opportunity to shift responsibility to the legislature, why did the Supreme Executive Council not take advantage of it? Its refusal to suspend the sentence of either Roberts or Carlisle pending the assembly's review of the clemency petitions may simply have been the result of its determination, reached as soon as the guilty verdicts were returned, to proceed with the execution of the two condemned men, come what may. All that followed, therefore, in the council's apparent willingness to consider the petitions urging clemency and to review the trial notes, would have been nothing but a cruel hoax. As late, however, as October 23, the prosecuting attorney for the Commonwealth, Joseph Reed, indicated that he was taking nothing for granted about the council's treatment of the clemency petitions. At the same time as the council sought to obtain McKean's trial notes, its vice president, George Bryan, dispatched a confidential letter to Reed requesting his assistance, if one may term it that, in deciding the fate of Roberts and Carlisle. Although we lack the letter from Bryan to Reed, we have Reed's artfully composed reply, sent from Newtown, then the county seat of Bucks County, where the justices of the Supreme Court had opened session to try other treason cases, as well as to dispose of more routine matters of court business.[29]

In a biography and collection of correspondence he compiled in the nineteenth century, Reed's grandson denied that Reed had maneuvered to ensure the execution of Carlisle and Roberts. He portrayed his grandfather as staying scrupulously aloof during the post-trial period. Other than a passing reference to the letter, William Reed ignored the potent message Reed had sent to Bryan, which had as its purpose and effect hastening the condemned to the gallows.[30] Above all, Reed's reply to Bryan needs to be appreciated for its political content, since Reed had been actively campaigning for a seat on the executive council in elections that took place on October 13 and that resulted in his being elected not only to the executive council but also to the assembly from the city of Philadelphia. In November he resigned his post in the assembly so as to fill the more prestigious office of councilor, and a few days after his resignation, the assembly and the council jointly met to appoint him to chair the council and assume the title of president of Pennsylvania.[31] Although still engaged as prosecuting attorney when framing his reply to Bryan, Reed anticipated the new role he would assume. He acknowledged receipt the evening before, on October 22, of "your Favour inclosing a Copy of the Petition of the Jurors on Roberts & Carlisle, & the Recommendation of the Judges thereupon." He then gave this revealing insight about the process under way:

> The former I allways expected [i.e., the jurors' petition], the latter I did not
> [i.e., the judges' recommendation]. I lament it the more as it has contributed
> largely to the Embarrassment which the Board must have upon the Occasion, &
> which taking into View all Circumstances must have been sufficiently great
> without this Addition. The Difficulties with which you are now surrounded

are too obvious, & I can only say that it appears to me nothing is left but a Choice of Difficulties, for proceed how you will, the Mouth of Faction & Censure will open upon you, either in a Charge of unfeeling Cruelty, mean Timidity, or false Compassion. If the Record had been sent you at an earlier Day as it ought to have been, or if there now intervened any considerable Space of Time before the Meeting of the Assembly, I should have no Difficulty in suggesting as my Opinion a speedy Execution of both the Criminals—but as there are only five Days (exclusive of Sunday) before the Meeting of the House (tho' I should do it with great Reluctance if I had the Honour of a Seat in Council) yet I think I should, under all the Circumstances of the Case, defer it for a few Days.

Reed addressed the procedural issue of what the assembly might properly do in exercising its power to intervene. He was "very clear"—clearer than the governing constitutional provision—that the assembly's only function was to provide the council "Advice or Representation," and not to grant relief on its own. Absent "considerable Unanimity" in the assembly, Reed saw no difficulty, as he put it, but "should it be with general Consent, the Voice of the People will certainly justify Council in any Act of Mercy, provided their own Consciences & Judgments are satisfied that it is the Voice of the People, & that such a Measure tends to the Happiness of the State, for otherwise neither Clamour, Fear of Offence, or Hope of Favour ought to influence the Judgment of the patriotick Senator."

If one lays aside any question about the propriety of a private communication between Bryan and Reed on the subject of granting clemency, Reed has thus far in his reply threaded his way through some delicate matters and provided evidence that the council remained at least theoretically open to persuasion. But what next followed in his letter seems professionally indefensible, for Reed reported that he had sought out the judges sitting in Newtown to obtain their opinion on the feasibility of hanging Roberts and Carlisle forthwith: "Without Communication of your Letter to the Judges, I have discoursed them on the Subject, They are unanimously of Opinion that the Trials were fair, & the Sentences just, & having shown me their Opinion as expressed when Roberts received his sentence, I have procured it for your Perusal with a request that it may be safely returned & not printed as being too inaccurately drawn for publick View—a Request which I hope will be attended to, as otherwise I could not have obtained it."

Bryan had also asked Reed about a record or records of Roberts's trial that the council might consult. Reed wrote that his notes and those of the judges were in Philadelphia, and that while he doubted that his notes, "taken with so much Haste & Inaccuracy," could be deciphered, he said that his wife would deliver them to Bryan "upon Request" and that "she will know them by looking among the Papers taken out of the Parlour closet." Because the attorney general, due to illness, withdrew at the outset of Roberts's trial, no notes, Reed added, could be expected of Mr. Sergeant.[32] It seems useless to speculate whether Bryan addressed a similar request for assistance to counsel representing Roberts and Carlisle.

It is now evident by what route the Supreme Executive Council obtained McKean's toxic sentencing statement, and under cover of what prejudicial message. It came not directly from the chief justice as the newspaper that later published it implied, but rather from an advocate-turned-politician, who, in obtaining the statement and sending it to Bryan as he did, had his own axe to grind. If the editor of the *Pennsylvania Packet* actually received McKean's imprimatur before publishing the sentencing statement, the chief justice should have given it with considerable reluctance—not because it remained "too inaccurately drawn for publick View," the reservation attributed to McKean in Reed's letter, but rather because its author may have come to realize that its prior delivery to the council had prejudiced the application for clemency that the trial jurors had made and that he had endorsed.[33]

On the same day, Friday, October 23, that Reed wrote his letter to Bryan, the Supreme Executive Council met and ordered that "John Roberts & Abram Carlisle be, agreeable to the sentence of the Court, executed on Wednesday, the fourth day of November next, & that a Warrant be issued for this purpose accordingly."[34] The council took that action presumably without having before it Reed's letter or the sentencing statement and trial notes of Thomas McKean. A necessary formality, the issuance of the order did not foreclose granting a reprieve, which in practice frequently came at the last moment. Council's receipt of Reed's letter may well have done so, however.

Reed was correct in telling Bryan that, in this awkward situation, the council was dammed if it did, and damned if it didn't. The "Clamour" that Reed feared came mostly from those petitioning for clemency, and yet a reprieve would have seemed the necessary and inevitable first step toward commuting the death sentence. Designing any kind of acceptable relief posed an almost impossible dilemma for the council, as granting it would have provoked outrage among the radicals whose reaction the council members dared not ignore. If the lives of these two Quakers, who had indisputably crossed the line of nonengagement that their religion so persistently preached were spared how could others under suspicion of having committed treason, awaiting their day in court, be effectively prosecuted and punished? The record that the council would soon be able to consult in Roberts's case, the more troublesome of the two convictions for treason, established through the testimony of his own witnesses that he accompanied the British on a punitive foraging expedition, which the council may have concluded alone justified hanging him. As for any referral to the assembly, that body was in transition, making any action on its part conjectural; in the statewide elections that occurred on October 13, a number of conservatives from Philadelphia were voted in whose presence undercut the Whig majority.[35]

However politically difficult it would have been to grant relief, hanging Roberts and Carlisle cannot pass as an example of statesmanship at work, not unless one watches sympathetically as men of state, under pressure, bow to political expediency. A commentator in modern times has approved in sweeping terms the justice of the sentences imposed after "a fair trial before a court of moderate men who showed themselves willing to hear every argument of the learned counsel engaged to defend them." The same author, while finding Roberts and Carlisle "proper objects of pity," remains unconvinced that they were deserving of mercy, and argues in strained logic that the "need for execution" was "exemplary." The sole exemplary value that carrying out the sentences might be perceived as having was to dissuade future juries from returning guilty verdicts in treason cases.[36]

As the last steps were taken toward execution day and all hope of saving Roberts and Carlisle vanished, Philadelphia averted its gaze from the looming spectacle of a public hanging. Once the trials began in late September, the two Philadelphia newspapers then in circulation reported the bare minimum on the proceedings and on the death sentences handed down. There was no sign in the newspapers of any gloating or rejoicing about what lay ahead. In marked contrast, when Samuel Lyons and Samuel Ford were shot as deserters two months before, the *Pennsylvania Evening Post* underscored the lesson their deaths should convey: "The number of spectators was very great, and it is hoped that the melancholy scene will have a proper effect upon the profligate and the thoughtless." It appears that only a small group of friends and relatives accompanied Roberts and Carlisle on their last journey. The same newspaper that reported the large crowd present at the execution of the two deserters published this inconspicuous notice three days after Roberts and Carlisle were hanged: "Last Wednesday was executed on the commons of this city, according to their sentence, John Roberts and Abraham Carlisle. The unhappy prisoners behaved with the greatest resolution."[37]

After receiving news of the deaths of Carlisle and Roberts, James Humphreys, Jr., the Tory publisher of the discontinued *Pennsylvania Ledger*, sent a letter from New York to Joseph Galloway, who had relocated to London. On leaving New York in October, Galloway had asked Humphreys to keep him informed of developments at home and to send him from time to time copies of "rebel newspapers." Humphreys had just obtained the brief newspaper reports of the hangings, which he passed along to Galloway with an expanded account of what happened at noontime on November 4 in Philadelphia:

> By the enclosed papers you will find that poor Roberts and Carlisle have been cruelly and wantonly sacrificed. They were walked to the gallows behind the

cart with halter around their necks attended with all the other apparatus that make such scenes truly horrible—and by a guard of militia, but with hardly any spectators. Poor Carlisle, having been very ill during his confinement, was too weak to say anything; but Mr. Roberts, with the greatest coolness imaginable, spoke for some time—and, however the mind sinks back and startles at the reflection of so tragical a scene, it is with pleasure that I can inform you they both behaved with the utmost fortitude and composure.[38]

The "pleasure" Humphreys took in informing Galloway of the stoic behavior of the two men may be interpreted as independent evidence from a loyalist source that they had been employed by the British, which would render them victims, in Galloway's eyes, of Whig vengeance. As for what Roberts said in his last moments, another Tory correspondent of Galloway's, Isaac Ogden, put words in the condemned man's mouth that he probably never spoke. "His Behavior at the Gallows," this loyalist friend wrote, "did honor to human nature. He told his Audience that his Conscience acquitted him of Guilt; That he suffered for doing his Duty to his Sovereign; That his blood would one day be demanded at their hands." Roberts then, according to this Ogden, turned to his children and exhorted them to remember his principles, "for which he died and to adhere to them while they had breath." If Roberts had uttered words like these, the "rebel papers" would have published them as an admission of guilt missing until then, rather than praising him for approaching his end "with the greatest resolution." Furthermore, in making such a declaration, he would have rejected the counseling he received in prison from his Quaker visitors and impaired any chance his family might have had of receiving more gentle treatment from the authorities in the years to come.[39]

The bodies of Roberts and Carlisle were left hanging in the commons for an hour afterward. That evening Elizabeth Drinker paid a visit to her neighbor, Carlisle's distressed widow, and recorded in her journal that Carlisle's body "looks placid & Serene—no marks of agony or distortion." Although not in Philadelphia on the day of the hangings, John Pemberton similarly noted in his diary that the two men had "dyed without Struggle, & almost in an Instant" and that afterward the "Countenances of the dead looked like persons in an easy Sweet Sleep, & no Distress appeared on them, nor blood on either abt their necks."

Separate funerals took place under Quaker auspices: for Carlisle in Philadelphia on November 5, and for Roberts in Lower Merion on November 6. Each drew a large number in attendance; if the Quaker establishment had refrained from public support of the two men during their imprisonment, it rallied to their visible support following their deaths. Humphreys told Galloway that Carlisle's body was "buried in the Friends' burying Ground, attended by above four thousand people in procession," a number that seems inflated without detracting from the size of the turnout. Elizabeth Drinker and her four children were among those attending this service, "a remarkable large Funeral, and a Solemn time," at which George Dillwyn and Samuel Emlen spoke, the former praying fervently, she wrote, in the burying ground located on the east side of Fourth Street, directly opposite College Hall where Carlisle's trial had occurred.

The next day Henry Drinker joined an assembly of Friends at Roberts's funeral. Nicholas Waln preached at length before John Roberts came to rest beside his ancestors in the graveyard of the Merion meeting, a mere stone's throw away from the farmhouse of Michael Smith and his wife.[40]

V

Doubt

Was John Roberts guilty of treason? That question can no more be answered now than it could have been in 1778 without confronting a second question: Did he deserve to lose his life because of conduct that put his country in serious jeopardy? In considering those questions, as to which, even under the trial record now available, there may be no clear-cut answer, one should avoid assuming that the Revolutionary generation was a bloodthirsty lot, willing casually to dispatch convicted criminals to death on the gallows. Although it is true that conviction for any number of crimes, ranging from murder to sodomy and counterfeiting, automatically resulted in a death sentence, that exposure frequently led juries to err on behalf of an errant defendant by returning a verdict either of acquittal or of conviction for a lesser offense.[1]

At the beginning of the Revolution, reformers in Pennsylvania anticipated an overhaul of the penal system to reduce reliance on the death penalty as a means of combating crime. The Pennsylvania constitution of 1776 contained two hortatory provisions, one calling for legislative reform of the penal laws as soon as possible to make punishments "less sanguinary, and in general more proportionate to the crimes," and a second for the establishment of houses of correction "[t]o deter more effectually from the commission of crimes by continued visible punishment of long duration." The war prevented progress from being made on either front, although the Walnut Street prison, constructed just before the war began, was envisioned as a means of promoting the second objective.[2]

After the war the movement toward reform gained traction, led by the perennial gadfly Benjamin Rush. At a meeting of the Society for Promoting Political Enquiries held at Benjamin Franklin's house in March 1787, Rush read a paper in which he defended the proposition that "all *public* punishments tend to make bad men worse," or as he made the point more memorably, "A man who has lost his character at a whipping-post, has nothing valuable left to lose in society." In this paper on converting public punishments to private, even secret, ones, Rush wandered far afield, so much so that he felt compelled at the end to clarify that his proposals should not be interpreted as countenancing the death penalty, whether carried out in public or in private, "because I consider it as an improper punishment for *any* crime."

Rush drew liberally, albeit erratically, on Beccaria's *Essay on Crimes and Punishments* published in 1764, which maintained that crime was deterred by the certainty of punishment, not its severity. This same theme was taken up in the early 1790s by William Bradford, attorney general of Pennsylvania, in urging legislative reform of the penal system and a more judiciously calibrated set of punishments for convicted criminals. At about that time Rush produced another paper directly attacking capital punishment—*Considerations on the Injustice and Impolicy of Punishing Murder by Death*—which represented his distinctive blend of political theory and scriptural exegesis.[3] These calls for reform culminated in legislation passed by the Pennsylvania legislature in 1794 that for the first time in the United States distinguished among degrees of murder, reserving the death penalty only for murder in the first degree. That statute began with a recital that Bradford would have applauded, though Rush, who advocated outright abolition of the death penalty, would have been slightly less enthusiastic about it:

> Whereas the design of punishment is to prevent the commission of crimes, and to repair the injury that hath been done thereby to society or the individual, and it hath been found by experience, that these objects are better obtained by moderate but certain penalties, than by severe and excessive punishments. And whereas it is the duty of every government to endeavor to reform, rather than exterminate offenders, and the punishment of death ought never to be inflicted where it is not absolutely necessary to the public safety.[4]

The act of 1794 dealt specifically with the crime of high treason. "Every person duly convicted of the crime of high treason," the legislation provided, "shall be sentenced to undergo a confinement in the gaol and penitentiary house of Philadelphia for a period not less than six nor more than twelve years." Of course, one might say that, as a result of the adoption of the United States Constitution, committing treason and its punishment had become academic concerns at the state level. In a criminal procedure act of 1790, Congress prescribed death by hanging as the penalty for treason committed against the United States. The framers had, however, specifically debated the matter and concluded that the federal constitution should not preempt the states from prosecuting treason. So, sixteen years after Carlisle and Roberts were hanged, the legislature in Pennsylvania substituted a much milder sanction than hanging for treason committed against the Commonwealth.[5]

Once the jury had convicted Carlisle and Roberts of treason, McKean was duty bound under the then applicable statute to impose the death sentence. Others may have thought differently, but Joseph Reed, as the prosecutor, never had any doubt that both defendants were justly tried, convicted, and executed.

The day after the hanging, he sent an outspoken message to his friend and recent comrade-in-arms, General Nathanael Greene. Having achieved his goal of election to the Supreme Executive Council, he no longer had any reason to hold back in expressing his views, a constraint that showed to some extent in the letter he sent to George Bryan of twelve days earlier when granting clemency to Roberts and Carlisle was still under consideration. Painting a picture for Greene of the current conditions in Philadelphia, Reed used language similar to that contained in the midsummer newspaper diatribe of Astrea de Coelis's against unrepentant Tories: "New characters are emerging from security, like insects after a storm [Astrea de Coelis: "swarming, like flies upon a carcase"]. Treason, disaffections to the interest of America, and even assistance to the British interest, is called openly only an error of judgment, which candour and liberality of sentiment will overlook." Reed had no patience with those seeking clemency for Carlisle and Roberts, who were, "[o]ut of the great Number of Pilots, Guides, Kidnappers, and other Assistants of the British Army, two of the most notorious." To grant them mercy would have been unthinkable, "for none could be more guilty—but these being rich and powerful (both Quakers) we could not for shame have made an Example of a poor Rogue after forgiving the rich."

Reed told Greene that he had just been elected to the Supreme Executive Council, "and shall now accept the Chair, if offered to me, with a tolerable salary." The council consisted, he wrote, of "Whigs to a man," whereas the assembly was of mixed composition: "a considerable majority of real Whigs in the House—a number of new converts to the Independence of America—and a few real inveterate, but concealed Tories."[6] The changing and less dependable composition of the assembly, Reed now confirms, may have been another reason why the executive council did not refer the clemency petitions to that body.

James Wilson, the principal lawyer representing Roberts, refrained from expressing any opinion after the trial about his client's guilt or innocence. Because Wilson had undertaken the defense of many accused of treason, it became necessary for him to defend himself, first by force of arms in October 1779 when he and other conservatives were attacked in Wilson's house at the corner of Third and Walnut Streets, and then in print the following year after having been savaged in the public press and elsewhere for alleged Tory sympathies. Acting as his own advocate, he sent a letter to the *Pennsylvania Gazette* in which he dilated on his history as a patriot during the past decade. Regarding the charge that, as a Tory in disguise, he had provided his professional support to traitors, he wrote that he had "indeed been council for many persons who were tried on indictment for treason. But have I, therefore, countenanced their crimes?" If the Commonwealth deemed it necessary to engage counsel learned in the law to present the prosecution's case, he argued, "Is it less necessary for the prisoner?" What detracts, one has to say, from Wilson's self-defense is the barely veiled admission that the people whom he defended in court, all but two of them successfully, were guilty as charged. "The trial of criminals," he reflected plaintively, "is neither the most profitable nor the most agreeable part of a Lawyer's profession."[7]

As for the twelve men who had the initial responsibility of deciding John Roberts's fate, we know that the jury did not easily reach its verdict. On the day McKean sentenced Roberts, the *Pennsylvania Evening Post* reported that the trial had occurred "about a fortnight ago, when the jury, after sitting near twenty-four hours, brought in their verdict guilty." By the standards of the day, twenty-four hours was an exceptionally long time to take to reach a verdict. In eighteenth-century England, a jury more typically either announced its verdict from the jury box, without retiring from the courtroom, or left only for a brief interval. To discourage protracted deliberations by juries that found it necessary to confer before reaching a verdict, the jurors were denied food or drink, fire or candle.[8]

Some sense of the pressure imposed on a jury is apparent in the case of Samuel Rowland Fisher tried during the following year of 1779 in the Philadelphia Court of Quarter Sessions. Fisher was charged with the lesser offense of misprision of treason because of letters he sent to his brother in New York allegedly providing information damaging to the patriot cause. He proved to be an intransigent presence in the courtroom—contesting the court's authority to try him at all, rejecting the advice of the presiding judge to accept William Lewis as his counsel, and representing himself effectively enough that the jury withdrew to consider at length its verdict, whereupon "some Constables were sworn to keep them without Meat or Drink." The jury twice sent word to the court that it had acquitted Fisher of the charges against him, only to receive a stern lecture from the bench about its duty to reconsider. One juror protested, as Fisher recorded in his journal, that "you may as well keep us here, for if we are kept six days & nights more I can never agree to any thing else without wronging my Conscience." But, under sustained bludgeoning, the jury finally capitulated and declared Fisher guilty.[9]

After McKean instructed them, and unable to report a unanimous verdict on the spot, the members of the jury in Roberts's trial would have adjourned to a separate room, presumably in the same building of the College of Philadelphia where the trial took place. Until they reached a verdict, they, too, would have been sequestered without food or drink. How they went about their task and what particular questions they may have debated among themselves are matters for conjecture only. The concept of reasonable doubt as a basis for acquittal, now firmly embedded in our constitutional law as an essential element of due process, would not have been available as a guide to help them in their deliberations. Not until the end of the eighteenth century did the beyond-reasonable-doubt standard crystallize in Anglo-American law so that judges regularly incorporated it in their instructions to the jury.[10]

Although the court would not have spelled out in so many words the burden of persuasion that the prosecution had to meet to convict Roberts, the jury knew that the accused was entitled to the presumption of innocence and that to find him guilty of treason, a capital crime, they had to agree, all of them, in good conscience that his guilt had been clearly established. Yet, the door of the jury room having shut behind them, they were subject to pressure, both inside and out. They could not have been impervious to the discontent voiced about Tory collaborators during the British occupation of Philadelphia and the corresponding demand that accounts now be settled with former adversaries. They knew, if only because two of their number had participated in the verdict, that Abraham Carlisle had already been found guilty of treason for acting as a gatekeeper issuing passes during the British occupation. Each of them would have brought a particular perspective, informed or not, to the events of the past twelve months that, quite apart from what was said in the courtroom during the trial, may have affected how the jury voted. The sanctity of a jury determination of guilt or innocence has historically rested, as Justice Oliver Wendell Holmes laid it down in dictum, on the theory "that the conclusions to be reached in a case will be induced only by evidence and argument in open court, and not by any outside influence," but this theory becomes fragile once a jury proceeds, unmonitored and in private, to consider and dispose of the case before it. No judicial instructions, however explicit, can keep a jury from reverting on occasion to the ancient model of twelve men whom the sheriff summons from the neighborhood where the crime has occurred to search their own memories and provide their own information concerning the accused and the circumstances surrounding the commission of the crime.[11]

If Joseph Reed, in writing to Nathanael Greene, had grounds for identifying Carlisle and Roberts as "two of the most notorious" who had aided the British, more than one member of the jury, living in Philadelphia, should have likewise been able, based on personal knowledge, to identify Roberts as a notorious Tory. By the same token, other members of the jury may have spoken up on his behalf, testifying in effect about knowledge they had of him and his family and friends, of good works he performed, and even of his troubled state of mind. Nor, in mitigation of Roberts's conduct, could the jurors have failed to understand from their own experience the conflicting pulls exerted by loyalty to the old regime and allegiance to the new.

We still must ask what caused the jury to hesitate as long as it did in coming to a verdict. While struggling with their own feelings about a war in progress whose outcome remained in doubt, the members of the jury would have returned to what they heard in the courtroom to test the strength of the case against Roberts and the credibility of the witnesses called by each side. How much, for example, should John Ellis's report of the recruiting effort in the tavern on Strawberry Alley count against Roberts when the assistance Roberts allegedly provided amounted to no more than a weak echo of the recruitment pitch, and when neither Ellis nor anybody else present succumbed to it? Then take the much heralded confession of Roberts at the Middle Ferry tavern on the Schuylkill: even if one believed Groves and Stroud rather than Pritchard— that, in inebriated company, Roberts had told of an attempt six months before to persuade General Howe to commit troops in the rescue of the Quaker exiles on the road out of Philadelphia—what possible military value could attach to the so-called intelligence he communicated to the British commander? Wasn't this just another example of Roberts's ineffectual performance, of the yawning gap between the treasonable activities he was charged with and the ability to carry them out? Twelve years later, when Alexander James Dallas was trying to piece together a report of the treason trials from various sources, he suggested that there was greater substance to Roberts's confession of contested admissibility by having Roberts travel before the Battle of Brandywine to the Head of the Elk, Howe's point of disembarkation in late August, to deliver information that might have mattered in the coming campaign. There is nothing in the trial testimony about a confession having that content.

But as George Ross, counsel for Roberts, had to acknowledge near the end of the trial, a serious problem remained. It was Mary Smith's testimony, supported by Andrew Fisher. Ross admitted that they were "the only witnesses to prove the overt act of joining the Army." Mary Smith's testimony was in this respect especially damaging. Were these witnesses, however, to be fully believed? Michael Smith made no bones about it that, almost from their first acquaintance four years earlier, he and Roberts clashed. Was there some deepseated grudge between them, having nothing to do with the Revolution, which shaped what he and his wife swore to in court? It is also possible that Andrew Fisher, a small-time farmer like Michael Smith, who said he had known John Roberts "for ten years past," had his own grievance with Roberts. In McKean's trial notes, Sebastian Ale, a neighbor of Fisher's in Blockley, is recorded as saying that Fisher told him he would trade his adverse testimony for one of Roberts's good cows (a proposed bargain that the Quaker reporter attributed to Michael Smith).[12]

Even after applying a discount because of personal bias or enmity and regardless of how many witnesses came forward to cast doubt on the reputations for truth-telling of the Smiths and Andrew Fisher, certain uncontroverted facts weighed heavily against the defendant. At a critical moment in the early fall of 1777, when the tide appeared to be turning against the American army, John Roberts left his home and his family and took refuge in Philadelphia for the entire duration of the British occupation, almost nine months, and during that period, by the testimony of both his own witnesses and the prosecution's, he was seen in the company of Lord Cornwallis's forces as they marched out to raid the countryside where Roberts, better than anyone else in occupied Philadelphia, was competent to guide them.

Whether based on their own knowledge or on common gossip, the jurors may have perceived another liability Roberts shouldered that was never expressly exposed at his trial, nor could it have been without violating the evidentiary rule then generally observed that prohibited testimony impugning the character of the defendant.[13] Many of the witnesses who testified for Roberts, as well as his friends and business associates, were suspect in their own right. We have already seen how, a year after the Roberts trial, Joseph Pritchard, whom the defense called as a witness to counter the testimony of Groves and Stroud, landed in the same prison where Roberts and Carlisle had spent their final days, convicted of the lesser offense of misprision of treason. Pritchard was charged with serving as a guard for the British at the Middle Ferry "to inspect all persons going in or out of the City," which, on the face of it, was not that different from the conduct that resulted in Abraham Carlisle's death. Pritchard spent two years in jail before the executive council issued a limited pardon releasing him from imprisonment.[14]

Frederick Kesselman as a witness made a negligible contribution to Roberts's defense. Although he testified that Groves and Stroud had bad reputations, he was forced to admit, in McKean's trial notes, that "he does not know any thing of them himself." Kesselman left Philadelphia not long after the trial, to join the British in New York and to suffer attainder by executive council proclamation in May 1779.[15] Owen Jones, who, with his wife, accepted Roberts as a long-term houseguest, had been the provincial treasurer of Pennsylvania, and the jurors at the trial would have had no trouble in recognizing him by reputation as a loyalist sympathizer.[16] Colonel Thomas Proctor, called as witness to establish that Roberts and his family frequently extended hospitality to American officers seeking overnight lodging, was something of a loose cannon, rumbling off whenever provoked. Though it could not have counted against his credibility with the jury in 1778, it may be taken as evidence of his questionable character that he had to face a court-martial in 1780 on the charge of fraud in mustering phantom soldiers in his regiment, a charge of which, one hastens to add, he was cleared.[17]

Robert Aitken, the printer who delivered the journals of Congress to Roberts for safekeeping, was elected an elder of the Scots Presbyterian Church in 1775. In the years that followed he scrupulously discharged his duties as a member of that church's session. Yet, while remaining in Philadelphia during the British occupation, Aitken stumbled badly when he swore allegiance to the British Crown. For these dour Presbyterian Scots who were doctrinally opposed to all oath-taking but strongly in favor of the Revolution, it was a close call which gave greater offense: the oath itself, or professing allegiance to the King of England. After a period of suspension, "having been broken up by the British army taking possession of the City," the church's session met and took under consideration a formal complaint lodged against Aitken, who pleaded in contrite reply that he had acted out of fear of imprisonment and had since moved to correct his error by taking the test oath Pennsylvania required. His fellow elders, not being fully satisfied, proposed rebuking him before the congregation, a sanction he persuaded them to forego "as he appre-hended it might do him a signal injury." This chastening experience for Aitken took place only three weeks before Roberts's trial, and the fresh memory of it may have limited how much he was willing to reveal in court concerning the relationship he had with Roberts.[18]

Roberts had incriminating connections tied to his fishing company about which there was contradictory testimony at the trial. That he was an avid fisherman, for personal pleasure and for profit, was amply and consistently established. His house and mills were located on a tributary of the Schuylkill River, and both Mill Creek and the Schuylkill were laden with a wide variety of fish, especially spawning shad in the Schuylkill in the spring months. In 1773 the Pennsylvania Assembly named "John Roberts, Miller," along with others, including David Rittenhouse, as a commissioner under a previously passed statute to ensure the navigability of rivers and the unobstructed annual migration of fish upstream to spawn. In other legislation the assembly had prescribed specific regulations designed to prevent overfishing in the Schuylkill through repeated use of "divers seines or nets in the same pool or fishing-place." After a winter of being cooped up in Philadelphia and with spring approaching, Roberts naturally gravitated toward the Schuylkill and the mem-bers of his fishing company or partnership. If the exact location of the fishing company's seine on that river cannot now be fixed, we may nevertheless be certain that, having familiarity with the river and the regulation of its use, he would have been of invaluable help in finding the best places to fish.[19]

Joseph Pritchard identified the members of the fishing company in the testimony he gave about the meeting at the Middle Ferry tavern that occurred after a long day of fishing on the Schuylkill. Three names stand out besides his own as examples of men of doubtful commitment to the Revolutionary cause. Once again trusting his ear, McKean took down "Abia Wright," as one such name, which is very close to Abijah Wright. The Wright of that name had been imprisoned since early July, on the combined charge of treason and burglary in forcibly entering before daylight on February 14, 1778, in the company of six other men, the house of Andrew Knox, Esquire, and having fired "sundry Balls thorough the door." Wright was convicted of the crime of burglary on November 11, and hanged the following month. In Samuel Rowland Fisher's opinion, Wright's principal offense was serving as a guide to the British; Fisher commented that McKean treated Wright very roughly at his trial and in delivering another sentence of florid dispatch.[20]

Two other members of the fishing company whom Pritchard identified appear to have been among those named in the conditional attainder proclamation of May 21, 1778. Jacob Richardson, a carpenter from Upper Merion, was accused of having acted as a guide in leading the British forces into Philadelphia at the end of September 1777, whereas James Stevens (or Stephens), a baker from Philadelphia, would later be brought to trial and acquitted of the charge of having committed treason by serving as a watchman for the British at the Middle Ferry.[21]

How much background information of this character filtered into the jury's deliberations we cannot tell. As the members of the jury hesitated over how they should vote, balancing the evidence against Roberts with the favorable testimony of the many witnesses who came forward to support him, they would necessarily have had to consider the consequence of a guilty verdict for someone whose conduct often seemed ambiguous and confused. If they had the option that juries in capital cases often have today, of rendering an initial verdict and then deciding, after they vote to convict, whether the evidence justifies the imposition of the death penalty, their task would have been an easier one. They had, however, an all-or-nothing choice, between conviction and acquittal. The terms of the indictment barred their returning a verdict for a lesser offense, like misprision of treason, which under the statute would have resulted in Roberts's imprisonment for the duration of the war and the loss of half his property, the penalty imposed on the prickly Samuel Rowland Fisher.[22] Furthermore, the prior conviction of Abraham Carlisle made it all the more difficult for the Roberts jury to acquit this wealthier Quaker who had also consorted with the British.

The jurors may have tried to navigate their way out of this dilemma by agreeing on a guilty verdict, but subject to the understanding that they would request clemency. Nothing appears in the record or the bare newspaper account of either Carlisle's trial or Roberts's that indicates that they made such a request in open court. Yet, in a system of draconian punishments, it was by no means unheard of that a jury returning a guilty verdict would simultaneously recommend mercy, or that a judge might thereafter apply to the executive authority for mitigation of the sentence mandated by the conviction. The American experience in granting clemency during that period has not been extensively charted, but it was an accepted feature of the administration of justice in England for judges to stay a sentence while applying for and often obtaining the King's pardon.[23]

The treatment of George Hardy provides a frightening example of the tardy dispensation of mercy in a Pennsylvania treason case. Hardy was convicted of high treason on April 8, 1779. McKean, joined by his two fellow justices, all the members of the jury who brought in the guilty verdict, and "divers reputable Citizens" petitioned the Supreme Executive Council for mercy "so far as respects his life," noting that his behavior, "during the several times he appeared before the court, and at and after the trial, was decent, respectful and penitential." The justices saw a prospect of reformation if his life was spared, while at the same time they thought his death "would afford little benefit by the example" since he was "a man of small note or consideration." One of the gaolers in the Old Jail told Samuel Rowland Fisher that Hardy (or Harding, as Fisher called him), who was imprisoned there, would be "condemned & reprieved either in the Dungeon or at the Gallows." True to that prediction, Hardy went to the gallows a month later where, on the verge of being "launched into eternity," he received a last-minute reprieve, to the reported satisfaction of the spectators "who were strongly moved by compassion towards the wife and children of this unhappy man." By that time it was recognized that Hardy couldn't be granted a pardon under the constitution until the end of the next session of the General Assembly; eventually the executive council pardoned Hardy, but on condition that his property be forfeited and that he accept permanent banishment from the state.[24]

An odd and combative Frenchman may have succeeded in prying open, at least a crack, the door behind which the Roberts jury remained closeted in protracted indecision. Brissot de Warville, one of a long succession of French observers who have found the study of America and Americans irresistible, came to this country for a six-month stay in 1788, full of idealistic preconceptions and with a particular devotion in the abstract to the Society of Friends and its principles. Prone to lose his head in argument, Brissot would later do so, via the guillotine, as a leader of the Girondin faction at the height of the Terror in the French Revolution.[25]

In the trip he took to America, Brissot had as a primary objective cancelling the critical comments of a predecessor of his, the Marquis de Chastellux, who several years before had written in his *Voyages dans l'Amérique Septentrionale* that Quakers affected a simplicity and candor in "a smooth and wheedling tone which is altogether Jesuitical." Chastellux expatiated on the charge of Quaker deceitfulness: "concealing their indifference for the public welfare under the cloak of religion, they are indeed sparing of blood, especially of their own; but they trick both parties out of their money, and that without either shame or decency." To make matters even worse in Brissot's eyes, the English translator of Chastellux's work had dropped at this very point in the text a long taunting footnote about the trials of Carlisle and Roberts and the treason that "these harmless quakers who would not *bear arms*" flagrantly committed. In view of the "evident necessity for making an example of these most dangerous of all enemies, lenity would have been as ill-timed as unjust to the suffering citizens."[26]

A modern editor of Brissot's attempt to correct the record and answer Chastellux has characterized the volume Brissot published on his return to France as "extremely tendentious, partisan, and ideological."[27] Yet one ought not lose sight of the investigation Brissot pursued while in the United States that focused on the Roberts and Carlisle trials. His account, tendentious and partisan though it might be, is intriguing because of the access he apparently had to inside information, one possible source of which may have been Miers Fisher, whom Brissot speaks of as his "good friend."

Some things Brissot got plainly wrong: for example, that the same jury tried both Roberts and Carlisle, and that Joseph Reed, as "the Quakers' worst enemy," hastened to become president of the executive council so as to forestall in that role the pardon that the council was otherwise ready to grant. But he did get something substantially right: a revelation we now know about only because it appears in the elusive trial notes of Thomas McKean and in the testimony that McKean alone recorded of Daniel Clymer and Robert Aitken. "He [Roberts] proved another point," Brissot wrote, "which attested his innocence, that at that time the secret papers and archives of Congress were hidden in his mill, where the English headquarters were located, and he never betrayed the secret." That piece of information had to come either from a person present at Roberts's trial or from someone who had detailed knowledge of what happened there, and Brissot's access to such an informant lends plausibility to his next disclosure: "Only two of the jurors thought Carlisle and Roberts guilty, and the ten others wished to acquit them. The two succeeded in persuading the other ten to change their votes only by promising that a pardon would be granted and by persuading the others of the necessity of a conspicuous example." One may take as added support for Brissot's version of what happened the admission Joseph Reed made in his letter to George Bryan, written twelve days prior to Roberts's execution, that as the prosecuting attorney Reed "allways expected" that, once the trial was over, the jury would petition for mercy."[28]

A persuasive basis thus exists for concluding that the Roberts jury did come to such a resolution and that the two members of the jury who abstained from signing the petition for clemency were the two who held out for conviction. Those jurors were James Hood and James Barnes, seated as the tenth and eleventh jurors; in spite of the serial service of jurors in the treason cases that followed, Barnes never served again, and Hood was a member of the jury in only three more cases.[29]

Of all the contemporary judgments reached concerning the fairness of Roberts's trial and its outcome, none was the subject of more careful deliberation than that of the committee of inquiry appointed by the Philadelphia Meeting for Sufferings. The original role of the Meeting for Sufferings was, in keeping with its name, to collect accounts of losses and hardships suffered by Friends because of adherence to Quaker testimonies. It came into existence in 1756 to provide relief to Friends who experienced difficulties because of their pacifist stance during the French and Indian War; eventually it would assume a larger responsibility as a kind of executive committee acting on issues of importance that needed to be addressed between sessions of the Yearly Meeting.[30] Although the Meeting for Sufferings was, in the structure of Quaker meetings, clearly the body to take notice of the trials of Carlisle and Roberts, both in and out of court, it refrained from any kind of official action until after their deaths.

The first entry in any Quaker record about the unhappy situation of either of the two prisoners was a late notation in the minutes of a committee that met at Merion on October 19, 1778, to the effect that, having devoted some attention to "the case of John Roberts–Miller now under Sentence of Death," the committee "thought best to apply to the Meeting for Sufferings in Philadelphia for their advice & assistance in his Distressed Situation." Four members of the committee were duly appointed to deliver this brief minute of referral to Philadelphia.[31] The Meeting for Sufferings was, of course, fully aware of the ordeal Roberts and Carlisle were going through. Quakers of high repute daily visited the prisoners as they neared their end, not only to offer religious support and comfort but also to set the record straight about the failure of the condemned men to adhere to Quaker principles. It was mainly solicitude about the Society's reputation that led John Pemberton, John Parrish, Samuel Smith, and Henry Drinker to engage Abraham Carlisle in deep conversation days before he died, pointing out "the burthen bro't on Friends by his omitting to pay due attention to some early hints & advice given him" and then noting, with a lawyerly satisfaction, Carlisle's apparent willingness, under the influence of their persuasion, "to acknowledge the same in Writing."[32]

Not until two weeks had passed after the deaths of Roberts and Carlisle did the Meeting for Sufferings give formal recognition to their cases, but again in language that seemed to mirror greater concern for the Society of Friends than for its two recently deceased members or for their bereaved families:

> The Reputation of Truth and our Religious Testimony having suffered by two late Sorrowful Instances of two of our Brethren in Religious Membership being put to Death in this City by those now in Power, Israel Pemberton,

John Reynell, James Thornton, James Pemberton, Henry Drinker and Nicholas
Waln are appointed to make Inquiry into the Circumstances of their cases to
be laid before the Meeting for further Consideration.[33]

A month later the committee reported on the initial progress it had made and
emphasized where its attention was directed: "Some profitable and Weighty
Observations were made upon this sorrowful and afflicting Dispensation tend-
ing to excite Friends to a deep and watchful Attention to the Testimony of Truth
and a vigilant Care over our Brethren for their Preservation from deviations on
either hand." Month after month in 1779 in the minutes of the Meeting for
Sufferings the matter was marked continued until, on the 16th 9th mo, the
committee appears to have laid its completed report before the meeting which
expressed "a concurrence with [its] General Tenor" but signaled that the
matter would be continued for further consideration. There the trail in the
minutes comes to an abrupt halt, no mention thereafter appearing in the
minutes for the next six years.[34]

In December 1785, the Meeting for Sufferings dusted off the report of the
committee of inquiry that James Pemberton had signed and submitted under
date of 8th mo 4th 1779, "as solidly attended to & calmly deliberated on." How
to explain this long hiatus when the committee saw as its urgent duty in 1779
"to obviate the misrepresentations and aspersions propagated by our adversaries
in order to vindicate their own conduct, or injure the cause of Truth"?[35] The
Meeting for Sufferings made no effort to provide an explanation. During the
Revolution its invariable practice was to speak out strongly and uncompromis-
ingly in defense of Quaker principles, and yet about these two unfortunate
members of the Society, it maintained a long silence that it may have decided
was the most prudent course to follow as long as other Friends were still
exposed to retaliatory measures.

The Meeting for Sufferings finally accepted the report and incorporated it
in its minutes in apparent response to a request for documentary material
from John Gough, a Quaker historian preparing a history of the Society of
Friends and its vicissitudes, although Gough's four-volume work, when published toward the end of the decade, contained no mention of this tragic
episode.[36] At any rate, if not the last word on the trials of Roberts and Carlisle,
the report represents measured Quaker judgment based on the testimonial
record kept by a friendly observer at each of the two trials. The notes taken
for Carlisle's trial, running to four compressed manuscript pages, appear to
be in the handwriting of Henry Drinker. There is no reason, however, to
believe that Drinker attended either trial, and more likely he simply transcribed
the notes someone else made. The notes for Roberts's trial run to eighteen
pages (excluding McKean's appended sentencing statement) and are in an
unrecognizable hand. Both sets of notes may be found today in the miscellane-

ous records of the Meeting for Sufferings, along with the final report of the committee of inquiry.[37]

Beginning with an acknowledgment of its task to inquire into the cases of "the two Members of our religious Society who suffered Death in this City by Execution," the committee moved on to put "this affecting Subject" in the context of the trials Friends had historically faced "in times of persecution" on account of "their stability and faithfulness to their Christian Testimony." Because of their faith, Friends had been compelled on painful occasion to surrender their lives at "the hands of deluded, & malicious men," which the committee accepted as heroic witness promoting "the cause of Truth & Righteousness in the Earth." In its next breath it deplored as "uncommon and sorrowful" when any are "brought to such an end while in membership with us, and not on the like account." Having obtained information about the court proceedings, the committee saw it as its solemn duty ascertaining to which group Carlisle and Roberts belonged: Were they victims of deluded men, and hence martyrs, or were they instead victims of their own deviation from the truth, and hence the subjects of prayerful reflection and pity?

The committee's report could not avoid being defensive in tone as it took on aspects of a lawyer's brief prepared to counter charges brought against two members of the Society of Friends for having visibly taken sides and provided aid and comfort to the British during the occupation of Philadelphia. The impression of discomfort may be increased for readers of the report today by the authors' recourse to an emollient Quaker vocabulary and idiom, which, in dulling the sharp edges of contentiousness, can also tend to obscure meaning.[38]

The committee stressed that Friends had been constantly reminded from "the early appearance of the commotions among the people in these Colonies" to steer clear of any involvement in warfare, "and divers weighty advices were given forth with pressing exhortations to this effect, which as occasions increased were repeated with earnest admonitions, & cautions to all among us, to beware of becoming parties in the public consultations, bustles, and disturbances prevailing." This emphasis by the committee constituted an essential part of the Society's own defense—that it had put all its members, Carlisle and Roberts included, on clear notice of what religious profession in the Society of Friends entailed. Yet in spite of these warnings, some Friends "have been overtaken, & ensnared by such plausible appearances that they have involved themselves in difficulties, and distress," and subjected their families "to great affliction and adversity." It was at this point that the committee made a significant concession by adding to the foregoing observation these words about two such Friends who had gone astray: "which is lamentably the case of the members now under our consideration, tho in some respects they vary from each other." To put it bluntly, the committee had concluded that it would not attempt to exonerate Roberts and Carlisle, not completely, and that in any event their cases needed to be treated separately.[39]

Having focused on John Roberts, this study has not pursued a thorough examination of Abraham Carlisle's trial and the evidence presented against him. The committee, under an obligation to consider both cases, recognized that Carlisle, "an Inhabitant of this City of a reputable moral Character," had been present at all times within the jurisdiction of the Philadelphia Yearly Meeting and the Philadelphia Monthly Meeting (Northern District). After the British had taken possession of the city in the fall of 1777, "he was prevailed upon," the committee wrote, "to accept an office to grant permits for persons to pass in & out." His undertaking to do so gave concern to Friends who "expressed their uneasiness to him, but their endeavours to convince him of his error, did not prevail with him to withdraw or decline from executing it."[40]

If indeed the meeting in Philadelphia took such steps to caution and dissuade Carlisle, it did so informally, leaving no entry in its records to that effect. When, not long before his death, Carlisle received a visit intended to be of a consoling nature from Samuel Smith and Isaac Catherall, he disconcerted these two weighty members of his own meeting by telling them that, in agreeing to guard the gates for the British, he believed he had simply done what Friends had advised him to do. Smith and Catherall instantly protested that he must have misunderstood: the most Friends could have properly suggested was that "he should do no more than be an assistance to facilitate the passing out or in [of] such that were known to be Inoffensive People." Carlisle yielded to persuasion, saying, according to a later report of the conversation, "he was very sorry if he had given any uneasiness to Friends as he had always had a Regard for the Society."[41]

From her vantage point as Carlisle's neighbor, Elizabeth Drinker lends credence to the notion of his limited responsibility as a watchman issuing passes to the needy when she records in her diary on November 24, 1777, "the poor people have been allow'd for some time past to go to Frankford Mill, and other Mills that way, for Flour, Abraham Carlile [sic] who gives them passes, has his Door very much crouded every morning." In contrast to this benign view, we know that Joseph Galloway, the year after Carlisle's death, told a parliamentary investigating committee that he had urged Carlisle to leave with the evacuating British forces because of the services he conspicuously rendered during the occupation of Philadelphia.[42]

In taking up Roberts's case, the committee disclaimed knowledge of any instruction he might have been given to avoid involvement in the prevailing commotions: "The other being a member of the neighbouring Monthly Meeting in the Country, we have not learned that any religious care or advice was seasonably extended to him." That statement was both literally true and disingenuous. Because of Roberts's rapid and unexpected decision to leave home and go to Philadelphia in early October 1777, the Radnor and Merion meetings would have lacked the opportunity to catch up with him, much less to extend "seasonably" any kind of religious care or advice. Nevertheless, although the members of meeting who were formally sanctioned for violations of the testimony against war continued to come exclusively from the ranks of those "going out in the Militia as Warriers [sic]," the Merion meeting went on record in the summer of 1777 with an admonition of unmistakable clarity to dissuade its members from participating in the conflict on either side. "[A]t this time of Singular probation," Friends were advised that they should "carefully guard against Joining in the present Commotion [in] any way."[43] In point of fact, if any Quaker meeting had the ability to caution Roberts directly, it would have been the Philadelphia meeting, alone in a position to observe what he was doing once he moved in with Owen Jones and his wife. To be fair about it, however, the Philadelphia meeting was not at full supervisory strength during this period, because many of its senior members had been sent away in an enforced absence.

Three out of the six members of the committee of inquiry, as originally formed, Israel and James Pemberton and Henry Drinker, were among the Virginia exiles. The committee therefore could express genuine indignation when referring in its report to the unjust apprehension and "banishment without an examination or hearing" of the Friends transported to Virginia and attributing to Roberts on their account "Suffering in his Mind by this arbitrary violation of Civil & religious liberty," enough that "he hastened away without previously consulting them [the banished Quakers] to give intelligence thereof to the General of the British Army then on their march towards this City, in the hope to frustrate the intention of sending them into exile." So, notwithstanding the effort of Roberts's counsel to minimize this story's impact, the committee accepted it, and went a step further. It alleged that, once this "proceeding of his" became known, it "gave sensible pain & concern to friends," a reaction that is nowhere else documented and that, moreover, appears to conflict with the testimony given at Roberts's trial by another Virginia exile, Miers Fisher, who said that he knew nothing at all about Roberts's supposed scheme to rescue the Friends on the road to Winchester.[44]

The committee acknowledged the second more damaging charge against Roberts: that "he was seen in company with the English Army, or parties of them in some of their marches or enterprizes not far distant from the City," but added that "he allways insisted this was against his will and that he was forcibly compelled to do it, which also appears by the evidences given at his tryal." In short, the committee found Roberts and Carlisle guilty of violating the Quaker code in "their deviation from that rectitude, & stability of Conduct which our Christian Peaceable principles require." Those errors necessarily restrained the Meeting for Sufferings or any other meeting "from interposing in their favour or vindication, as is our duty & usual care, when our brethren are subjected to suffering or persecution for righteousness sake, & the testimony of a Good Conscience." Violating the Quaker code was one thing; being convicted of treason and sentenced to death was quite another. The committee did not hesitate to pass its own judgment on the harsh treatment accorded both Roberts and Carlisle, and especially on the executive council's refusal to act favorably on the many petitions submitted for clemency. In the full perspective that the passage of time has provided, it is hard to take issue with the measured conclusions the committee reached:

> Having perused a Copy of the evidence taken at their trial, we find them to be very contradictory, & discover clear indications of a party Spirit, and that they were prosecuted with great severity & rigour is also apparent, the punishment inflicted far exceeding the nature of their offence; and that this was the general Sense of the people was demonstrated by great numbers of all Ranks uniting their interest & influence for saving their lives by petitions, & divers personal applications to the persons in power who held the authority over them, but they proved inexorable alledging political reasons for rejecting those ardent solicitations.[45]

As the day set for the executions approached, John Pemberton and Henry Drinker paid a visit to George Bryan, the acting president of the executive council, and the next day the two of them, joined by John Parrish, went to see another member of the council, Joseph Hart. In whatever appeal they made, the representatives of the meeting would not have attempted to retry the cases of the two men facing death by claiming their innocence. Even taking the most charitable view, Carlisle and Roberts had departed from the Quaker code that the Philadelphia meeting had so insistently proclaimed, to the recurrent impatience of the members of the council whom these high Quakers now sought out. To have any chance of success, theirs had to be a plea for compassion and clemency, added to those that so many others had already requested in the petitions to the council. But John Pemberton recorded in his diary that they came away from these interviews "with little or no reason to expect mercy." After the second meeting with a member of the executive council, a delegation consisting of Pemberton, Drinker, Parrish, and Samuel Smith carried the sad intelligence to Roberts and Carlisle in prison, whom they found, Pemberton wrote, "in a thoughtful disposition, & tender, particularly J.R."[46]

The statement that politics controlled the council's decision ought to have come as no surprise. The stronger than expected showing of the conservatives in the recent election for the assembly caused the members of council to be especially attentive to their political base that demanded retaliatory justice. Joseph Reed may have accurately reflected the concern of those in power when he told his friend Nathanael Greene that, unless all Toryism, however flagrant, was to go unpunished and the whole attainder apparatus collapse, Roberts and Carlisle were the prime candidates for hanging.[47] Bryan and Hart would not, of course, have been this candid in explaining the council's political decision; yet one wonders whether their Quaker supplicants pressed for something more in the way of an answer. If they did, they risked hearing how the militant preaching of pacifism in time of war made it politically impossible to rescue two wayward members of the Society of Friends who had failed to remain neutral.

VI

Toward Forgetting

Forgiving usually precedes forgetting, as in the familiar injunction, "Forgive and Forget." One represents an exercise of willpower, whereas the other is a benefit that time may confer. If forgetting were to come first and wipe away entirely the memory of the wrong committed, nothing would be left to forgive. That the two concepts are, however, related is evident once we shift from words of Old English derivation to those of Greek: *amnesty* and *amnesia*.

It may be useful to distinguish, as the French philosopher Paul Ricoeur has done, between pardoning and amnesty. The right to grant pardons is the traditional prerogative reserved to the sovereign, the "residue of a quasi-divine right" usually exercised for the relief of individuals accused or convicted of crimes. Amnesty is, in contrast, what Ricoeur calls an "institutionalized form of forgetting," typically broader in scope, not dependent on a prior finding of individual criminal conduct or culpability, and customarily granted by legislative act. Amnesty in this light becomes a means of reconciling enemies and promoting civil peace.[1] Yet the boundary between granting a pardon and granting amnesty can become a blurred one, just as for the boundary between forgiving and forgetting. We have seen in an earlier chapter the uncertainty that existed in the period after Roberts's conviction when petitions for clemency were submitted on his behalf and Abraham Carlisle's. To whom should the petitions be addressed? Who in the improvised institutional framework established under the Pennsylvania constitution of 1776 had the ability to grant relief: the Supreme Executive Council, a plural executive having hedged powers, or the unitary legislative body, having enhanced ones? In a long newspaper column "Rectifier" had forcefully argued that a petition circulated for Abraham Carlisle mistakenly sought forbearance from the assembly when the power to intervene by way of pardon belonged alone to the sovereign.[2]

Regardless of who had the power to grant pardons, the eighteenth century understood the relationship between forgiving and forgetting when referring to pardons as "acts of oblivion." Ricoeur reaches even further back in time to the extraordinary formulation in the Edict of Nantes proclaimed by Henry IV, king of France, that the memory of preceding religious troubles "remain

111

extinguished and dormant as something that has not occurred" and forbidding "any of our subjects to retain any memory thereof." In modern times the exercise of the pardoning power has often had the opposite effect from mandated amnesia by stirring up continuing controversy.[3]

The challenge for the Revolutionary generation was how to come to grips with the loyalist phenomenon while at the same time, as Sarah Purcell has put it, "creating a usable national memory based on gratitude for patriotism." Among Americans, achieving independence had not been a universal aspiration; despite the "long train of abuses and usurpations" that the Declaration assigned to him, as many as one out of every five Americans, an estimated half million in all, would have elected to remain subjects of Britain's king. In Gordon Wood's useful reminder, by a multiple of six, more loyalists left America during the Revolution per one thousand of population than fled France during the French Revolution. The exodus of loyalists counts in Wood's view not because of their sheer number but rather because of the positions many of them had previously occupied as "well-to-do gentry operating at the pinnacles of power and patronage." Their forced departure led, he has written, to "ramifying disruptions" in the preexisting social order, being one more factor in making the American Revolution a transformative and radical experience. Wood cites as evidence of such disruption in Pennsylvania the banishment of members of elite family groups like the Shippens and the Chews.

And yet the counterargument may be made that, through what one might call "deliberate forgetting," many suspected of loyalist sympathies, like the Shippens and the Chews specifically, were reinstalled in the postwar power structure and that the disruption of the old order was not everywhere quite as radical as Wood would have it. The "reintegration of Loyalists into society," as Sarah Purcell has pointed out, "required an extensively delicate balancing of remembering and forgetting." That the process of reintegration was "highly selective" and incremental does not, however, detract from the general direction in which postwar society often found it convenient to move.[4]

True, it would take more than a full decade in Pennsylvania before Tory sins were largely forgiven, if not forgotten, and even then not every sinner was pardoned, not when the spirit of forgiving collided with the still live memory of past wrongs. Pennsylvania could not bring itself in the 1790s to pardon General Howe's superintendent of police during the British occupation of Philadelphia, Joseph Galloway, who, strange to say, had acquired in Thomas McKean a sympathetic supporter. Galloway's attorney had petitioned the legislature for a pardon, but judging the unfavorable lay of the land, he withdrew the petition in 1790 before it was voted down. In a letter to McKean of 1793, more magnanimous than resentful, Galloway thanked McKean for volunteering to help procure a pardon "in case I should return to Pennsylvania" but expressed regret that objections made on his particular account had excluded from the benefit of a general amnesty others similarly situated "who during the late contest with America deserted her cause." Unable to fathom why objections should apply with such force against him, he proceeded to give McKean "a brief state of my conduct, during the war, dictated by a religious regard to truth." The work of a practiced advocate, it failed in this instance to be persuasive.[5]

Exceptions to the harsh treatment of attainted loyalists occurred much earlier, coming not infrequently as the result of having privileged access to persons in power. The case of Tench Coxe provides one such example. Coxe had sided with the British during the occupation of Philadelphia and profited as a merchant from engaging in illegal trade. Named in a proclamation of attainder two weeks after Carlisle and Roberts were similarly charged, he escaped a treason trial by turning to Thomas McKean, a longtime friend of the Coxe family, who is credited with obtaining Coxe's discharge.[6]

In March 1778, the Pennsylvania Assembly included Nathaniel Vernon, the former Chester County sheriff who joined the British forces and continued on in the British service through the surrender at Yorktown, among those whom it condemned and whose property was subject to forfeiture for committing "divers treasonable acts without any sense of honour, virtue, liberty, or fidelity to this State."[7] To stay in Philadelphia after the British decided to leave the city was never an alternative for Nathaniel Vernon, who, with his son Nathaniel, Jr., resettled in Nova Scotia after the war. His four other sons, Thomas, Job, Frederick, and John, were unabashed Whigs, and two of them fought with the American army. These four sons petitioned the assembly for relief from confiscation of their father's estate, and in October 1779 their request was granted in special legislation, which provided, however, that the revesting in them of title to their father's estate should not affect such parts of his personal property "as have been sold before the passing of this act in pursuance of the said act of attainder." That proviso was essential because in the prior month sundry cattle and sheep jointly owned by Vernon and John Roberts had been sold at public vendue, with the Commonwealth realizing from the sale the sum of three hundred ninety-five pounds.[8]

Elizabeth Graeme Ferguson, a woman of spirit, intelligence, wealth, and literary talent, secretly married in 1772 Henry Hugh Ferguson, ten years her junior, whose conspicuous attachment to the Crown—he, too, was named as a traitor—threatened to result in the confiscation of her inherited real estate. Despite her intelligence, Elizabeth Ferguson was notably lacking in prudence, agreeing to deliver messages from sources that cast doubt on both the wisdom and the patriotism of the messenger. The Reverend Jacob Duché enlisted her to convey a bewildering letter to George Washington advocating surrender, a letter that its recipient characterized as a "ridiculous, illiberal performance," while reprimanding the messenger for "the intercourse she seemed to be carrying on," which he expected to be discontinued posthaste. Not sufficiently chastened by this experience, Mrs. Ferguson served as a conduit the following year for a proffered bribe to Joseph Reed from a member of the Earl of Carlisle's peace commission.[9] Even so, the assembly, when petitioned to confirm her title to the family property outside Philadelphia, free of the taint of her husband's defection to the British and his proclaimed attainder, obliged by finding that "the said Elizabeth appears to have acted a friendly part to the cause of the United States and to be in such a peculiar situation as to deserve the protection and indulgence of this commonwealth."[10]

No such generous act of forgiveness or oblivion would be forthcoming to alleviate the distress of John Roberts's survivors. Nor were they themselves permitted to forget the outcome of the trial. In the near term, nobody could forget that Carlisle and Roberts had been hanged in the public commons on the charge of having given aid and comfort to the forces of their recent sovereign. The juries that continued to sit in treason trials during the remainder of 1778 and in 1779 had learned their lesson about the consequence of returning a guilty verdict, even when accompanied by a plea for compassion. In the unlikely event that the public officials responsible for prosecuting Roberts and carrying out his punishment had any second thoughts, they soon overcame their misgivings and proceeded with the confiscation of the convicted traitor's property (Figure 6.1).

Moreover, were Jane Roberts and her children of a mind to forget, forgetting was scarcely a tolerable option for them. In the years ahead they were repeatedly compelled in their own self-interest to relive the memory of John Roberts's trial and hanging. Within weeks after his death, they applied for legal protection, and the one body that by everyone's understanding lacked the constitutional power to grant clemency—the court in which Roberts had been tried—came to their rescue. The first person to relent, and perhaps partially to repent, may have been Thomas McKean, whose self-indulgent sentencing statement, when delivered to the executive council as purporting to reflect the court's considered opinion concerning Roberts's guilt, eliminated any realistic chance of his obtaining clemency. Jane Roberts, Roberts's widow; her son Thomas; and Roberts's maiden aunt, Gwen Lloyd had petitioned the Supreme Court to exclude from the sale of Roberts's goods and chattels, scheduled at his house for Monday, November 30, 1778, a broad range of articles they claimed they were entitled to, either as a matter of separate ownership or for necessary support. The court under McKean's leadership entered a temporary restraining order that carved out of the sale, pending a final judicial determination, all of the items the petitioners had identified, and in the spring of the following

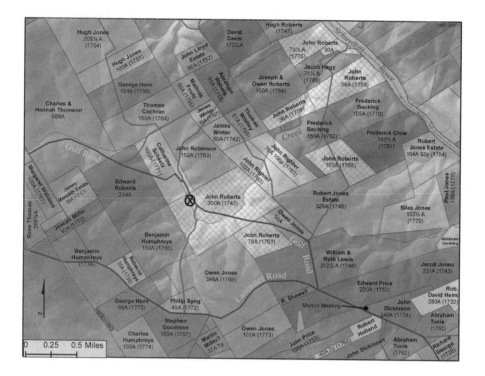

Figure 6.1 Map of Roberts properties along Mill Creek. The Supreme Court of Pennsylvania decreed that John Roberts had effectively transferred to his son Thomas the three parcels closest to the Schuylkill River. The site of Roberts's gristmill, built in 1746 on the south side of Gulph Road slightly west of his house, is marked by a circled x.

year, the court issued a blanket ruling granting the petitioners, without exception, the relief they requested.

Among the many valuable articles that Jane Roberts was thus able to retain for her support and maintenance and that of her underage children were a desk and bookcase, a clock, beds, miscellaneous furniture, kitchen ware, and a stove. Although less obviously tied to support and maintenance, the court also awarded her the cider and the whiskey in the cellar, a substantial quantity of harvested hay and wheat, a wagon and cart, the bay gelding, the pigs, and the cow. Thomas Roberts, the older of the two Roberts sons, received the second wagon, the four beehives in the garden, and additional furniture from the house.[11] The maiden aunt, an aged sister of John Roberts's mother, who had moved in with the Roberts family and occupied a second-floor bedroom, was allowed to keep a chest of drawers and looking glass, her bed and bedding, a half dozen cups and saucers and a tea pot, and one spinning wheel.[12]

At the auction sale that took place on December 1, a day later than originally scheduled, Jehu Roberts, the younger son, was the successful bidder on such articles as his father's map of Philadelphia for more than twice its appraised value, some but not all of his father's fishing gear, the copper boiler in the shed for a fraction of its appraised value, the staves in the cooper shop for a third of their appraised value, and the ten tons of hay in the barn at the value specified by the appraisers. From the auction sale the Commonwealth realized three hundred twenty-eight pounds, ten pence; of that sum, Jehu's total contribution far exceeded what all the other purchasers paid. In short, while it was undoubtedly heart-rending for the family to part with as much as they had to, they managed by one means or another to salvage a great deal.[13]

Under the Supreme Court's restraining order issued before the sale, Jane Roberts also received temporary permission to use, as she requested, "the Messuage, Plantation & Mills whereon we now live." In its ruling of the following spring, the court permitted her to continue in occupancy for another year or until the sale of the property and, while there, to sow and reap fifty acres of grain. Because the principal real estate John Roberts owned on Mill Creek would not be sold until the middle of 1780, it appears that his widow remained undisturbed in her possession of the property (Figure 6.2) for all of this period. So Thomas Roberts testified some years later: "His Mother was never driven from her House. She had permission to live there for a year or a little more after his Father's Death. She had the use of the whole Plantation, except the paper Mill."[14]

In November 1779 the Roberts family submitted a petition to the assembly requesting that Roberts's confiscated real estate not be sold and that the family be permitted to retain title to it. When the assembly failed to act on the petition, Jehu Roberts renewed the request on behalf of himself and his seven sisters by addressing a petition to the executive council, asking in language reminiscent of the clemency petitions submitted for his father that the threatened sale of the property be suspended until the next meeting of the assembly. The executive council, now presided over by Joseph Reed, again turned out to be unyielding; it rejected the plea on the day it was presented, clearing the way for the auction sale to proceed.[15]

For many months, it had been unclear exactly what property or properties Roberts had owned, and when those holdings might safely be offered for sale. The confusion was understandable inasmuch as properties in Roberts ownership were scattered at different locations throughout the Mill Creek Valley. In April 1779, Timothy Matlack, the secretary of the Supreme Executive Council and the Keeper of the Register for Forfeited Estates, notified the public that the real estate previously owned by various persons attainted for treason would be "speedily sold by public auction or vendue." Creditors of the traitors were accordingly put on notice that they should come forward and

Figure 6.2 John Roberts's house today, as restored and maintained in private ownership. The lower section of the house to the left is thought to have been built by Roberts's grandfather in the last decade of the seventeenth century; Roberts added the section to the right in the early 1750s.

Reproduced by permission of The Lower Merion Historical Society.

assert their claims in timely fashion. At the end of July it was announced that some of the forfeited properties would be offered for sale at the courthouse in Philadelphia beginning on August 25, including a parcel of one hundred acres that Roberts had owned, on which a house and barn stood, located near Frederick Bicking's land and the Schuylkill River.[16]

Nevertheless the bulk of Roberts's holdings remained unsold until June 1780. Contradictory notices appeared in the newspapers about the properties available for purchase. In anticipation of a scheduled sale on December 15, 1779, which did not occur, two properties of Roberts were specified in the advertisement:

> No. 1. three hundred acres in Lower Merion township, one large and sundry other dwelling houses, two grist mills, a sawmill and a paper mill, with barns, stables, and a great number of other buildings of divers kinds, all in excellent order. No. 2. Seventy eight acres adjoining the above; a dwelling house, barn, &c thereon.

As late as May 1780, a third property was included in the notice of a prospective sale: "No. 3. A Tract of Land on Schuylkill, containing 300 acres, adjoining Frederick Bicking land, with three dwelling houses, a powder mill, and oil mill, and a saw mill thereon, with other improvements." Concerning this third property, the agent for confiscated sales erred on two grounds: the aggregate size of the holding was less than two hundred acres, and by court decree the greater portion of it was excluded from the sale of Roberts's confiscated assets. Thomas Roberts, the older Roberts son, had succeeded in persuading the Supreme Court that prior to the cutoff date of July 4, 1776, his father had effectively transferred to him ownership of this land close to the river, with its dwelling houses and other improvements, which therefore removed it from sale as part of Roberts's forfeited estate.[17]

Who purchased the confiscated property? The agent who conducted the auction sale on August 25, 1779, recorded the name of the successful bidder for the 100-acre parcel, the first of the Roberts properties to be sold, as "Daniel Climer and Company." This was the same Daniel Clymer whom Roberts's lawyers called as their star witness, and to whom, after the trial was over, Roberts turned for help. He was also the same person who signed a tepid and tardy clemency petition, conceding in so many words that Roberts and Carlisle were guilty as charged.[18]

In the year following Roberts's death, and with or without any information he may have gained as a lawyer, Clymer seized on the opportunity to acquire forfeited estates. A month after buying Roberts's one hundred acres, he submitted a successful bid for seven lots in Roxborough across the Schuylkill River that Christopher Saur, an attainted Tory printer, had owned.[19] With regard to the Roberts purchase, Clymer announced at the sale that he was not acting alone. His silent partner, William Eckhardt, a biscuit baker in Philadelphia, later had to step forward to make a required deposit at a time when Clymer had serious trouble of his own to contend with. On October 6, Eckhardt paid the sum of two thousand ten pounds on account of the purchase price of four thousand five hundred ten pounds that Clymer had bid at the sale, and it was Eckhardt who would ultimately take title to the property in a conveyance from Clymer.[20]

Two days before Eckhardt made that payment, Clymer had joined others in coming to the aid of Roberts's beleaguered lead counsel, James Wilson, whose house at the corner of Walnut and Third Streets, afterward known as Fort Wilson (Figure 6.3), was stormed by an angry mob protesting Wilson's representation, successful more often than not, in defending Tories accused of treason. Shots were exchanged, and casualties counted, before the president of the executive council, Joseph Reed, summoned troops and arrived on the scene to restore some semblance of order. Clymer played a large part in the

RESIDENCE OF JAS WILSON KNOWN AS FORT WILSON.
THIRD AND WALNUT ST
1779

Figure 6.3 Fort Wilson, James Wilson's residence at the southwest corner of Third and Walnut Streets, where Wilson and others were attacked by an armed mob in October 1779.

Reproduced by permission of The Historical Society of Pennsylvania.

defense of Fort Wilson; he managed to transport ammunition from the arsenal located at Carpenters' Hall to those holed up under siege in Wilson's house. As a consequence, at the very time money was due on account of the Roberts purchase, Clymer had to post his personal bond of five thousand pounds to ensure his appearance in court in the event that charges were pressed against him; one of the two sureties on the bond he posted was the merchant John Chaloner, a witness for the defense at Roberts's trial.[21]

In another of the many twists of fate in the story of John Roberts, Clymer would be the beneficiary of a sweeping pardon that the Pennsylvania Assembly granted all those who participated in "a tumult and breach of the public peace wherein sundry persons were unhappily killed in and near the house of James Wilson, Esquire, in Walnut Street for which the several parties concerned therein stand bound by recognizance to answer in due course of law." The assembly found that, in the time since that disturbance occurred, "a cordial quietude has taken place" that rendered rigorous prosecution inexpedient "inasmuch as it may tend to perpetuate enmity and discord between the citizens of the same state, when union and harmony are so necessary against the common enemy." Contrary to the assembly's finding, the act of oblivion that it passed did not erase the memory of past grievances. Though the assembly might congratulate itself on witnessing in 1780 the restoration of "a cordial quietude" in Philadelphia, James Wilson felt under continuing pressure in that same year to defend himself in the public press against those who remained vocally up in arms because of his defending Tory clients.[22]

The sale of Roberts's two major holdings occurred on June 21, 1780. There had been a number of false starts, explained perhaps by Thomas Roberts's effort to claim as his own the acreage lower down on Mill Creek that his father had supposedly given him. In the mid-May advertisement of the sale of the remaining Roberts properties scheduled for June 21, this acreage was included, but then, within a short time, apparently excluded. Jehu Roberts's petition to the Supreme Executive Council submitted on June 3, requesting for his sisters and himself suspension of the pending sale, pointedly states that Thomas Roberts was not seeking to establish a share in his father's remaining property, "having received part of the said Estate, by a Decree of the Court." Though the date of the court's decree is missing, it may have been entered several months earlier, since, in a conveyance he made years later of this property he received from his father, Thomas Roberts recited that he submitted his claim to the court on December 4, 1779.[23]

The record purchaser of the main parcel of approximately three hundred acres on which the Roberts house and mills stood and the adjoining parcel of about seventy-eight acres was Edward Milner, a miller by trade from New Britain Township in Bucks County, who had recently moved to Philadelphia. The deed to him from the executive council, dated December 16, 1780, recited a consideration of 271,600 pounds "subject to the yearly rent of 135 bushells and four-fifth part of a bushel of good merchantable wheat, payable to the trustees of the University," which, at the conversion rate of seven shillings, six pence per bushel of wheat, worked out to annual payments to the University of fifty pounds, eighteen shillings, six pence. As in the case of the previous sale of Roberts property to Daniel Clymer, Milner seems to have been acting as agent for the real party or parties in interest, for he immediately turned around and conveyed these two properties to John Maxwell Nesbitt, John Donaldson, and William Erskine, in whose ownership the properties remained until 1797. Milner, the father-in-law of Donaldson, appears to have stayed on site as agent for these wealthy Philadelphia merchants.[24]

Even after the sale in 1780, Thomas Roberts remained in possession of part of his father's property. He testified before a parliamentary commission in

Figure 6.4 Merion Meetinghouse, to the left, and the surrounding area, at the beginning of the nineteenth century, including a field in the distance that Michael Smith may have farmed as John Dickinson's tenant. The covered wagon is heading eastward on Lancaster Road toward Philadelphia.

From Robert Sutcliff's *Travels in Some Parts of North America in the Years 1804, 1805, & 1806* (1811).

Reproduced by permission of The Lower Merion Historical Society.

England in 1786 that "he first rented it in the year 1781 for £250 per ann. for the Mercht Mill, Saw Mill, Grist Mill and part of the Land." He may have sublet the paper mill and an adjoining meadow needed in its operation for seventy-five pounds per year. From the income realized through these arrangements, he said that "he supported & still supports his mother and such of the Children as were than and are now unmarried & unprovided for." His testimony provides an unexpected disclosure: As of 1786, his mother was still living on the part of the property that he had leased.[25]

Beginning in mid-1777, Jane Roberts had endured punishing changes beyond her imagining. She lost her husband, first as her protector at home and then as a traitor condemned to death. That eight years after her husband's death she and her unmarried daughters, deprived of many of their possessions, were living at holdover sufferance in a corner of the family property that her son leased, offered her little consolation. The proximity to their former house daily reminded her of the steep descent from comfortable prosperity to straitened circumstances that she and her children had experienced. Nor, to make matters worse, could she find religious solace in attending the Merion meeting, not when she knew that Michael Smith and his sons were farming the property just beyond the meetinghouse wall (Figure 6.4).[26]

121

The March 1778 act of attainder provided that the justices of the Supreme Court "may and shall order and appropriate such part of the forfeited estates, for the support of such traitor's children, or wife and children, if any, as to them may appear sufficient." On May 6, 1779, the court awarded Jane Roberts a lifetime annuity of seventy-five pounds, the first payment falling due on the first of April a year later. The state defaulted on that obligation, and it took legal action culminating in a 1783 court decree for Jane Roberts to obtain the back payments owed her; in that year she received the total sum of two hundred twenty-eight pounds, ten shillings, and three pence, which included the costs of suit for recovery of the delinquent annuity payments.[27] Nor did she thereafter receive this annual payment automatically. In April 1786, "the relict of John Roberts, Late of Lower Merrion," submitted a formal memorial and petition to the Supreme Executive Council referring to the court's determination in her favor, "now on your files," and requesting the executive council to pay her the sum of seventy-five pounds in specie due as of April 1. The comptroller general then certified to the council that the pension amount had been paid to Jane Roberts "up to the first of April 1785 at £75 per Ann. & no longer." Until her death in 1795, the procedure of applying for and obtaining payment was repeated each year, in a ritual of remembrance that the state may have regarded as providing necessary proof that the executed traitor's widow was still living.[28]

As the war drew to an end, the Roberts family might have hoped that its trials would lessen. In 1782, the representatives of Great Britain and the United States met in Paris to negotiate the provisional terms of a peace treaty. One issue that sharply divided the delegations was how to provide, if at all, for the loyalists whose properties had been confiscated because of their adherence to the Crown. The failure to come to a resolution threatened to prolong the conflict between Britain and America. The British representatives insisted on restoration of the loyalists' confiscated properties as a condition to signing the treaty, whereas the American representatives were equally adamant in opposing any such requirement.

Finally, the stalemate was broken and a compromise agreed upon that permitted the British to save face. Article 5 of the provisional treaty of peace signed in December 1782 gave cold comfort to the loyalists: It was agreed that Congress would "earnestly recommend" to the legislatures of the several states that they provide for the restitution of all confiscated properties "belonging to real British subjects" and also of persons resident in the districts in possession of the British army who had not borne arms against the United States. It was further agreed that "persons of any other description" would be given free liberty to come to the United States and for a period of twelve months proceed "unmolested" in using their best endeavors to obtain restitution of their confiscated properties. The treaty again pledged that Congress would "earnestly recommend" to the states that they undertake a reconsideration and revision of all confiscatory legislation "so as to render the laws or acts perfectly consistent not only with justice and equity but with that spirit of conciliation which on the return of the blessings of peace should universally prevail."[29]

On neither side could the peacemakers have seriously believed that the incantation of "earnestly recommend" had any binding effect or that Article 5 would lead to the restoration of confiscated property in an irenic modification of prior laws directed against loyalists and their property. Under the Articles of Confederation, Congress lacked power to compel the states to honor treaty obligations, assuming that Article 5 contained any element of a commitment. After the definitive treaty of peace was signed in September 1783, it became apparent that Article 5 was nothing more than a rhetorical device, the means used to arrive at a necessary end.

Joseph Galloway, the loyalist in permanent exile in Britain, had no illusions about Article 5. When it first surfaced in the provisional treaty, he dismissed its value and instead placed on the British Government the responsibility in good conscience for compensating the loyalists.[30] Similarly, Benjamin Franklin, Galloway's friend and confederate before the Revolution and, among the members of the American delegation negotiating the peace treaty, the most outspoken in his opposition to compensating the loyalists, held nothing back in a reply to a British correspondent who protested the injustice of America's failing to restore the loyalists' confiscated estates. This exchange occurred in June 1785 when Franklin was about to end his long embassy in France and return to Philadelphia. To welcome home the loyalists (Franklin preferred the term "royalists") and restore their property, Franklin said, would be to invite "anarchy and confusion." They had played "a deep game, staking their estates against ours," and winding up unsuccessful in the wager. Yet they were not without recourse in the promises "from your government, of indemnifica-tion in the case of loss," as to the likely fulfillment of which Franklin voiced no objection, concluding with barely concealed glee that "though still our enemies, they are men; they are in necessity; and I think even a hired assassin has a right to his pay from his employer."[31]

Franklin was aiming, in that last thrust, at the work of the commission appointed by parliament in 1783 "to enquire into the losses and services of all such persons who have suffered in their rights, properties, and professions during the late unhappy dissensions in America in consequence of their loyalty to his Majesty and attachment to the British Government." Because of a not unjustified suspicion concerning the validity and extent of many of the losses claimed, the commission required that evidence be presented and witnesses examined to substantiate the requests for compensation. Not all of the loyalists who sought compensation received it, and few who received it got as much as they applied for, or may even have reasonably expected.

Most of the claims came from loyalists in exile, either in Britain or in Canada. Those still living in America had a better chance of obtaining compensation if they traveled to London to present their cases in person before the commission, which represented an investment in time and money that cut down on the number of successful claimants from the United States. By the time that the commission issued its final report in 1790, £3,033,091 had been awarded in compensation on aggregate claims of £8,216,126, or payment close to thirty-seven percent of the total claimed. Of 206 Pennsylvania loyalist claims that have been analyzed, thirty-five percent were for £500 or less, and thirteen percent for over £5,000; as a general rule, the smaller the claim, the more likely it was that the commission would authorize payment at close to par. A majority of the Pennsylvania claimants (about fifty-four percent) were from residents of Philadelphia. Only twelve of the total number from Pennsylvania identified themselves as Quaker loyalists who suffered losses, giving arguable statistical support for Quaker neutrality during the war. In the final reckoning, it has to be conceded that the payout to claimants was not intended to be immediate, but rather spread out in sixteen semiannual installments at so modest an interest rate that converting the government debentures into present cash entailed taking a steep discount from their face value. Yet, over all, the procedure was a fair one; the compensation was significant; and the settlement of these claims, despite the sometimes keen disappointment of those who submitted them, had the effect of promoting reconciliation on both sides of the Atlantic.[32]

The Roberts family nominated Thomas Roberts to go abroad for that purpose, and in gathering together the various documents he needed to take with him, he turned for help to a critically positioned member of the Quaker community, Abel James. James had been Henry Drinker's senior partner in the mercantile firm of James & Drinker, which, in 1773, incurred patriot wrath for trying to import taxed tea into Philadelphia.[33] What recommended him in early 1786 as an intermediary acting for the Roberts family was a prior connection he had with the newly elected president of the Supreme Executive Council, recently returned from France, Benjamin Franklin.

Years before Franklin had entrusted to his then friend Joseph Galloway the manuscript of his unfinished autobiography. That document remained in the possession of Galloway's wife after Galloway had left Philadelphia with the departing British forces in June 1778. Grace Galloway subsequently died, and as executor under her will, Abel James came upon Franklin's manuscript. In 1782 he sent Franklin in Paris a copy of the unfinished memoir, accompanied by James's warm endorsement of the work and a strong plea to Franklin, with whom he had previously been on friendly terms, to complete the narrative: "Life is uncertain, as the Preacher tells us; and what will the World say if kind, humane & benevolent Ben. Franklin should leave his Friends & the World deprived of so pleasing and profitable a Work; a Work which would be useful & entertaining not only to a few, but to millions?" In particular, James believed that Franklin's autobiography, when completed, would be of inspiration to the youth of the country: "I know of no Character living, nor many of them put together, who has so much in his Power as thyself to promote a greater Spirit of Industry & early Attention to Business, Frugality & Temperance with the American Youth."[34]

In a petition addressed to "Benjamin Franklin Esquire, President, and the Supreme Executive Council of Pennsylvania," dated 25th 2nd Month 1786, Abel James identified himself as "employed by Jane Roberts the Widow of John Roberts late of Merion deceased, and their Surviving Children to prepare the necessary Papers and Writings to enable Thomas Roberts the Eldest Son of the said John Roberts, and certain other Persons as their Attornies," to apply for and receive all such sums of money as the commissions sitting in England "shall think it just and be pleased to allow for the Losses Forfeitures & Misfortunes of the aforesaid Family, the Widow and Children of the aforesaid John Roberts." Most of the papers had been assembled and attested to in an acknowledgement made before a local judge. The two final steps, technical formalities, were the focus of James's petition. They entailed annexing a certified copy of the entire legal proceeding against Roberts, including the condemnation, the warrant of execution, and the sheriff's return of the execution, and, second, confirming the power to act of the judge who had taken the acknowledgment and the master of the rolls and the recorder of deeds who had supplied exemplified copies of original documents—"All which your said Petitioner humbly represents he is well and fully informed are necessary to make the said papers effectual to the End intended."[35]

Thus, two months after the Meeting for Sufferings committee had finally released its report, in the protracted exercise of caution, on the trials of Carlisle and Roberts, one of Philadelphia's most prominent Quakers, the long-time business partner of a member of that committee, found it possible openly to support the Roberts family in documenting Roberts's sad end. Choosing words of great deference, James applied to the Supreme Executive Council, asking it to certify the entire proceeding that ended in Roberts's death, and to do so for the fully disclosed purpose of assisting in the attempt to obtain compensation from the British Government for the losses that followed from that proceeding. Irony compounds in witnessing the cooperation achieved between a Quaker grandee and the executive body in Pennsylvania, which in the past had been the source of so much grief for the Roberts family, cooperation whose transparent objective was to mitigate the consequences of Roberts's treason conviction, or what the committee of the Meeting for Sufferings had decried in its report as his "deviation from that rectitude, & stability of Conduct which our Christian peaceable principles require." But the winds had perceptibly shifted: revolutionary fervor had subsided; former Tories were no longer ostracized; and Quakers of high rank, like Abel James, had recovered status and respectability. Rather than forgetting what had happened between countrymen divided by the Revolution, these strange bedfellows were now engaged in a studied effort to recall it.[36]

The formalities requested in James's petition were promptly completed. "His Excellency, Benjamin Franklin, Esquire," president of the Supreme Executive Council, signed the necessary verifications under date of February 28, 1786, with the great seal of the Commonwealth affixed thereto. Elizabeth Drinker noted in her diary on March 5 that "Tommy Roberts" had set off that morning with Captain Robinson as a passenger bound for Dublin on Robinson's ship. It is entirely possible that Thomas Roberts stayed as an overnight guest at the Drinkers along with his cousin Jacob Downing, who in the following year would marry Sarah Drinker, the Drinkers' oldest child.[37]

Armed with these and other authenticated documents, Thomas Roberts arrived in England on April 28, 1786, "after enduring many hardships and a most tempestuous passage." In requesting that the parliamentary commission grant a speedy hearing, he recited in a memorial addressed to the commissioners that his absence from home would be "attended with the greatest inconvenience, the nature & conduct of the Estate whereby the said Family is to be supported requiring his constant presence and attention, as the same consists of Mills among other things, in the management of which your Memorialist's superintendance is indispensable."[38]

In the memorial and petition she addressed to the commissioners, Jane Roberts recited that she had been

> reduced to a State of deep Distress and Affliction in the Loss of an Affectionate and tender Husband, who thro' the Severity of Certain Laws passed in this Government during the late unhappy Contest between Great Britain and her Colonies, and the inflamed Temper of Persons active in the Execution of those Laws, was arraigned, tried, condemned and executed for continuing to manifest a respectful Attention to the British Government, and coming into the City of Philadelphia during the time it was possessed by the British Army in the year 1777.

What, she said, added to her sorrow as an impoverished widow of sixty-four years of age was the measurable realization that her nine children "who had before them but a short time since the flattering prospect of a Life of Plenty" were now "her Partners in this Scene of Indigence."[39]

Thomas Roberts gave detailed testimony before the commissioners about the land his father owned, the improvements he had made on it, and the market value of the property if offered for sale in good times. He located the land at approximately nine miles from Philadelphia, describing it as "good but hilly"; the portion under cultivation yielded, he said, better than sixty tons of hay a year and three hundred odd bushels of wheat. In itemizing the losses incurred during the Revolution at the hands of the American forces, he accounted for all of the cattle (fat cattle, horses, working oxen, milch cows, sheep, hogs), which were missing in the inventory that the appraisers completed immediately after his father's conviction. One awkward problem of proof he had to face was the absence of any deeds establishing his father's ownership of the confiscated real estate. He explained, in what seems to have been a strategy recurrently used for protecting valuable documents, that the deeds "were buried underground in a Wood Box and when they were taken up the wet had got in and defaced them entirely."[40]

To help him get over this and other hurdles, Thomas Roberts received the support as witnesses in the proceeding of Samuel Shoemaker, John Potts, Colonel William Rankin, Abraham Pastorius, and Phineas Bond, Esquire, all of whom, Tories attainted for treason, had sought refuge in England, and three of whom, Shoemaker, Potts, and Bond, would later be pardoned by the Commonwealth. Each of them testified that he knew Roberts and was familiar with his property holdings, which had the value the Roberts family claimed.[41]

William Rankin, a former colonel in the York County militia, is of particular interest. He said that he had visited the Roberts property "before the Rebellion" and described the land as "very good" and the farm "well stocked," which, with the several buildings all of stone, formed "quite a Village." The main property in his opinion would have sold prior to the war for eight thousand pounds, a sum he would have willingly paid for it. Like Samuel Wallis, Rankin had played a double game in the Revolution, pretending as a colonel in the militia to be a patriot while secretly plotting to organize a loyalist uprising on the frontier. After he showed his true colors by deserting the militia and joining the British army, Rankin was arrested and thrown into prison in York County. If he had not succeeded in escaping from prison in 1781, his certain trip to the gallows would have deprived the Roberts family of the helpful testimony he gave in England five years later. Although not a matter of record in his treason trial, John Roberts had formed a connection with two men who were never brought to trial but who were guilty of treason of the deepest dye. A triangular relationship uniting the three of them may be established if, as Carl Van Doren suspects, Samuel Wallis and Rankin communicated with each other during their undercover work for the British.[42]

The total amount of the Roberts claim for compensation before the royal commission came to 9,432 pounds, 10 shillings, in Pennsylvania currency, or

5,780 pounds sterling. The commissioners took their time in deciding how much of the claim they would recognize in an award to Jane Roberts. As the summer dragged on in London without any word from the commission, Thomas Roberts became apprehensive and addressed a letter to the commissioners in which he requested that they inform him "whether the evidence I have offered has or has not been satisfactory, or what other proofs you will desire in order to establish our Claim for relief, as my sole Motive in coming to England, where I have been some time detained, was to solicit the Justice of this Nation." He sought this reassurance as he was about to sail for Philadelphia in the hope that he might be able "to satisfy my Family that nothing on my part has been wanting to obtain them that satisfaction we flatter ourselves we so justly merit."

Thomas Roberts sailed for home, after the commission apparently indicated that nothing more was needed from him. When, however, another year went by without a decision, the only Roberts family representative left in England felt compelled to determine from the commission "what is likely to be done in the Business." William Dillwyn, a Quaker businessman and an early abolitionist, reviewed in a letter of tactful inquiry the history of the claim's submission and the investment that the family had made in sending Thomas Roberts to London to testify on their behalf. Over the years, lawyers have learned the hard way that pressing a dilatory tribunal for judgment often produces an unwanted result, but Dillwyn found a formula for deftly managing that risk: "I would regret," he wrote in ending his letter, "the omission of anything in my Power, which would tend to the Relief of a distressed Family; and if, from reasons I am unacquainted with, they are not likely to receive any Compensation, I am desirous their sufferings may not be increased by an improper Dependance on it."[43]

The commissioners finally awarded Jane Roberts the sum of 3,931 pounds sterling, or roughly two-thirds of the amount claimed. In 1787, Abraham Carlisle's widow, Ann, and her son submitted their claim for compensation on account of the loss of the house and lot on Front Street next to Henry Drinker's property. They pleaded financial inability to make the trip to England, but on the basis of a written submission, supported by certificates from Philadelphia, the commissioners granted them compensation in the full amount claimed of six hundred pounds sterling.[44]

Sometime after receipt of the royal commission's award, the Roberts family decided to cut its ties to Lower Merion Township. In 1792 Thomas Roberts sold the property his father gave him and a few years later moved to a house in Philadelphia at Second Street above Vine. For a long time he had as his close friend and drinking companion Joseph Price, a Quaker from Lower Merion and a man of many parts: a carpenter by trade, a farmer, an innkeeper, a sawmill operator, and a coffin maker who unfailingly accompanied his customers to their final resting places. Best of all, though, Price was a diarist of erratic spelling and syntax who would record over a period of four decades events, big and small, occurring in his extended domain. After escorting the bride-to-be from Lower Merion to Philadelphia, Price obtained a marriage license and a parson for the hastily arranged wedding of Thomas Roberts and Polly Cochran in March 1796. He would chart with concern his friend's subsequent decline in illness, ending in Thomas Roberts's death in May 1799. True to one of Price's several vocations, he went to Philadelphia the morning of Roberts's funeral and "helpt, to Screw him up & put him in the Coach" for delivery to the Merion meeting burial ground that afternoon.[45]

In 1791 Jane Roberts, her daughters, and her son Jehu obtained a certificate from the Merion meeting directed to the Uwchlan Monthly Meeting permitting them to relocate to West Whiteland Township in Chester County, near the place of Jane Roberts's birth. Through the ubiquitous Joseph Price, we learn that Jehu Roberts, his schoolmate, then in his early forties, married in November of the following year. Jehu and his wife, Elizabeth, had two children, a son and a daughter. One cannot help but feel that it was more than a Roberts family tradition that inspired the parents to name their son John.[46]

"Old Jane Roberts," as Price referred to her, died and was buried in Uwchlan on November 1, 1795. The will she signed a week before her death was not, however, the will of a destitute widow. She gave her son Thomas the sum of one hundred pounds "from motives of natural affection notwithstanding he is well-provided for out of the Estate of the Family Property," presumably a reference to the property of his father that the Supreme Court awarded him. To her younger son, Jehu, who had stayed by her side during all her trials, she gave the sum of fifty pounds and objects that she had succeeded in holding back from the forced sale: "my clock, desk [and] bookcase, and firehearth Stove." Her daughters were to receive her wearing apparel and the remaining household goods and furniture, as well as equal shares in the proceeds realized from the sale of certain assets she directed her executors to complete "to the best advantage" within a year after her death. Those assets consisted of "all my Several Tracts & Shares in tracts of backlands wheresoever situated which were established to me in fee by Act of Assembly some Years past" and any dower right she had in the Elk Iron Works.[47]

Something must have somehow fallen through the cracks to cause Jane Roberts to believe she had a dower claim in her husband's partnership interest in the Elk Iron Works. How such an expectation might have arisen may be gleaned from tracing a complicated land transaction through a later confirmatory conveyance that had the potential of inadvertently protecting Roberts's interest from confiscation.[48] As for the other assets, "the tracts of backlands," the Pennsylvania Assembly, in what seems a hesitant move toward amnesty and contrition, had passed special legislation in 1792 providing that title to confiscated properties that John Roberts had owned but that the Commonwealth had not yet disposed of should revest in Jane Roberts, her heirs and assigns.

Epilogue

By the turn of the nineteenth century, much had been forgotten, whether deliberately or not. John Roberts's case had receded in public memory, and only a few were left who could have retained it in private memory. Of those seven ordinary people who testified against him at his trial (eight, if one counts a final rebuttal witness), we can't be sure whether any survived, but we do know for a recorded fact that Michael Smith, Roberts's most outspoken antagonist, died in 1786.[1] Joseph Reed, who vigorously prosecuted the case for the Commonwealth and then maneuvered behind the scenes to secure Roberts's execution, died in 1785. James Wilson, Roberts's lead trial counsel, went on to become a member of the first United States Supreme Court, but suffered an ignominious end, dying on the southern circuit in a frantic flight from his creditors. By a prank of history, Samuel Wallis, the undiscovered traitor who had acted as a go-between in the British negotiations with Benedict Arnold, was Wilson's partner in disastrous land speculation; Wallis succumbed to yellow fever in September 1798 on his way back home from Edenton, North Carolina, where he arrived too late to confer with Wilson before the latter died there.[2]

Thomas McKean belongs in the survivor class. In 1799 he stepped down from the office of chief justice that he had occupied for more than twenty years to become the elected governor of Pennsylvania under the constitution of 1790, adopted, after so much bitter partisan controversy, in replacement of the radical constitution of 1776. To succeed him as chief justice, McKean appointed Edward Shippen, Jr., who was the father-in-law of Benedict Arnold and suspected of loyalist leanings during the Revolution. Shippen's full reinstatement as a respected lawyer and jurist may be taken as one more sign of the ongoing policy of amnesia and reconciliation that began once the war was over.[3]

Another official present at Roberts's trial also survived. Edward Burd had continued to serve as clerk to the Pennsylvania Supreme Court, or its prothonotary, to use the distinctive title that Pennsylvania has conferred on the holder of that office. A lawyer in practice for only a few years, he rejoiced when he

131

received his commission on September 2, 1778, just as the treason trials were about to get under way. One of the perquisites the prothonotary enjoyed was collecting, on a piecework basis, substantial fee income from managing the business of the court. With the full calendar of trials looming up in the fall term of 1778, Burd wrote expectantly to a friend on the day he took office, "I have received no fees yet tho' some are in Embryo." The money he received in fees would come in handy as he looked forward to his marriage at the end of the year to his attractive first cousin whom he had long courted, a daughter of Edward Shippen, and the soon-to-become sister-in-law of Benedict Arnold.[4]

Almost twenty-five years to the very day after John Roberts's trial for treason began in College Hall in Philadelphia, Edward Burd found himself once again under an obligation to retrieve in formal fashion the record of that proceeding. When Thomas Roberts went to England to present his mother's memorial and petition to the royal commission, he took with him as an essential document an exemplified copy of the proceedings against his father certified to by Edward Burd, as prothonotary. Now, in 1803, Burd would be called on in his official capacity to return to the treason trial and produce another copy of that record, this time to aid in the disposition of a case pending before two justices of the Pennsylvania Supreme Court sitting on circuit in a remote county seat more than one hundred fifty miles from Philadelphia. In carrying out this assignment, Burd might have paused to recall the testimony he had listened to at Roberts's trial and the atmosphere of doubt and concern that prevailed in Philadelphia prior to the deaths of Carlisle and Roberts. If he did so, his recollection may have been clouded not simply by the passage of a quarter of a century but by his occasional inattentiveness while then in court, for we have a letter of Burd's written on a personal matter in which he remarks, "I write this in Court when we are just going on with the Tryal of John Roberts."[5]

The case that required reviving the record of the treason trial arose as a consequence of the Pennsylvania legislature's passing a statute revesting title in Jane Roberts and her heirs to certain land that remained unsold out of her late husband's confiscated estate. The committee of the legislature that examined the petition requesting this action was careful not to concede too much for fear of undermining the forfeiture and appearing to grant some kind of posthumous pardon. It emphasized that "the critical circumstances of the late contest" afforded "an ample justification" for the forfeiture of Roberts's property and that "the committee would deem it inexpedient and impolitic upon the mere suggestions of commiseration and compassion to restore an equivalent to the attainted person or his surviving representatives."

Yet, the application before it allowed the legislature, "in the indulgence of its benevolence and humanity consistently with the policy of the government, and without establishing a precedent that can be productive of any dangerous consequences," to grant the petitioner's request and restore to her "no more than that remnant of property which hath not been thought of sufficient importance, during the lapse of near 14 years, to be seized by the public." Such compliance with Jane Roberts's request would "in the present season of peace and prosperity" derive added support, the committee philosophized, when viewed in relation to the provision in the state's constitution of 1790 ensuring that "no attainder shall work corruption of blood, nor, except during the life of the offender, forfeiture of estate." And so the legislature proceeded to enact legislation that confirmed title in Jane Roberts, "and her heirs, executors, administrators and assigns forever," to "such part of the estate, real and personal, of the said John Roberts as hath not heretofore been seized, sold, aliened or otherwise disposed of, by and on account of the public."[6]

The focus in the petition to the legislature and in the committee's report was on a tract of about thirty-six acres on the lower reach of Mill Creek in Lower Merion Township that for whatever reason had escaped public sale. In carrying out the family relocation plan, that remnant now also could be sold and the proceeds allocated for the benefit of Jane Roberts in her final years.[7] The sweeping language of the confirmatory statute reached, however, more remote holdings of her late husband to which Jane Roberts alluded in her will when she directed her executors to sell "all my Several Tracts & Shares in tracts of backlands wheresoever situated which were established to me in fee by Act of Assembly some Years past." The wheel of fortune would thus turn again, requiring a trial in Lycoming County at the beginning of the nineteenth century to determine who was entitled to the 300-acre tract of "Merion," located in Muncy Township, Samuel Wallis's home territory, which had been surveyed in 1774 pursuant to a warrant issued in the name of "John Roberts Miller."[8]

The Roberts family brought an action in ejectment, the traditional means of resolving title disputes that pitted fictitious parties against each other, alleging a forcible ouster from possession by Richard Roe of John Doe. John Doe was the stand-in for the Roberts claimants, whereas Richard Roe represented William and Barnet Barelow, who had apparently leased a portion of the property from the real party in interest, one Stacy Potts.[9] In the person of Stacy Potts, we are summoned to return to that early moment in the Revolution when the American army was on the brink of disastrous defeat. By common account, as night approached on Christmas Day, 1776, Johann Rall, the Hessian commander at Trenton, had sat down to an agreeable game of checkers with a Quaker tradesman in whose house Rall had established his headquarters. During the surprise battle that followed ending in an American victory, Colonel Rall fell mortally wounded, and was carried back to Stacy Potts's house to die.[10]

An entrepreneur years before that term came into vogue, Potts owned at the time of the Revolution a tannery, ironworks, and a papermill in Trenton.

In 1776 he and John Fitch, the original steamboat inventor and operator, were partners in manufacturing files and in general iron-working. Later Stacy Potts would join others in supporting Fitch's pursuit of an exclusive patent right for his steamboat. In the 1780s, lured by the prospect of land investments westward, Potts put his Trenton properties up for sale and relocated to Harrisburg, Pennsylvania, where in short order he became a leading citizen and a member of the Pennsylvania legislature. He acquired property along the east branch of the Muncy Creek in Northumberland County (soon to become Lycoming County), to which he recruited tenants to lease and improve, but without Potts's having the least hint that he was subject to an adverse title claim. Only when the Pennsylvania legislature passed the redeeming statute for the benefit of the Roberts family did the basis of that claim emerge. The committee in reporting out the statute had mistakenly concluded that in granting Jane Roberts's petition "no injustice will be done to any individuals."[11]

After all that had happened, to recapture this acreage originally surveyed in John Roberts's name, in a remote corner of the state, came as a windfall for his heirs. However, the windfall wasn't theirs right away; the suit in ejectment that the sons brought dragged on for years in two courts until 1804 when the case was called for trial before a jury and two justices of the Supreme Court sitting on circuit, "the Honorable Edward Shippen Esqr. Doctor of Laws, Chief Justice of the said Supreme Court, and the Honorable H. H. Brackenridge Esqr, his associate." So as to establish the sequence of events, the record of the treason trial and of Roberts's conviction and execution became material evidence, relied on by counsel for the defendants to prove that Roberts's property had been lawfully taken by the Commonwealth. Edward Burd's certified account of the proceeding would have been read to the jury, ending, as it did, with the guilty verdict and the judgment of the court "that John Roberts be hanged by the neck till he be dead." In punctilious concern, Edward Burd or his clerk added as a last-minute insertion in the certified record the Latin abbreviation that followed the formidable entry of judgment: "*int. comr.*," or "*interim commitur*," "meanwhile let him be committed," a status for John Roberts that would figuratively last beyond his death as he remained a prisoner in memory and time.[12]

Though Stacy Potts had the stronger equitable claim, based on his good-faith lack of knowledge, the jury found for the plaintiffs. It awarded the Roberts family the nominal sums of "six pence damages and six pence costs," but what really mattered was the jury determination that John Roberts's successors had legal title. Potts's tenants and purchasers were forced to depart the premises.[13] The result understandably didn't sit well with Stacy Potts, and in 1806 he applied to the Pennsylvania legislature for relief. His petition, mild in tone, was the kind of an appeal one might have expected from a Quaker who felt wronged but who also in the previous decade had been a member of the legislative body from which he was now seeking redress.

He began by stating that, "under the laws and authority of the Commonwealth of Pennsylvania," he had become possessed of these lands and that, "after much pains and many fatiguing journies" he had succeeded in attracting settlers who were willing to improve the property located in what had been until then "an uninhabited wilderness." He had proceeded "[w]ithout any intimation or fear that his title could be in any way affected." Were it not for the act of the assembly passed in 1792 restoring title to unsold properties in Jane Roberts, he would have realized handsomely on his investment. In the face of "a solemn decision of the judicial power of the government" against him, he deemed it unbecoming "to suggest a doubt as to the justice and propriety of the decision," but he nevertheless thought it only fair that the Commonwealth should reimburse him for the money he was obligated by law to pay those parties claiming under him who had been displaced by the court's judgment.[14]

Stacy Potts never obtained from the public treasury the compensation he sought for his losses. Instead, the Commonwealth of Pennsylvania concluded that the time had come at last to close the books and let John Roberts and his treason trial slide into oblivion.

APPENDIX A

Note: The framework for this consolidated perspective is supplied by the Quaker note-taker whose account is often more complete than Chief Justice McKean's trial notes. Nevertheless, McKean was a constant presence at the trial and recorded testimony from witnesses whom the Quaker reporter sometimes missed; McKean's legal expertise also contrasts with the Quaker's lack of it. The chief justice's contributions in supplementing or clarifying the Quaker record are shown below in bracketed italics.

❋ ❋

[Respublica Pennsylvania   *Philadia Septemr 30*[th] *1778*
         v   *Indictment for treason.~*
John Roberts   *Nomina Juratorum – ~ Wm Adcock, Isaac*
                           Powell, David Pancoast, Cadwalader Dickinson
                           (stricken),
Challenges 33   *John Steinmetz, Andrew Forsyth, Andrew*
                           Buchart, John McNeil, John Campbell
                           (stricken), William Rigden, John Drinker, James
                           Hood, James Barns and Thomas Corjie —
                           sworn & affirmed.~
    Mr. Attorney General,
         Opens the evidence — P. endeavored to rescue Persons sent to
      Virginia. ~ &c. ~]

Republica
      vs   Indictment for High Treason
John Roberts

        1st In endeavouring to procure a party of Light horse to rescue those banished to Virginia
         2ndly Acting as a Guide
         3dly Being at Offices under the King & causing People to be imprisoned as Rebels.

4th That he endeavoured to persuade people to inlist under Captn James.

5thly That he lived in the Country and joined the Enemy in the city —

Test for the

State . . . . Mary Smith [*sworn*], deposeth & Saith that early one morning in december last when the Enemy were going up the road to catch General Potter, a Colo. of Light horse rode up the lane to the house, and ask't if they were friends to Government, enquired for the Old Rebel & his son and was told they were gone to take the horses away, upon which those at the lane End among whom was John Roberts, & no other Countryman called to him to come out of the Rebels hole upon which the Colo. galloped back to the road and she ran after him, and as he was on a full Gallop She called to John Roberts [*Mr. Roberts, Mr. Roberts*], who was as at about the distance from here [*where she stands*] to the [4th] Street for assistance, that Jno. Roberts could hear her, but would not. & gave no answer [*P. could hear her, but would not hear her*], that she heard the Colo. ask the crowd twice, and once as he rode by Jno Roberts if they were friends to Governmt., that to be sure Jno Roberts spake to him, but she did not hear him [*P. when she called to him for help pulled his hat down—she called as loud as she could hollow—he must have heard her*], that no other Country people were present; that after this the horn was blown, upon which the Troop rush't forward [*into the house to search for her husband— they cried out "shew him no favor"*], beat her, tore off her cloaths [*they stripped all her clothes off except her under-petticoat*], & plundered the house, that she was at this time in the house, and did not see Mr Roberts after the Enemy rode to the house [*this was about 2 & 1/2 miles from P.'s house*], that they stript the cloaths off of Eleven beds [*all the stock had been taken by the enemy before. Her husband & son were driving off the horses and hogs*], that Roberts could as well have prevented their being plundered, as the other neighbours; that this is the only time she saw Mr. Roberts with the Enemy; — that three days after this her son was made prisoner of [*by the British horse*], & she came to the New Jail to see him [*she got a Pass from Colo. Morgan, by the General's permission, to come to Town*]; that on the day the Enemy took their cattle, the British Commissary [*Eldor*] gave an order, or Certificate to get the mony which she brought into the city, went to Mr Roberts, enquired the way to the paymasters, upon his asking what she wanted there she told him to get paid for their Cattle, & shew'd him her Certificate he laughed & said we don't pay no Rebels; she then went to Mr Galloway's and was told by him upon hearing that she was a neighbour of Mr Roberts, that she could not get a better man, & went to him, & ask't if he could speak a word in order to get her Son out of prison 'till he should get better, & was told by him that he should never come out unless the old rebel & his son Mich would come out of General Washington's Army and take the oath of Allegiance, he refused to assist her, altho she begged for God's sake that he would; that she went to Mr Roberts again in the afternoon, & next morning & took her brother in law who left town last night or she would have brought him, to him at Owen Jones's, that in the afternoon Roberts was not at home, upon which she got a petition wrote to Genl Howe & delivered it when Roberts was there, & went into the parlour to Genl Howe and she heard him talking with him, that Roberts went in to get a pass for a man to carry out some thing she thinks Salt, [*P. got a pass, wch. the man shewed in his hand, she believes it was to carry salt out ~She followed P. out of Genl Howe's the back door, over some steps, she shewed her petition to P.*] that at Genl Howes she shew'd her petition to Mr Roberts who look't over it & handed it back without saying anything; — Mr Roberts on her asking him which was Major Belfour look't in for him, but not seeing him he went away; — when she first saw Genl Howe he kep't the petition to peruse and said her son should be out of jail for a few days [*but he had not the time to read it then, he would read it in the evening, and bid her call in the morning*] but the next morning he refused; that as she went away she overtook Mr Roberts [*near to Owen Jones's*], & ask't him to go up with her the next day, & speak for her son, & was answered as the day before [*P. told her again if her husband & son did not come from the rebel army, & surrender themselves up, Bill should never come out ~*]; that evening she got a cart & horse to take her son, but on the next morning was ordered at Genl Howe's to be gone in a minute or they would put her to jail to her son, that she did not see Mr Roberts on this day, that her son continued in goal for seven months, that she never saw, or spoke to Mr Roberts during her son's imprisonment, being afraid to go to him, lest she should be sent to Jail, that John Roberts told her that thirty thousand Russians would come & kill us all, and therefore her husband, & sons had better come, & deliver themselves up; that she knows not whether Jno Roberts ever convey'd any hard mony to her son; — that the General cast his eye quite under [*either squints or has a cast in one of his eyes*] and wore a Golden Star [*on his breast*] but knows not whether there was a ribbon on, that John Roberts was dress'd as ususal, that she knows nothing at law about whether Gen. Howe was pitted with the small pox [*this was the person P. told her was G. Howe. ~*]

[*John Ellis — produced to prove pr. attempted to inlist him, & others ~ Ross/ Objected to by P. Counsel, Haw. ch 35 sec. 17 ~ by inlisting or persuading others to inlist for the purpose of joining the army of the Enemy. Atty Gen/ Mr. Reed Foster 200-207 ~ loose words, not relative to any act or design, persuading to inlist without the actual inlisting, may not be treason, but it may shew Quo Animo the P. joined the B. Army. ~*]

Mr. Wilson — Persuasion, means prevailing, or advising successfully. ~
where no actual inlisting, there can be no persuasion to inlist. ~
Court over-ruled the objection, so far as testimony tended to shew quo animo
P. joined the British army. ~]

John Ellis [*sworn*]; Says that he has known John Roberts [*very well*] for 5, or
6 years past, was going along Strawberry alley last winter, and went into a
room allmost full of people at Moyers tavern, & some of them very full of
liquor; — Captn James was endeavouring to procure them to inlist, the
Deponent saw Jno Roberts come in, & said to James, you seem to have a
fine parcel of people here, you will make out well in recruiting to day, Jno
Roberts said it is a fine corps Lads, if you have a mind to inlist you could
not get into a better [*corps*], said no more to the people. — Lieutn Vernon
said to the Dept you appear like a stranger, & set [*sit*] by your self, &
endeav'd inlisting him [*then said you are a strong looking man, will you
inlist in the service ~Ws. replied no*], & told him that if he would, he
should be quartermaster to the Troop; Jno Roberts said my friend it is a
very good offer, if you have a mind to engage, I don't know how you could
better yourself, — the Depont said no more [*said he had no intention to
engage, & he soon after went away.~*], & went away with Mr Roberts
without saying anything more ~

Ann Davis [*sworn*], That she knows Jno Roberts well, that sometime past
some cattle were taken [*from Ha(ve)rford*] by her brothers, after which she
[*& her* sister] came into the city [*about some clothes they had been
plundered of and when they did not find them, they were returning to the
Middle Ferry, and there were taken and carried before*], and upon her return
was taken at the Ferry & detained, & taken before a magistrate [*one Potts*],

and after examination was ordered to prison by Justice Potts unless she [*they*] could find bail [*he asked her if she was acquainted with any Body in Town, she said yes, John Roberts*]; upon telling Mr Potts that she was acquainted with Jno Roberts who happen'd to come in immediately, that upon this Mr Potts ask'd what she had to say of Mr Roberts, that the Witness told Roberts who she was, he said he knew them well [*he replied he knew her father well*], & was sorry to hear the Character they bore; Mr Potts ask't him if he knew that they were aiding in taking up the cattle, and was answer'd by Mr Roberts that he heard even the Mother had assisted, Mr Potts ask't the Prisoner if the family were Rebels before this time [*of taking the cattle*], and was answer'd by Roberts that they were, and he need go no further for evidence; [*upon which they got James Harris to bail them, & they then went away, upon condition they would ansr. when called upon — this was in the Beginning of April*] that when they were plundered she did not see Jno Roberts ~

Michael Smith [*sworn*]; — That he [*lives in Lower Merion,*] hath known Jno Roberts for about four years, & that to his sorrow; that on the day the Enemy came to Philadelp' he came down Lancaster road near the five mile Stone having seen a terrible smoke towards Philada, & returnd towards the black Horse, and the Prisonr came out of a lane [*at the 6 mile stone he saw the P. come out of a lane*] into the road in sight of the black horse, went to the black horse, & dismounted from his horse, & seeing the Witness said to him what do you think of yourself now you Old Rebel, I will have you hung [*hanged*], because you ordered your son to load his gun with a ball & shot to shoot him for not paying the Three pounds fine, which the Depon never did [*the British army were just then marched into Philadia.~*]; that he is the husband of Mary Smith, that he knows nothing of Jno Roberts discouraging people from taking up arms; — that he never saw the prisoner with the British Army ~

Andrew Fisher [*sworn*] That he hath known Jno Roberts for ten years past, [*he lives in Blockly township*] that in the last Fall, but can't say in what month he saw Jno Roberts with the British army that he knows not what he was doing with them, but was on horse back, & the Army was going up to the Gulph mill, that this was [*Ws. was at his own house*] between 7, & 8 oClock a.m. and many of the British Light horse were with him [*P. was riding with a good many L. Horse—they came to his house & took 5 cows, 9 sheep, £ 9, hard money, £ 50, Congress-money & some linen*], that Mr Roberts stop't for a small time at the blacksmith's shop, that a Soldier presented his gun at the Witness bosom, called him, & his sons rebels, & said he would shoot them, that no more of the neighbours were wth the Enemy, that he was not disguised, cant say whether he had his hat flap't, had no arms [*The soldiers came to him and said you are an old Rebel, you have two sons in the Rebel Army, you are a prisoner — Don't remember how P. was dressed or whether armed ~*], that the Witness was brought to Philadelp about 4 or 5 weeks after this, & put in the Old Jail where Mr Roberts came Roberts said he would help him out if he would bring his two sons in [*and put them there ~ his sons were then in General Washington's army ~ P. came alone ~ Frederick Vernor kept the old goal ~ he was 6 mos. in the old goal & 1 in the new, & then carried to New York*], that Roberts frequently came to the prison to look for Friends, that he was seven months in jail, & then carried to New York, that he was very often at Mr Roberts to help him out [*P. said he would help him out, if he would bring his two sons out of the Rebel Army*], that the Dept lives two miles this Side Michael Smith, that at the time he saw JRoberts with the Enemy they were going toward Roberts's house [*Ws. Was exchanged*] ~

[*Edward Stroud & Michael Grove — to prove P.'s confession.*
Mr. Ross/ objects to any evidence of the P. confession — Conviction must be by two witnesses.

143

Mr. Wilson/ reads the Act of Assembly — no evidence of confession can be admitted 2 Hawk. 256 ~ 5 & 6 Edwd. 6th ~ 7th Will. 3.~ Foster ~ pa. 11 ~ ibid 241. 2 & 3. ~ Eden, Penal Law 149 ~

Mr. Reed/ A dozen Judges have settled this Point — Confessions may be given in evidence to corroborate other proofs of overt acts by two witnesses. ~

Mr. Ross/ ~ replies ~

Court over-rules the objection — it being proper evidence to explain and corroborate the testimony of the two witnesses. ~]

Michael Groves [*sworn*] — deposeth; [*Has known the Prisoner many years —*] that about the middle of April last he was in company and drinking with Jroberts at the middle ferry when a number of his acquaintcs were present [*they were conversing upon public affairs*], & heard him say, what a shame it was that such a number of our fellow Citizens should be taken away by the Rebels in the manner they were meaning [*Israel*] Pemberton Fisher, & those others who were taken off by an American Gaurd just before the battle of Brandywine, that just before their going away he went to them, ask't them if they would condescend not to go [*with the rebels*], and some of them had answer'd they did not like his question for that it might occasion bloodshed and was not agreeable, but that others seemed desirous of accepting a mode to Stop them, that upon this he sat [*set*] off home [*that evening*], and when he got home he got a fresh horse to try to get into the lines of the Enemy, that on the next night the friends [*Pemberton and the rest of them*] were to lodge at PottsGrove, that by the assistance of a friend he got who lived in Chester County he got within the lines of the Enemy in Chester County, he inquired for Mr Galloway [*his friend Galloway*], found him, & told him his errand, that he wanted a party of Light horse to rescue those worthy good friends who were hurried [*dragged*] away from their families by the Rebels, & were to lay that night at PottsGrove, Mr Galloway said he would serve him as soon as possible by applying to Gen. Howe, and accordingly did, & received for answer from the Genl that the horse were very much fatigued, not fit, and that he would give him an answer in two hours whether he would furnish them, or not, that he waited at Mr Galloways till the answer came, did not go much out for fear of being seen as there was a terror on his mind [*he did not like to go out much in publick, lest he should be known, & therefore stayed in the house until he got the General's ansr.*]; that the answer was that he could not furnish any troop, but his prime troop which would hurt him greatly in case they should be lost [*that he could not spare as troop unless it was his prime troop, wch. Would weaken him much, & that he did not care to trust them so far in an Enemy's country*], that Roberts said he knew the situation well [*he knew the country well*], and told Galloway that with 25 horse he would engage to bring them within the Lines that night at the risque of his life, that Galloway desir'd him to stay but he refused, & went home [*and let the matter rest there, as he did not care to stay within the British lines, lest somebody should know him — —*], join'd them when they came near his house, & then came into the city with them [*and stayed with them all winter*]; & said had it not been for that one act [*he had done*], he never would have come to town with them; that of the Witness's own knowledge Jno Roberts came into the city with the Enemy [*he saw P. the first time, a few days after the Enemy came into Town*], that he frequently saw him examining people in the market; that another [*a certain*] John Roberts came for Salt [*and afterwards applied to Ws. who referred him to S. Shoemaker for a pass —*], and the prisoner said to the Deponent tho' not in the other's hearing he was not worthy of a pass he was so great a Rebel, this not said to Shoemaker; — that he heard the prisoner say frequently that there was no doubt but that if the friends of Government would exert themselves but they would drive the Rebels far

enough [*and soon conquer them*], — that he knows no instance of the
prisoner's keeping people in jail, or from getting out of town, that he knows
of but one Instance of examination, & then Roberts ask't him if he knew
the situation of the Rebel army [*Ws. saw a man, whom P. asked where the
rebel army lay*], that he never had any dispute, or quarrel with Mr Roberts,
never saw the prisonr in arms, or march, or come in with the Enemy
[*Never had a dispute with P. nor had any occasion ~ had a sein with P. and
others, has fished with him.~*], — that this conversation passed in the Barroom [*front room*] at the middle Ferry house, with 12, or 15 people present
— viz [*Present*] Edwd Stroud, Joseph Pritchard Jesse Sturges, Jams
Stephens, Arthur Mullan, & talk'd to about three or four, that it was
between 7, & 8 oClock in the evening, that he talk't so loud, all in the
room might hear, that he seem'd to address all who were there, that
Roberts appear'd most intimate with Pritchard & Stephens, & directed his
discourse particularly to them, that Pritchard appeard to be in liquor [*and
said, he was sorry that he had done this one action*] ~

Edward Stroud [*affirmed*], — [*Has known P. 20 years* —] That about the
15th of April last, he was in company with Mr Roberts at the middle Ferry
in company with Jos Pritchard, Mich Groves & others five or six in the
whole, hear'd him say it was a shame such a parcell of reputable men
should be taken from their families, & sent to a distant part of the Country,
that he had apply'd to them to know if he should go to the Enemy's Camp
to get a gaurd to rescue them, that some of them objected as it might
occasion bloodshed, & others seem'd satisfied that he should do so, upon
which he went home that night, and the next morning got a fresh horse,
was ask't by his wife where he was going, & said to take a ride, that he rode
about 15 miles and then called at a friend's house, told his errand, & his
friend said he would ride with him, which he did to Genl Howe's quarters,

[*Edward Richardson was there ~*]& enquired for Mr Galloway met with him, & told his errand, that Galloway said he would apply to Howe for some Light horse, & went accordingly, that Howe was busy but would give an answer in two hours, which he did, viz that his horses was very much fatigued & low, and if he sent any, he must send his best troops & therefore declined, as they might be taken, that Mr Roberts Said if he had 25, he would head them at the risque of his Life, & return'd home, that he knows no instance of Roberts's behaviour during the last winter, that Roberts directed his discourse principally to Jos. Pritchard, that it was in the Bar-room, that he never had any difference with Roberts, that he never saw the prisonr in arms, that they were in partnership in a fishing company, & had no quarrel or difference whatsoever, nor was there any among the partners, — that Mr Pritchard was present the whole time but so much intoxicated as not to be able to stand straight ~

[McKean skipped much of this testimony and noted simply: *Says the very same with Michael Grove. ~*]

[*Prisoner's defence. Mr. George Ross for Prisoner/ Being barely seen in Philadelphia or with the British Army is not treason, he ought to have been concerned in some act of hostility. —*]

[*Daniel Clymer, Esquire, sworn/*

On 3d January last he came from General W to Genl. H ~ with a flag on the subject of the exchange of Prisoners ~ he visited the new goal, saw P. come up, who said he would be glad to speak to him alone; Ws. told him he could not without Mr. Ferguson heard it — he however got an opportunity & told him he was unhappy being in Philadia. — that he was afraid to return home on acct. of some of his neighbours, that he had neither taken the oath to the King, or to the State, but wanted to remain neutral —

he said, he was forced to conduct Lord Cornwallis to the Gulph Mill — he told Ws., that the Journals of Congress were on his plantation, & he wished he would tell Genl. Washington of it, or they might fall into the Enemies hands — Ws. did so, & they were removed, also some things belonging to ws.— P. told him to lodge at his house — Colo. Proctor lodged there, but Ws. lodged at Mr. Penn's with Mr. John Ladd Howell — Ws. told P. they would all three lie at P. house ~ B. light horse came out that night & came by P. house next day, when Colo. Proctor was there, but did not call. ~]

Colo [*Isaac*]Warner [*affirmed*] deposeth that generality of People do not think Smith to be a man of credit~ [*Michael Smith lived near him this winter — is a warm, hot-tempered, rash man — knows nothing of his character as to his veracity — *]

John Zell [*affirmed*]. The general Character of Smith & his wife to be bad neighbours, of wicked dispositions, & of very indifferent characters ~

Jesse Thomas [*affirmed*]. The general character of Michael Smith and wife is bad [*indifferent, it is a bad one.*] ~

David Zell [*affirmed*]. The general character of Michael Smith & his wife is very bad through the neigbourhood ~

Jacob Jones [*affirmed*]. The general character of Michael Smith & wife is very bad, that he is not a man to be believd when he takes an oath, that John Roberts is generally thought well of~

Joseph Pritchard [*affirmed*]— Remembers being at the middle ferry with [*Edwd. Stroud, Michael Grove & others*] John Roberts, & divers others in

the month of April, or beginning of May, but doth not recollect, nor can
he believe that any conversation passed respecting the banished friends
[*who were sent to Virginia—it would have been improper*] as it was a mixed
company [*& he thinks P. had more prudence than to speak in that manner*];
that if such a conversation had happen'd in his hearing, he should recollect
it [*they had been fishing, & returned in the Evening to the tavern at the
Ferry, and went into the Barr-room,*] — that they met about their fishery; —
there were about fifteen in company [*10 were concerned in the Seine*]; that
[*this was the first time of the company's meeting (Abt. 6 weeks after*] there
was a difference between Jno Roberts & Stroud and Groves respecting their
Seine & fishery; that the general character of Stroud & Groves is bad, and
deficient in veracity, never heard Jno Roberts say a word about attempting
to rescue the friends [*the Quakers who were sent to Virginia, or any thing to
that purpose*].

    [McKean notes at this point in Pritchard's testimony: *Edwd. Stroud/
Joseph Pritchard was very much in liquor — Grove says the same. ~*]

    that J[*oseph*] Edwards, Jno Calin, Abia Wright, Jno Hastings, Jesse
Sturges, Jacob Richardson, [*John Roberts*], Jas Stephens, [*Edwd. Stroud and
Michael Grove were the company. ~*]

Colo [*Thomas*] Proctor [*sworn*], That on the 2nd of Jany he conducted a flag
[*with Colo. Clymer*] toward the city, & stop't at the house of Jno Roberts
with whom he had not a personal acquaintance, but understood that he
was in Philadelpa, that he went to the lines, slept that night at the
Governor's house, and at Jno Roberts's on the Second night [*and was told
there was no danger. ~*]

Miers Fisher [*affirmed*], Knows nothing of John Roberts ever making an
application to the Friends at the Lodge for permission to apply for Light

horse to rescue them; — never knew or hear'd of it, till Roberts was before the Chief Justice to be bailed ~

Frederick Kesselman [*sworn*]; That the general Character of Stroud, & Groves is very bad ~ [*Knows Edward Stroud and Michael Grove — they have a bad reputation — he does not know any thing of them himself. ~*]

John Chaloner; That about the middle of Janry he came into the city with flag, & brought live bullocks for the prisoners, upon his way down he lodged at Jno Roberts at night, came into the city & finishd his business, and upon his return, met John Roberts at the Ferry who ask'd him, if he thought he could be permitted to return home, & was told by the Depnt that he thought he could not as he had been in the city, & was reported [*he would not be permitted to come out of the city & remain between the lines, and also because it was reported & generally believed*] he had been a guide [*to the British Army*], that at this Mr Roberts seem'd distresst & repeated his wish; that JRoberts acknowledgd he had been up with the army but said he was forced, that he was kep't in the custody of a Sergt & not permitted to stir any distance; — [*Ws. asked P. why he came into the city*] that Roberts told him the reason of his coming into the city was because his brother millers had been taken up, & confined without a hearing, & Some of his illdisposed neighbours had threatened to take him up also, to avoid which he fled to the city; that on the evening of the day our Army crossed Schuylkil to meet the Enemy near the White horse, he & the Advocate General came to Mr Roberts, & ask'd for Lodgings, & was told they were wellcome to such as his house afforded, and treated them, Colo Boudenot & several other Officers with great hospitality ~ [*On the day the British Army crossed the Schuylkill, Mr. Lawrence, Judge Advocate General & Ws. lodged at P. house that night, & P. ordered their horses hay — many other Gentlemen of our Army also lodged there — next morning he would take no pay from any one — ~]*

Mrs. Susanna Jones [*affirmed*]; That on the night the Ld. Cornwalis crossed Schuylkil she thinks on the 12th [20th] of decemr Jno Roberts lodg'd at their house, a person knockt at the door about 2 oClo. am, & called him up, he went out, & returned in a little time, less than an hour, said [*told her daughter*] they wanted him to go out with them, but he refused to go; that at about 3 oClo, they were knockt up again, & she arose askt what they wanted, & who they were, & was answer'd Jacob James who said that Lord Cornwallis has sent for Jno Roberts & he would have him: — that at this time a numbr of Light horse were drawn up before the door, she call'd Jno Roberts up, & he went to the door [*he went with them*], as soon as he return'd he said that as soon as he got on [*over*]the Bridge they put him under a Gaurd [*an orderly Serjeant*], & kep't him so all day; he express'd great uneasiness at being forced out, but said as it was so he had done all the good for the Inhabitants in his power; that as he went on he requested Gaurds to be plac'd at the Inhabitants houses [McKean began abbreviating with : "*&c &c*"], & mentioned many places regularly along the road to prevent plunder, occasion'd much plunder to be return'd, for that the distresses, & cruelties were more than his nature could bear: — that he express'd the greatest uneasiness at being a witness of such scenes of distress, that in the Evening he returnd, told her that he had repeatedly refused going with them; that the general conduct of J.Roberts was that of a constant friend to the distress'd Inhabitants who came in from 50 to 100 per day for pay for cattle &c — that the reason of his coming to the city was for fear of loss of life from some malicious neighbours, & particularly Mich Smith & wife; that she was repeatedly up the road after Smith's son was taken prisoner, Smith's wife very frequently sent mony by her to be

deliver'd to Jno Roberts for her son which was accordingly done; — that
Smith's wife said she had a confidence in JRoberts, & was sure if the
mony &c [*money, linen, a great coat*] went to him, her son would get it;
that Roberts told he had a gaurd plac'd at the door of Captn Hastings who
was in the American Army ~

Owen Jones [*affirmed*]; [*When Lord C. went over the Schuylkill, the 11th or
12th of Decemr., P. went away early in the morning & returned early in the
Evening, & told him the scene of distress he had gone thro' that day was too
great to bear, he was taken to the Bridge & there an ordinary Serjeant was
placed over him—that the army had plundered without mercy—that he had
remonstrated with L. C. abt. it, & prevailed to get guards placed at every
house to prevent it if possible, but it availed little.~*] That he (JR) placed
Gaurds at, & assisted all without distinction; — that he came to the city
12th or 14th of Octobr [*came to Town abt the 12th of October, & lodged with
him from that time for 4 months*], — in the city assisted people employ'd in
the American Service, & that with chearfulness to the astonishment of the
Deponent for the relief of his enemies; — that he was lookt upon as an
Offender, & troublesom in doing more than he ought to do; — never
heard the prisonr call Americans Rebels; he believes it to be the
American & British Armies that Roberts called them ~

Philip Syng [*Sing*][*sworn*]; [*Has known P. 7 years ~*] That at the time Lord
Cornwallis was up the Country John Roberts prevail'd on his Lordship to
place a gaurd [*a centinel*] at his Gate ~
[*Reuben Haines ? (stricken)*]
John Smith [*sworn*]; When [*L. C. and*] the English Army march'd up
Conestego road, they came by his house, the gaurd came there, & took
him prisoner along with them into the road, when he got there he saw Jno

Roberts under a gaurd, & he was put under the same gaurd, and they were march'd up the road together, when the[y] came up to the road which leads to Jno Roberts house he stept up to Lord Cornwallis, & begg'd leave to go see his family, but was deny'd by Cornwallis, who order'd the Sergeant to take care of them, & not let them go out of the road; they march'd as far as the Gulf Mill, and there halted; — they took one American Lieutent Evan Jones with one or two others [*John Jones (Millwright) & Wm. Evans, who had been a Lieutnt in the militia, and some others, were taken prisoners*]; — they apply'd to JRoberts for assistance, he went under gaurd to Ld Cornwallis, told him that they were peaceable and he believed has never been out, & got them discharg'd [*he got L. C. & Genl. Grant to release them, as neighbors of his, and that they had never been with the Rebel army that he knew of*]; knows not whether John Roberts knew him to be a Lieuntenant or not; — From this they march'd to Matson's ford & kept the prisoner & Depont under gaurd 'till they encamp'd at near Derby Creek [*abt. ten miles off*]; — As they went along Jno Roberts made a very heavy complaint, said they took him out of his bed at 2 oClock that morning, & he could not for all he was worth be witness to Such Scenes [*he was distressed at the mischief they had done*]; — says he I shall suffer hereafter for being out, but God knows I could not help it; — In the evening JRoberts endeavour'd to his utmost to get both discharged but could not either: — They ordered the Depnt to take a letter for Jacob James's wife at about 8, or 9 oClock, & he made his escape & left Jno Roberts there; delivered the letter to an American Major; that they went by Michael Smith's lane end with Jno Roberts under gaurd without stoping [about this and the testimony to follow, McKean recorded only: "*They went by Michael Smith's & Prisoner was undr. Guard—the soldiers were abt. the house*"]; that he did not see Mich Smith wife altho' he was close along side of Jno Roberts; that no Officer rode up to Speak with Jno

Roberts, did not hear MSmith's wife call nor hear or see any of the family, was not in the Lane; — that JRobts did not direct, or guid the Army at all; — that no Colo. of Light horse spoke to John Roberts; that tears came from his eyes to see the distresses of the Inhabitants; — a gaurd at PSyng's and at Cap. Jones, that Cap. Jones must have known this; — that JRoberts & the Witness were marchd about the middle of the Army; — that Roberts had gone up stairs half an hour before the Depnt went with the letter, & he supposed him to remain there when he went away — that the Troops were about Smith's house before he, & Roberts came opposite the house ~ [*Michael Smith is a malicious and spiteful man.. ~*]

Andrew Murr[*a*]y [*sworn*],

That when the Enemy march'd up the Lancaster Road he was made prisoner & put under the same gaurd wth JRoberts, & Jno Smith; Mr Roberts said he was forced out, & that nothing should have tempted him; that Jno Roberts was kind to the Inhabits in general; that at the request of the Depnt JRoberts apply'd three, or four times to Ld. Cornwallis [*P. got leave from Serjeant to speak with L. C.*] to procure his discharge, & at length effected it altho' Roberts knew him to belong to the Continental Service ~

Robert Shewell [*Sewell*] [*sworn*], On the 29 of decemr last Mr Roberts & his daughter came to the Depnt, & handed him a letter from Captn [*Stephen*] Hopkins of Colo. Moylan's Light Dragoons; Roberts hesitated at asking him where Hopkins was, & look'd at his daughter; Shewell said he had a Sincere friendship for Hopkins, & might be trusted [*P. told him he was forced to go with the army ~*]

Mary Price [*affirmed*], That when the Enemy march'd to the Gulph Mill
Jno Roberts was at their house under gaurd; she desired him as an old
neighbour, but he was hurried along a gaurd left at their house. — Great
deal of property belonging to Fugitives from the city was there & saved by
the gaurd placed there at the instance of JRoberts, she heard him say that
nothing troubled him so much as being forced out ~

    [For this witness, McKean recorded only: "*Nothing to the purpose. ~*"]

Jonathan Robeson [*Roberts*]; that at the time the British Army march'd up
to Merrion, Mr Roberts there was at his house & Farm about 100 loads of
wheat, Rye hay &c & about 100 bbls of flour, Types & printing press &
about 50 tons of barr Iron. John Roberts knew all this, that the Army was
within a mile of Roberts's house ~

    [For this witness, McKean likewise limited himself to: "*Do. ~*"]

Obadiah [*Obediah*] Wilday — says he received favours & assistance from
Jno Roberts when he came to the city, altho' JR knew him to be a
Lieutenant in the Militia, — heard a militia man threaten to shoot Jno
Roberts.

    [McKean amended an initial "*Do* " by adding this testimony, "*On 12*th
*Decemr. last, the day the army came up the Lancaster road, heard a
firing ~*"]

Lydia Shelden [*Sheldon*] [*sworn*], says her brother was taken up 7th of
Decemr when Jno Roberts march'd through Derby and after being
confined at Wilmington for a time was put in goal there, being sick applied
to Jno Roberts tho a stranger, & told him his case and he enter'd Security
in £150 sterling.

William Young [*affirmed*] was taken prisoner by Refugees JRoberts not only relieved his sick Grandson; but he has also known of his relieving many poor Whig prisoners ~ [*Latter end of March, a party took his son-in-law & two grandsons prisoners — afterwd. they took him prisoner — he got acquainted with P. by chance — they got out on parole by P. means. ~*]

Peter Trapler [*Drexler*] [*sworn*]; The Rebels [*Regulars*] took 34 head of Cattle from him, Jno Roberts assisted him in getting some, and payment for others —

Sebastian Hall [*Bostean Ale*] [*sworn*], That Michael Smith said, that if John Roberts would give him a good Cow he would not swear anything against him ~ [*Andw. Fisher told him if John Roberts would give him a cow he would not swear agst. him. ~*]

Captn. [*Israel*] Jones [*affirmed*], — Altho' the Guns were found at his house and he was a Captn. of the Militia, and had been out; yet Jno Roberts had a gaurd placed at his house [*Ld. Cornwallis came out by his House ~ when they had all past almost, when the rear came in, & plundered, he was sick ~ they found his gun ~ two of them afterwd. told him, he had a friend with them, or we would have burned your house and barn & every thing — he supposed it was P. ~*]; — JRoberts also offered him [*his wife*] mony, or other Services while he was out with the militia [*to support her in his absence*] ~

[*Robert Aitkin, sworn. P. took care of the Proceedings of the Congress & other things, books, & printing types ~ and told him he would be true to his trust. ~ P. came to justify himself to the Whig-club — Pelatiah Webster, Walter Shee, &c. ~*]

[*Mr. Ross. Have got over every charge of treason. Michael Smith, his wife &*
Andw. Fisher, the only witnesses to prove the overt act of joining the
Army ~]

[*Mary Miller. She saw P. at home that day of the battle of Brandewine abt.*
Sunset — or the Evening after. ~]

[*Jacob Beary (Berry?). John Roberts was at his house abt. 11 oclock the day*
after the battle of Brandewine. ~]

[*Mr. Lewis/ Cites Foster 13. 14. ~Who an Enemy 3 Inst. 10. 11. ~ Cro. Car.*
247 ~ Appeal of Murder]

[*Lewellin Young. 23d Sept. 1777 he was taken prisoner — was put in goal*
— Sometime in April last he was in sick Quarters — P. told him he was a
busy meddling fellow, had collected the £3.10.0 fines, and ought to lie in
goal, that there were 100 rebels walking the streets, who ought to be in goal
also, that General Howe was too tender to the Rebels.]

[*Mr Wilson/ ~ Foster 13. 14 ~*

Mr. Reed/ Principal charge viz. Knowingly and willingly aiding & assisting
the Enemy — by joining their armies. Coming from the Country into
Philadia., whilst in possession of the enemy, is very different thing from being
surprized, or dwelling in Phila. & not having it in their power to remove
when the Enemy arrived. ~]

APPENDIX B

Note: McKean's sentencing statement, published in the *Pennsylvania Packet* on November 7, 1778, three days after John Roberts's execution, was preceded by a disclosure that the chief justice apparently dictated. Provided for its declared purpose, it effectively denied John Roberts any hope of a reprieve.

* *

The following is a copy verbatim of the sentence of the Court upon John Roberts, pronounced by his Honour the Chief Justice, which was sent to the Supreme Executive Council, at their request, about ten days ago, to shew the opinion of the Court respecting the conviction. It is now published by permission of the Chief Justice, with this observation, that it was originally written to help his memory, and not for the public eye.

John Roberts, You have been indicted, and after a very long, a very fair, & impartial tryal been convicted of High Treason. ~ You have had all the Indulgence and advantage that the law would allow you; you have had a copy of your indictment, and of the pannel of the Jury, and sufficient time for your defence and challenges.

The Jury who have found you guilty, were such as may be justly said that you yourself approved of, for though the law gives a liberty to challenge thirty five, you have challenged but thirty three so you allowed the rest to be an indifferent Jury to pass between the State & you upon your life & death; your Council have moved for a new trial, and the Court have disallowed that motion, being fully satisfied you have been convicted upon legal and clear evidence; their next Step is to proceed to judgment;

159

and sorry I am, that it falls to my lot to pronounce the dreadful Sentence, but I must discharge my duty to my Country.

Treason is a crime of the most dangerous & fatal Consequence to Society; it is of a most malignant nature; it is of a crimson colour, and of a scarlet dye. Maliciously to deprive one man of life merits the punishment of death, and blood for blood is a just restitution. What punishment then must he deserve who joins the enemies of his Country, and endeavours the total destruction of the lives, liberties, and property of all his fellow-Citizens, who willfully aids & assists in so impious a cause, a cause which has been complicated with the horrid & crying sin of murdering thousands, who were not only innocent, but meritorious; and aggravated by burning some of them alive, and starving others to death. ~ it is in vain to plead that you have not personally acted in this wicked business; for All who countenance, and assist are partakers in the guilt. Your junction gave encouragement to the invaders of your Country; your example occasioned the defection of others, and you exerted yourself in forwarding their Arbitrary designs. ~ It is in vain to plead that you fled to the Enemy for protection against some of your neighbours, who threatened your life, because they thought you a Tory; for you might have applied for, and obtained protection from the Civil Magistrate, or from the Army of your own Country. ~ It is in vain to plead that you intended to relieve some Friends who were ordered under a guard to Virginia, for Government was then doing a necessary and usual Act in like cases for its preservation; the restraining men whose going at large was thought dangerous to the Community, and putting them for a time under gentle confinement. Your offering to put yourself at the head of a troop of horse of the Enemy, and to effect their rescue at the risque of your life was a strange piece of Conduct, in one who pretended that he was consciously scrupulous of bearing Arms in any case. Alas! happy had it been for you had you fallen under like indulgent restraint and been sent also to Virginia.

It is true, and I mention it with pleasure that your interest with the Commander in Chief of the British Army was frequently employ'd in acts of humanity, charity, and benevolence. This must afford you some comfort, and your friends some consolation; but a good General would have done the same things to a vanquish'd Army, and they can by no means compensate for Treason. ~

You will probably have but a Short time to live. Before you launch into Eternity, it behoves you to improve the time that may be allowed you in this world; it behoves you most seriously to reflect on your past conduct; to repent of your evil deeds; to be incessant in prayer to the great and merciful God to forgive your manifold transgressions and Sins, to teach you to rely upon the merit and passion of a dear Redeemer, and thereby to avoid those regions of sorrow; those doleful shades, where peace and rest can never dwell, where even hope cannot enter. It behoves you to Seek the conversation, advice, and prayers of pious and good men; to be importunate at the Throne of Grace; and to learn the way that leadeth to happiness. May you, reflecting on these things, and pursuing the will of the great Father of light and life be received into the company and society of Angels, and Arch Angels, and the spirits of just men made perfect, and may you be qualified to enter into the joys of Heaven; Joys unspeakable and full of Glory.

The Legislature of this Commonwealth, agreeable to the lenity evinced by all their Laws, have thought proper to direct, that persons guilty of High Treason should be dealt with and proceeded against, as in other capital cases; And therefore the solemn judgment in Treason heretofore prescribed by the Laws of Pennsylvania is, now done away.~

The Judgment of the Court therefore is, "You shall be taken back to the place from whence you came, and from thence to the place of execution, and there to be hanged by the neck until dead."

May God be merciful to your Soul.

APPENDIX C

Note: The minutes of the Monthly Meeting for Sufferings held in Philadelphia on the 15th of the 12th mo 1785 began with an explanation that certain papers of the Philadelphia Yearly Meeting had been gathered together to forward to John Gough, a Quaker historian in England, such "as appeared proper for the work he has in hand" — that work eventually being published as *A History of the People Called Quakers*, 4 vols. (Dublin: Robert Jackson, 1789–1790). In the course of searching for appropriate material to send Gough, the meeting decided to return to and revive "the Consideration of the Report made in the year 1779 on the Case of John Roberts & Abraham Carlisle," which has been "solidly attended to and calmly deliberated on." The report of the committee appointed to look into the matter was then finally entered in the minutes of the meeting as follows.

To the Meeting for Sufferings in Philadelphia

The Committee appointed to make enquiry respecting the case of the two members of our religious Society who suffered death in this city by execution on the fourth day of the eleventh month last, having obtained information of the proceedings of the Court against them, and the grounds of the charges upon which they were tryed & condemned; now give the meeting a brief account thereof as the matter appears to us ~

On a weighty consideration of this affecting subject in all its circumstances, we apprehend the reputation of Truth, & our religious profession will be found greatly interested not only in the sorrowful event, but the causes which in some measure produced it ~

The History of friends gives us an account of many of our worthy predecessors having suffered severe undeserved punishment in times of persecution for

163

their stability, & faithfulness to their Christian Testimony, and of some who on that account had their lives taken from them by the hands of deluded and malicious men, whereby the cause of Truth and Righteousness hath been promoted & advanced in the Earth; but that any should be brought to such an end while in membership with us, and not on the like account is uncommon, and sorrowful; it therefore seems necessary, and we apprehend our duty to be acquainted with the occasion, & reasons alledged in support of so extraordinary a proceeding, and as far as the reputation of our Christian profession requires, endeavour to obviate the misrepresentations and aspersions propagated by our adversaries in order to vindicate their own conduct, or injure the cause of Truth.

In the early appearance of the commotions among the people in these Colonies, a religious exercise attended the minds of friends for the preservation of our fellow members in a conduct consistent with the peaceable principles of our Christian profession, and divers weighty advices were given forth with pressing exhortations to this effect, which as occasions increased were repeated with earnest admonitions, & cautions to all among us, to beware of becoming parties in the public consultations, bustles, and disturbances prevailing, and to avoid being concerned in any public office, or employment, or taking of the tests prescribed, & enjoined by the powers at variance during the present contest, and unsettled state of public affairs; from a firm persuasion that our union & safety consisted in steadily abiding under the direction, & instruction of the Spirit of Christ the prince of Peace which will lead & preserve us in a quiet & peaceable life, and we have faith to believe will in the Lord's time further prevail among mankind so as to put an end to Strife Contention and wars and in the room thereof bring in everlasting Righteousness; but through inattention hereto divers making profession of the Truth with us have been misled & become entangled in the confusions prevailing, whose example hath contributed to promote, & strengthen the errors of others still more incautious, & inattentive to the Divine principle, so that some have manifested open & active deviations from our antient peaceable testimony, which have afflicted their brethren, & occasioned much painful labour to friends in many places for their restoration & recovery, and where it has proved ineffectual, meetings have in general been under the necessity to maintain our Discipline against them; but so various have been the devices, & temptations which have presented, that some have been overtaken, & ensnared by such plausible appearances that they have involved themselves in difficulties, and distress, become obnoxious to party resentment, and their families subjected to great affliction, & adversity, which is lamentably the case of the members now under our consideration, tho' in some respects they vary from each other ~

One of them was an Inhabitant of this city of a reputable moral Character who after the British Army took possession thereof in the fall of the year 1777 was prevailed upon to accept of an office to grant permitts for persons to pass in & out; his acceptance of which station, & acting therein giving concern to friends they expressed their uneasiness to him, but their endeavours to convince him of his error, did not prevail with him to decline or withdraw from executing it ~

The other being a member of a neighbouring monthly meeting in the Country, we have not learned that any religious care or advice was seasonably extended to him; he resided at Merrion, maintained a reputable character among men, was well respected for his hospitality, benevolent disposition, and readiness to serve his neighbours & friends, and to administer relief to the afflicted or distressed ~

In the ninth month 1777 Several friends & others of their fellow Citizens being unjustly apprehended, imprisoned and afterwards Sent into banishment without an examination or hearing, Suffering his mind to be too much moved by this arbitrary violation of Civil & Religious liberty, he hastened away without previously consulting with them to give intelligence thereof to the General of the British Army then on their march towards this City, in hope to frustrate the intention of sending them into exile, which proceeding of his when it became known gave sensible pain & concern to friends; Sometime after his return from this Journey he was seen in company with the English Army, or parties of them in some of their marches or enterprizes not far distant from the City, but he allways insisted this was against his will and that he was forcibly compelled to it, which also appears by the evidences given at his trial; but these parts of his Conduct furnished occasion for the prosecution against him.

After the British Army evacuated this City in the sixth month 1778, their Opponents returned, & resuming their power, these two members were in a short time araigned with divers other persons, for High Treason, and after a tryal were by a Jury declared guilty, Sentenced to be executed and their Estates confiscated to the Government ~

Having perused a Copy of the Evidence taken at their tryal we find them to be very contradictory, & discover clear indications of a party Spirit, and that they were prosecuted with great severity & rigour is also apparent, the punishment inflicted far exceeding the nature of their offence, and that this was the general Sense of the people was demonstrated by great numbers of all Ranks uniting their interest & influence for Saving their lives by petitions & divers personal applications to the persons in power who held the authority over them, but they proved inexorable alledging political reasons for rejecting those ardent solicitations.

Notwithstanding they were members of our religious Society whom we respected, & commiserated in their distressed situation, yet as by their inadvertence to the principle of Divine Grace, and overlooking the repeated advice, & cautions given forth by friends, they were suffered to fall into such error, & deviation which occasioned great trouble of mind, & affliction to their brethren, and affected the reputation of Truth; This meeting or any other was restrained from interposing in their favour or vindication, as is our duty & usual care, when our brethren are subjected to suffering or persecution for righteousness sake, & the testimony of a Good Conscience; Nevertheless we were sensibly touched with much sympathy towards them, which was manifested by the repeated visits of divers friends who were religiously concerned for their well-fare, some of whom have informed us, that through the merciful visitation of Divine kindness they were favoured with a sense of their deviation from that rectitude, & stability of Conduct which our Christian peaceable principles require, and John Roberts at one time with earnestness expressed, "that he had gone beyond the line, & seen his deviation, and if his life was spared he should spend it differently." ~ and Abraham Carlisle said, "that he saw the Station he had filled, & acted in, in a different light, and that he had been under a cloud when the thought he was doing right," and on some further conversation respecting the concern, & burden he had brought on friends by omitting to give attention to some early hints, & advice, he appear'd disposed to acknowledge his error in writing, and at another time expressed that "he was very sorry he had given any uneasiness to friends as he allways had a regard to the Society": — it also appears that near the close of their time, from the disposition of mind attending them, there is ground to hope, & believe, they were through Divine mercy prepared for their awful solemn change, expressing their resignation thereto, forgiveness of those who sought their destruction, and their desire that all men might timely, & happily experi-ence redemption from the evils of the world, evidencing by their Sentiments, and the tranquil state of their minds, that they were not left comfortless in the hour of extremity.~

Submitted to the Meeting & Signed on behalf of the Committee Philada 8th mo 4th 1779.

Jams. Pemberton

Docketed "Report of the Committee of the Meeting for Sufferings on the case of John Roberts & Abraham Carlisle, 1779," Philadelphia Yearly Meeting, Meeting for Sufferings, Miscellaneous Papers (1779), Quaker Collection, Haverford College Library, box B.5.3, item 72.

Notes

Abbreviated References

Bell, *Patriot-Improvers*
Whitfield J. Bell, Jr., *Patriot-Improvers: Biographical Sketches of Members of the American Philosophical Society*, 3 vols. (Philadelphia: American Philosophical Society, 1997–2010).

Claims Commission
Records (microfilm) of the Commission Appointed for Enquiring into the Losses and Services of the American Loyalists (see Chap. VI, n. 32)

Colonial Records
Colonial Records of Pennsylvania, 16 vols. (Harrisburg, PA, 1838–1853)

Committee Report
Report of Committee of Philadelphia Meeting for Sufferings, Appendix C (see Intro., n. 16)

Diary of Elizabeth Drinker
The Diary of Elizabeth Drinker, ed. Elaine Forman Crane, 3 vols. (Boston: Northeastern University Press, 1991)

Futhey & Cope, *History of Chester County*
J. Smith Futhey and Gilbert Cope, *History of Chester County, Pennsylvania* (Philadelphia: Louis H. Everts, 1881)

Haverford
Quaker Collection, Haverford College Library, Haverford, PA

GSP
The Genealogical Society of Pennsylvania

HSP
The Historical Society of Pennsylvania, Philadelphia, PA

"Journal of Samuel Rowland Fisher"
Anna Wharton Morris, ed., "Journal of Samuel Rowland Fisher," *PMHB* 41 (1917):145 passim

Pennsylvania Archives
Pennsylvania Archives, First Series through Ninth Series, 119 vols. (Harrisburg, PA, 1853–1935) (see Intro., n. 6).

PMHB
Pennsylvania Magazine of History and Biography

Price Diary
Diary of Joseph Price, accessible online (see Chap. I, n. 12)

Scharf & Westcott, *History of Philadelphia*	J. Thomas Scharf and Thompson Westcott, *History of Philadelphia, 1609–1884*, 3 vols. (Philadelphia: Louis H. Everts & Co, 1884)
SEC	Supreme Executive Council
Sentencing Statement	Sentencing of Roberts by Thomas McKean, Appendix B (see Intro., n.1)
Statutes at Large	*Statutes at Large of Pennsylvania From 1682 to 1801*, 16 vols. (Harrisburg, PA, 1896–1911)
Swarthmore	Friends Historical Library, Swarthmore College, Swarthmore, PA
Trial Notes	Combined Trial Notes of Thomas McKean and Quaker observer, Appendix A (see Intro., nn.15 and 16)
Works of James Wilson	*The Works of James Wilson*, ed. Robert Green McCloskey, 2 vols. (Cambridge, MA: The Belknap Press of Harvard University Press, 1967)

Introduction

[1] The sentencing statement of Chief Justice Thomas McKean, as published in the *Pennsylvania Packet* (Philadelphia) on November 7, 1778, is set forth in its entirety in Appendix B hereto; it will hereafter be cited as the Sentencing Statement and by page number reference in Appendix B, as in this instance, App. B, p. 159.

[2] A fragmentary report of Roberts's case, limited to the legal issues raised at his trial, appears in the first volume of the reports prepared by Alexander J. Dallas, under the name of *Respublica v. Roberts*, 1 Dallas 39 (1778). Although the first volume contained "Reports of Cases Ruled and Adjudged in the Courts of Pennsylvania Before and Since the Revolution," the next three Dallas volumes would become the progenitor of a continuous series of official reports of cases decided by the United States Supreme Court. The first volume, published in 1790, necessarily drew on the notes and recollections of others as resources available to Dallas in his attempt to reconstruct the past proceedings in Pennsylvania; the result is not therefore an entirely trustworthy guide to arguments made in court or to judicial opinions. For background on Dallas's reports, see Julius Goebel, Jr., *Antecedents and Beginnings to 1801*, vol. 1 of the Oliver Wendell Holmes Devise, *History of the Supreme Court of the United States*, gen. ed. Paul A. Freund (New York: The Macmillan Company, 1971), 663–65, 720–21.

[3] Sentencing Statement, App. B, p. 161. McKean's engrained sense of self-importance is occasionally visible in John M. Coleman's truncated biography, *Thomas McKean: Forgotten Leader of the Revolution* (Rockaway, NJ: American Faculty Press, 1975), and more clearly so in G. S. Rowe, *Thomas McKean: The Shaping of an American Republicanism* (Boulder, CO: Colorado Associated University Press, 1978).

[4] Sentencing Statement, App. B., p. 161. The Pennsylvania treason statute applicable in John Roberts's trial was the Act of February 11, 1777, "An Act Declaring What Shall be Treason and What Other Crimes Against the State Shall be Misprision of

Treason," which provided in section 4: "And all persons . . . charged with any crime or crimes by this act declared to be treason against the state shall be dealt with and proceeded against as in other capital cases are by law directed." *Statutes at Large*, 9:45–47; regarding the traditional punishment for treason, see *Works of James Wilson*, 2:668–69. The 1777 statute superseded legislation passed in September 1776, before Pennsylvania adopted its new constitution, which was more moderate in the punishment of treason. For the history of the law of treason in Pennsylvania at the time of the Revolution, see Henry J. Young, "Treason and its Punishment in Revolutionary Pennsylvania," *PMHB* 90 (1966): 287–313; Bradley Chapin, *The American Law of Treason: Revolutionary and Early National Origins* (Seattle: University of Washington Press, 1964), 39, 55–59; Willard Hurst, "Treason in the United States," *Harvard Law Review* 58 (1944): 246–72.

⁵Catherine S. Crary, comp. and ed., *The Price of Loyalty: Tory Writings from the Revolutionary Era* (New York: McGraw-Hill, 1973), 237 (quoting from letter of James Humphreys to Joseph Galloway, Nov. 23 [1778]). The hanging took place in Center Square, at the intersection of Broad and Market (or High) Streets, then at some distance from the inhabited part of the city. See Scharf and Westcott, *History of Philadelphia*, 3:1843; and "Journal of Samuel Rowland Fisher," 326–27, for the hangings of Dawson and Chamberlain in the Philadelphia commons. See also Whitfield J. Bell, Jr., ed., "Addenda to Watson's Annals of Philadelphia, Notes by Jacob Mordecai, 1836," *PMHB* 98 (1974): 152.

⁶The record of the cases of Roberts and Carlisle, including the clemency petitions submitted, was published in *Pennsylvania Archives*, First Series, ed. Samuel Hazard (Philadelphia: Joseph Severns & Co., 1853), 7:21–58. Over almost a century's time, beginning in 1838, the Commonwealth of Pennsylvania published an extensive collection of historical documents in ten multivolume series under various editors, the first in order (but not in series numbering) being *Colonial Records*, followed by nine consecutively numbered series (hereafter cited as *Pennsylvania Archives*, with reference to the particular series, volume, and page number or numbers). None of the clemency petitions can be found today in the Pennsylvania State Archives in Harrisburg, as the author confirmed by his own trip to the archives and subsequently in a letter dated March 26, 2008, received from Aaron McWilliams, Assistant Archivist, Bureau of Archives and History, Pennsylvania Historical and Museum Commission.

⁷Those condemning the result include: Scharf & Westcott, *History of Philadelphia*,1: 394–95; Isaac Sharpless, *A Quaker Experiment in Government*, 2 vols. in one (Philadelphia: Ferris & Leach, 1902), 2:193–97; Futhey and Cope, *History of Chester County*, 115; Howard M. Jenkins, ed., *Pennsylvania Colonial and Federal: A History, 1608–1903*, 3 vols. (Philadelphia: Pennsylvania Historical Publishing Association, 1903), 2:67–68; and John F. Reed, "Truth Unmasked: The Story of John Roberts," *The Bulletin of the Historical Society of Montgomery County* 19 (1975): 318–19 ("judicial murder"). Those approving the result include: Benson J. Lossing, *The Pictorial Field-Book of the Revolution*, 2 vols. (New York: Harper & Brothers, 1860), 2:57 ("if it was ever expedient to take the life of a dangerous citizen, Roberts and Carlisle suffered justly"); Chapin, *American Law of Treason*, 57–58. Those straddling the fence, approving the verdict but not the denial of clemency, include Anne M. Ousterhout, *A State Divided: Opposition in Pennsylvania to the American Revolution* (Westport, CT: Greenwood Press, 1987), 188–90, and Stephen R. Boyd, "Political Choice–Political Justice: The Case of Pennsylvania Loyalists," in Michael R. Belknap, ed., *American*

Political Trials, rev. ed (Westport, CT: Greenwood Press, 1994), 45–56 (Roberts and Carlisle: "victims of politicized justice"). See also Peter C. Messer in " 'A Species of Treason & Not the Least Dangerous Kind': The Treason Trials of Abraham Carlisle and John Roberts," PMHB 123 (1999), 303–332, who argues that the executions of Carlisle and Roberts were influenced by conflicting views of salvation and redemption and the contest stirred up by the Great Awakening between the Old Lights, in favor of execution, and the New Lights, in favor of clemency; Messer's deterministic approach permits him to avoid any sustained consideration of the trials or the justice of their outcomes.

[8] Council ("T. M.," for Timothy Matlack, acting as secretary) to Thomas McKean, Oct. 21, 1778, Pennsylvania Archives, First Series, 7:21.

[9] "Petition of the Jury in the Case of John Roberts," Oct. 18, 1778, Pennsylvania Archives, First Series, 7:24–25; "Memorial of Jurors and Judges in Favor of Ara'm Carlisle, 1778," Oct. 18, 1778, ibid., 52–53.

[10] Minutes of the Supreme Executive Council of Pennsylvania (the Supreme Executive Council hereafter cited in these notes as "SEC"), Nov. 2, 1778, Colonial Records, 11:613.

[11] Minutes of SEC, Nov. 3, 1778, Colonial Records, 11:614.

[12] See pages 87–89 herein.

[13] For a view in an English context of the utility of trial notes in clarifying a meager and sometimes misleading record, see James C. Oldham, "Eighteenth-Century Judges' Notes: How They Explain, Correct and Enhance the Reports," The American Journal of Legal History 31 (1987): 9–42; and John H. Langbein, "Historical Foundations of the Law of Evidence: A View From the Ryder Sources," Columbia Law Review 96 (1996): 1172, 1176–78. As for the distinction between official court reporters, on the one hand, who, paid to prepare verbatim transcripts of court proceedings, may be liable for their failure to do so in timely fashion, and judicial note-takers, on the other, who, operating on their own and for their own purposes, are shielded from any such liability, see the opinion of Mr. Justice Stevens in Antoine v. Byers & Anderson, Inc., 508 U.S. 429 (1993). The evolution of the ability to produce verbatim reports of trial proceedings is traced in John H. Langbein, The Origins of Adversary Criminal Trial (New York: Oxford University Press, 2003), 180–190, and in Alan G. Gross, "Appreciating the Changing Factual Meaning of 'Verbatim,' or Battling the Curse of the 'Verbatim' Assumption," The Justice System Journal 25 (2004): 1–19.

[14] "Notes of C. J. McKean in case of Ab'm Carlisle, 1778," Pennsylvania Archives, First Series, 7:44–52. As for the acknowledged absence in the state archives of the trial notes in Roberts's case and the sinister explanation given by others for that absence, see ibid., 21 n. and 52 n.; James Bowden, The History of the Society of Friends in America, 2 vols. (London: Charles Gilpin, 1850), 2:329 (quoted in the text); Futhey & Cope, History of Chester County, 115; and Charles H. Browning, Welsh Settlement of Pennsylvania (1912; repr., Baltimore: Genealogical Publishing Company, 1967), 469–70.

[15] Morristown National Historical Park, Lloyd W. Smith Archives, microfilm reel 47, under "Roberts, John." A clue to the location of the lost McKean trial notes first appeared in Charles Page Smith, James Wilson: Founding Father, 1742–1798 (Chapel Hill: University of North Carolina Press, 1956), 121–22, 399, as later faintly echoed in Coleman, Thomas McKean, 290 n191, where Coleman mistakenly implies that the notes are "quite illegible." Page Smith, as Wilson's biographer, looked at the

McKean record and incorporated a limited portion of the trial testimony in his narrative. Jude M. Pfister, chief of cultural resources at the Morristown National Historical Park, has advised the author by e-mail that Lloyd Smith did not catalogue his collection and that he often acquired material in bulk purchases.

[16] There are two sources for this previously unexplored record: on microfilm, Philadelphia Yearly Meeting Records, Meeting for Sufferings, Miscellaneous Papers, 1779–1780, item 70, MR-Ph 507, at Swarthmore; and the original manuscript record of twenty-two pages (including McKean's sentencing statement) docketed as "Copy of the Evidence taken at the Tryal of John Roberts, 9 mo 1779 [sic]," under the same identification, box B5.3, at Haverford.

[17] A large debt remains outstanding to nineteenth-century authors of local and regional histories, of which no finer example exists than the Scharf and Westcott's three-volume *History of Philadelphia* published in 1884. Both local history per se and ordinary people have their defenders in academe. For local history, see Carol Kammen, ed., *The Pursuit of Local History: Readings in Theory and Practice* (Walnut Creek, CA: AltaMira Press, 1996). For ordinary people, see T. H. Breen, *American Insurgents, American Patriots: The Revolution of the People* (New York: Hill and Wang, 2010); Alfred F. Young, *Liberty Tree: Ordinary People and the American Revolution* (New York: New York University Press, 2006); and in a class-driven analysis, Steven Rosswurm, *Arms, Country, and Class: The Philadelphia Militia and "Lower Sort" During the American Revolution, 1775–1783* (New Brunswick, NJ: Rutgers University Press, 1987). Biographical entries for the members of the American Philosophical Society may be found by consulting the master index in Bell, *Patriot-Improvers*, 3:629–72.

[18] T. H. Breen gives two New England examples of nastiness in his *American Insurgents, American Patriots*, 14–16; see also Maya Jasanoff, *Liberty's Exiles: American Loyalists in the Revolutionary World* (New York: Afred A. Knopf, 2011), 22–23, 28–29, 131.

[19] The combined perspective is provided in Appendix A by using the Quaker record as template and inserting, by way of clarification and supplement, bracketed italicized text taken from McKean's notes; citation will hereafter be made to Trial Notes, App. A by page number herein.

[20] The report of the committee appointed by the Philadelphia Meeting for Sufferings is found on microfilm at Swarthmore, Philadelphia Yearly Meeting Records, Meeting for Sufferings, Miscellaneous Papers, 1779–1780, items 72 and 72a, MR-Ph 507, and in original manuscript at Haverford, under the same identification, in box B5.3. The full text of the committee report is set forth in Appendix C, to which reference will hereafter be made by page number herein, as in this instance, Committee Report, App. C, p. 164.

[21] *Extracts from the Diary of Christopher Marshall, Kept in Philadelphia and Lancaster During the American Revolution, 1774–1781*, ed. William Duane (Albany, NY: Joel Munsell, 1877), Dec. 28, 1777, 152.

Chapter I —From Immigrant to Refugee

[1] Charles H. Browning, *Welsh Settlement of Pennsylvania* (1912; repr., Baltimore: Genealogical Publishing Company, 1967), 175, 178–80; Rufus M. Jones, *The Quakers in the American Colonies* (London: Macmillan, 1911), 441–43; *The First 300: The*

Amazing and Rich History of Lower Merion (Ardmore, PA: The Lower Merion Historical Society, 2000), 14, 64–68, 72-75; Gloria O. Becker, *Mill Creek Valley: Architecture,
Industry, and Social Change in a Welsh Tract Community, 1682–1800* (Ann Arbor,
MI: University Microfilms International, 1984), 181–82. Becker's doctoral dissertation
is a thorough, in-depth study of the Welsh Tract and its inhabitants, with particular
attention given to the Mill Creek Valley and the succession of the three John Roberts
who lived there. The total area of the Welsh Tract has been variously recorded; from
a minimum figure of thirty thousand acres, it may have surveyed out to something
closer to fifty thousand. See Browning, *Welsh Settlement*, 249.

[2]The marriage certificate of John Roberts and Elizabeth Lloyd, 2nd 11th mo 1690
(Feb. 2, 1690/91), on microfilm at Swarthmore in "A Record of Marriages, Certificates
of Removal, and Births & Deaths, 1683 to 1730," MR-Ph 530, pp. 75–76; the children's
birth dates (Rebekah, 2nd 8th mo 1691; John, 17th 6th mo 1695; and Mathew, 23rd 4th
mo 1698), ibid., but at pp. 6, 11, and 17 of a separately identified "back of book";
and "Elizabeth wife of John Roberts (age 32) buried in Merion," 31st 8th mo 1699,
ibid., pp. 493–94. The spelling of the names of Rebekah and Mathew seems to vary
at the whim of whoever was making the entry.

[3]Will No. 127, admitted to probate March 11, 1704, and recorded in Philadelphia
in Book B, p. 343. The will is available at HSP, both on microfilm and in photostatic
copies of the original will and inventory in a bound volume of the Collections of
GSP, Philadelphia Wills and Inventories, Book B, Nos. 94–1129, 1701–1704. In the
account found in the estate file (see note 4 below), David Lloyd is recorded as receiving
one pound for advice and for drawing the will and also perhaps eighteen shilling for
probating it. If this David Lloyd was the sometime attorney general of the province,
later to become the chief justice of the Provincial Supreme Court, the first John
Roberts received expert deathbed assistance in framing the provisions in his will.

[4]Jonathan Roberts, "Memoirs of a Senator from Pennsylvania: *Jonathan Roberts,
1771-1854*," ed. Philip Shriver Klein, *PMHB* 61 (1937): 455–56. A photostatic copy
of the overseers' account, covering the period 1703 to 1715, and docketed as "Accot
agt ye Estate of Jno Roberts Deces'd," may be found in the same GSP bound volume
as cited in note 3 above. Two of the overseers, Mathew Roberts and Edward Roberts,
were brothers of the decedent whom he also named his executors. It does appear that
the overseers ran somewhat fast and loose in their accounting, especially the principal
overseer who at the end of the account claimed a lump-sum reimbursement for "52
Days Spent in Going to Town and other places with ye Charges of mySelf and horse"
at a per diem rate of four shillings, and a further charge, to top it off, of eight pounds
for keeping and settling the account.

[5]Becker, *Mill Creek Valley*, 201. For the Quaker formalities attending the marriage
of John Roberts and Hannah Lloyd, see Radnor Monthly Meeting, Minutes, 1684–
1733, 8th 7th mo and 10th 9th mo 1720, Swarthmore (microfilm), MR Ph 540, pp. 236
and 238; the marriage certificate dated 3rd 9th mo 1720 (Nov. 3, 1720), is found in
Radnor Monthly Meeting, "A Record of Marriages, Certificates of Removal, and
Births & Deaths, 1683 to 1730," Swarthmore (microfilm), MR-Ph 530, pp. 361–62.

[6]Becker, *Mill Creek Valley*, 202–204. The will was probated on May 17, 1721, and
recorded in Philadelphia as Will No. 217, Book D, page 187; Roberts provided by
codicil that, if he had no issue, his wife might elect to exchange her share in his
estate for the payment of one hundred forty pounds. The inventory, together with the
will and codicil, may be found at HSP in Collections of GSP, Philadelphia Wills and

Inventories, Book D, Nos. 206–246, 1720–1722. John Roberts III's birth date is entered in Radnor Monthly Meeting, "A Record of Marriages, Certificates of Removal, and Births & Deaths, 1683 to 1730," Swarthmore (microfilm), MR-Ph 530, p. 40.

[7] For the marriage to Paschall, see Radnor Monthly Meeting, Minutes, 1684–1733, 11th 8th mo, 8th 9th mo, and 13th 10th mo 1722, Swarthmore (microfilm), MR-Ph 540, pp. 258–60; the marriage certificate, in Radnor Monthly Meeting, "Record of Marriages, etc." Swarthmore (microfilm), MR-Ph 530, pp. 379–80. For the marriage to Osborne, see marriage certificate dated 6th 4th mo 1734, Goshen Monthly Meeting, Marriages, 1722–1787, Swarthmore (microfilm), MR-Ph 197, p. 47. See generally, but not always for consistent information, Futhey & Cope, *History of Chester County*, 714; R. Louis Lloyd, comp., *A Record of the Descendants of Robert Lloyd Who Came from Wales and Settled in the Welsh Tract at Merion Pennsylvania About 1684* (n. p.: [1947]), 3–9; Thomas Allen Glenn, *Merion in the Welsh Tract with Sketches of the Townships of Haverford and Radnor* (Norristown, PA: Herald Press, 1896), 83–84. Of Tory concentration there, Timothy Pickering wrote that Chester County was "the most disaffected in Pennsylvania." Octavius Pickering, *The Life of Timothy Pickering*, 4 vols. (Boston: Little, Brown, 1867–73), 1:192.

[8] Becker, *Mill Creek Valley*, 31–46; *The First 300*, 16–21, 44-45; and Browning, *Welsh Settlement*, 431–44, 533–40. Lancaster Road became Old Lancaster Road after a more direct route between Philadelphia and Lancaster was authorized by the legislature and completed in the 1790s. In its meandering course, Old Lancaster Road still runs parallel, here and there, to the Lancaster Turnpike (now Lancaster Avenue, or Route 30), and sometimes intersects it.

[9] For a representative sample of the activities of Roberts at meeting leading up to the Revolution, see Radnor Monthly Meeting, Abstract of Minutes, 1773–1778, 9th 9th mo 1773 (assist in forming "an account of the Settlement of these Meetings"), 10th 10th mo and 10th 11th mo 1775 (bequests of Margaret Williams), 14th 3rd mo 1776 (notify John Tucker and John Lloyd of disownment), Swarthmore (microfilm), MR-Ph 540, pp. 408, 445, 447–48, 452. Earlier, in 1763, Roberts appears to have been named as a trustee for the purchase of land for the Merion meeting.

[10] Futhey & Cope, *History of Chester County*, 173, 525–26, 714; the marriage certificate (dated 1st 4th mo, or June 1, 1743, in the old calendar) in Goshen Monthly Meeting, Marriages, 1722–1787, Swarthmore (microfilm), MR-Ph 197, p. 94.

[11] Futhey & Cope, *History of Chester County*, 714; Radnor Monthly Meeting, Births, 1682–1806, Swarthmore (microfilm), MR-Ph 530, pp. 63–79. Thomas Roberts provided these same birth dates for himself and his surviving siblings when he testified before a parliamentary commission in London in 1786. See Claims Commission AO/12/42/79-80.

[12] On Quaker encouragement of total abstinence, see Jack D. Marietta, *The Reformation of American Quakerism, 1748–1783* (Philadelphia: University of Pennsylvania Press, 1984), 105–8. The best evidence of Thomas Roberts's straying from the Quaker code, in his late marriage and in his frequent tavern visits, comes from the diary of his friend Joseph Price, a fellow Quaker (Collection 1657 at HSP), accessible by year in transcribed form on the Web site of the Lower Merion Historical Society at http://www.lowermerionhistory.org/texts/price/ (hereafter cited by date with reference to the online transcribed version as Price Diary). See e.g., Price Diary, Dec. 10, 28, and 31, 1791; May 1 and 18, and Dec. 9, 1793; Dec. 12 and 28, 1794; and Sept. 8 and 25, 1795. Thomas Roberts became a less dependable drinking partner after his move to Philadelphia and his marriage in 1796, as arranged by Price on Mar. 14, 1796.

[13]*Pennsylvania Archives*, Third Series, 14:99 (provincial tax of 1769); Becker, *Mill Creek Valley*, 295; Charles R. Barker, "Old Mills of Mill Creek, Lower Merion," *PMHB* 50 (1926): 3–4. Thomas Roberts and others testified in London in 1786 about the properties his father owned and the improvements constructed thereon. See Claims Commission, AO 12/42/77, 76–78, 79–83.

[14]*Pennsylvania Gazette*, Dec. 16, 1762, Jan. 13 and 27, 1763 (Lightin); May 31, 1764 (Rhoads); and July 30, 1767, June 18 and Nov. 30, 1769, March 16 and Aug. 17, 1774 (Dunning, also known as Duning and Downey).

[15]Roberts, "Memoirs of a Senator," 465; George Johnston, *History of Cecil County, Maryland* (1881; repr., Baltimore, MD: Genealogical Publishing Co., 1989), 347-48, 509; *Pennsylvania Gazette*, Oct. 12, 1769. In the mid-eighteenth century David Davis operated a fulling mill and perhaps a sawmill on the Mill Creek. Barker, "Old Mills of Mill Creek," 6; and *The First 300*, 59 (mistakenly refers to "Donald Davis"). Davis died unmarried in 1768, leaving a will in which he named his sister Mary and "my friend John Roberts, miller," as his executors. Will No. 188, dated Mar. 13, 1767, probated on July 27, 1768, and recorded in Philadelphia County in Will Book O, p. 244.

[16]*Pennsylvania Archives*, Third Series, 25:280–81. On the New Purchase of 1768, see David W. Maxey, "The Honorable Proprietaries v. Samuel Wallis: 'A Matter of Great Consequence' in the Province of Pennsylvania," *Pennsylvania History* 70 (2003): 367–68. This property would later become part of newly formed Lycoming County.

[17]Roberts, "Memoirs of a Senator," 446, 455, 469–70. Becker paints a rather flattering portrait of Roberts's growing involvement in religious and public affairs in the years leading up to the Revolution, *Mill Creek Valley*, 388–90, but evidence is missing that he occupied a position of significant responsibility in either sector. The author of a highly colored but undocumented article about Roberts dismissed him in an unkind cut as "mostly an historical nonentity" until his downfall during the Revolution. John F. Reed, "Truth Unmasked: The Story of John Roberts," *The Bulletin of the Historical Society of Montgomery County* 19 (1975): 302.

[18]*Pennsylvania Gazette*, June 22, 1774. Appearing in this same issue of the *Gazette* was the address of the William Smith to his fellow committee members.

[19]Act of Jan. 28, 1777 ("An Act to revive and put in force such and so much of the late laws of the province of Pennsylvania as is judged necessary to be in force in this Commonwealth, and to revive and establish the courts of justice and for other purposes therein mentioned"), *Statutes at Large*, 9:29–33; and *Pennsylvania Gazette*, Mar. 26, 1777 (for "friends of liberty"). For the chaotic conditions in Pennsylvania in the absence of state governmental authority in 1777, see Robert H. Brunhouse, *The Counter-Revolution in Pennsylvania, 1776–1790* (Harrisburg, PA: Pennsylvania Historical Commission, 1942), 27–38; and Steven Rosswurm, *Arms, Country, and Class: The Philadelphia Militia and "Lower Sort" During the American Revolution, 1775–1783* (New Brunswick, NJ: Rutgers University Press, 1987), 138–40.

[20]G. S. Rowe, *Embattled Bench: The Pennsylvania Supreme Court and the Forging of a Democratic Society* (Newark, DE: University of Delaware Press, 1994), 130–35; *Pennsylvania Gazette*, Aug. 20 and 27 and Sept. 3, 1777. The Court of Quarter Sessions met on June 3, 1776; then next on September 1, 1777; and once again on September 7, 1778, as, following the British evacuation, it was at last able to return to its normal schedule. Docket, Quarter Sessions Court, 1773–1780, Philadelphia City Archives; Scharf & Westcott, *History of Philadelphia*, 3:1736-37 n3. McKean's

appointment was confirmed as of July 28. He and his two colleagues on the Supreme Court were commissioned on Aug. 16 and 19, but subject to taking an oath that gave a double meaning to the commitment to serve faithfully; they were called on to declare their belief "in one God the Creator and Governor of the Universe, the rewarder of the good and the punisher of the wicked" and to acknowledge that the "the scriptures of the old and new testament [are] given by divine inspiration." Minutes of SEC, *Colonial Records*, 11:254, 270, 271, and 304; *Pennsylvania Archives*, First Series, 5:621 (the text of McKean's oath on Sept. 1).

[21] *Respublica v. Chapman*, 1 Dallas 53, 58 (1781); Act of Feb. 11, 1777 (treason statute), *Statutes at Large*, 9:45–47; Sentencing Statement, App. B, p. 160. See also Henry J. Young, "Treason and its Punishment in Revolutionary Pennsylvania," *PMHB* 90 (1966): 287–88, 299–302; and Carlton F. W. Larson, "The Forgotten Constitutional Law of Treason and the Enemy Combatant Problem," *University of Pennsylvania Law Review* 154 (2006): 879–82. As to the dilemma faced by one in search of protective allegiance at the outset of the Revolution, Mr. Justice Jackson captured it perfectly in his opinion in the landmark case of *Cramer v. United States*, 325 U.S. 1, 11–12 (1945): "Many a citizen, in time of unsettled and shifting loyalties, was thus threatened under English law, which made him guilty if he adhered to the government of his colony, and under colonial law, which made him guilty if he adhered to the King." For the Revolutionary War as a civil war, see Lawrence M. Friedman, *Crime and Punishment in Early American Society* (New York: Basic Books, 1993), 65, and Maya Jasanoff, *Liberty's Exiles: American Loyalists in the Revolutionary World* (New York: Afred A. Knopf, 2011), 21–53, 131.

[22] *Works of James Wilson*, 2:666.

[23] For Lewis's argument, see "Notes of C. J. McKean in the Case of Ab'm Carlisle, 1778," Sept. 25, 1778, *Pennsylvania Archives*, First Series, 7:50. Thomas Hobbes, *Leviathan*, ed. Richard Tuck (Cambridge: Cambridge University Press, 2008), 484.

[24] Pennsylvania constitution of 1776, in *Statutes at Large*, 9:585 (also available at http://www.duq.edu/law/pa-constitution/). On learning of the British decision to evacuate Philadelphia, Lord Richard Howe's secretary recorded, "I now look upon the Contest as at an End. No man can be expected to declare for us, when he cannot be assured of a Fortnight's Protection." Ambrose Serle, May 22, 1778, *The American Journal of Ambrose Serle: Secretary to Lord Howe, 1776–1778* (San Marino, CA: Huntington Library, 1940), 296. In patriotic rhetoric and in constitution-making, allegiance and protection were repeatedly invoked as reciprocal obligations underpinning civil society. See Philip Hamburger, "Beyond Protection," *Columbia Law Review* 109 (2009): 1834–47.

[25] Rosswurm, *Arms, Country, and Class*, 52–61, 135–36, 230–31; Marietta, *Reformation of American Quakerism*, 236–42; Brunhouse, *Counter-Revolution in Pennsylvania*, 38–41. Act of March 17, 1777 ("An Act to regulate the militia of the Commonwealth of Pennsylvania"), Act of June 13, 1777 ("An Act obliging the male white inhabitants of this State to give assurances of allegiance to the same and for other purposes"), and Act of Oct. 12, 1777 (supplementing the aforesaid Act of June 13, 1777), in *Statutes at Large*, 9:75–94, 110–14, and 147–49. In testimony before the parliamentary commission after the war, Thomas Roberts stated that he and his brother "never conformed to the measures of the Insurgents [and] never paid a fine." Claims Commission, AO 12/42/80.

[26] Brooke Hunter, "Wheat, War, and the American Economy During the Age of Revolution, *William and Mary Quarterly*, 3d ser., 62 (2005): 509–14; Thomas M.

Doerflinger, *A Vigorous Spirit of Enterprise: Merchants and Economic Development in Revolutionary Philadelphia* (Chapel Hill, NC: University of North Carolina Press, 1986), 199–223.

[27]Trial Notes, App. A, p. 152; Browning, *Welsh Settlement*, 76–77; John W. Jordan, ed., *Colonial Families of Philadelphia* (New York: Lewis Publishing Company, 1911), 1:630–31; *The First 300*, 41. The location of the Jones house in Philadelphia is established in Owen Jones's will dated 11th 10th mo 1791, probated as Will No. 405 on Dec. 5, 1793, and recorded in Philadelphia in Will Book W, p. 670. An unresolved mystery is where Roberts stayed in Philadelphia after lodging with Owen Jones and his wife.

[28]Trial Notes, App. A, p. 144; Sentencing Statement, App. B, pp. 160–61. For the Virginia exiles, see Isaac Sharpless, *A Quaker Experiment in Government*, 2 vols. in one (Philadelphia: Ferris & Leach, 1902), 145–71; Theodore Thayer, *Israel Pemberton, King of the Quakers* (Philadelphia: The Historical Society of Pennsylvania, 1943), 216–31; and Robert F. Oaks, "Philadelphians in Exile: The Problem of Loyalty During the American Revolution," *PMHB* 96 (1972): 298–325. The Masonic Lodge was a three-story brick building on the south side of Lodge Alley, between Walnut and Chestnut Streets, just west of Second. See Scharf & Westcott, *History of Philadelphia*, 3:2063.

[29]Trial Notes, App. A, pp. 144–45; Thomas J. McGuire, *The Philadelphia Campaign*, 2 vols. (Mechanicsburg, PA: Stackpole Books, 2006 and 2007), 1(*Brandywine and the Fall of Philadelphia*): 268–69; Futhey & Cope, *History of Chester County*, 115.

[30]Trial Notes, App. A, pp. 146–47.

[31]Trial Notes, App. A, p. 149.

[32]Trial Notes, App. A, pp. 149–50. In September 1777, McKean had issued a writ of habeas corpus on behalf of the Virginia exiles; the writ was first disregarded by those having custody of the prisoners and then overruled by the Pennsylvania Assembly, which suspended the writ. The Virginia exiles, released after seven months of confinement, returned to Philadelphia in late April 1778. Marietta, *Reformation of American Quakerism*, 240–42; Anne M. Ousterhout, *A State Divided: Opposition in Pennsylvania to the American Revolution* (Westport CT: Greenwood Press, 1987), 165–68. Henry Drinker's daughter Sarah would provide a Roberts family connection when she married Jacob Downing, the nephew of John Roberts's wife, but that marriage did not occur until 1787. *The Diary of Elizabeth Drinker*, ed. Elaine Forman Crane, 3 vols. (Boston: Northeastern University Press, 1991), 3:2137 (s.v., "Downing, Jacob"). Roberts was obviously close to Owen and Susanna Jones, whose son Owen Jones, Jr., was among the Virginia exiles.

[33]Committee Report, App. C, pp. 165–66.

[34]Sentencing Statement, App. B., pp. 160–61.

[35]A reliable account of this foraging expedition remains S. Gordon Smyth's "The Gulph Hills in the Annals of the Revolution," in *Historical Sketches: A Collection of Papers Prepared for the Historical Society of Montgomery County, Pennsylvania* (Norristown, PA: Herald Printing and Binding Rooms, 1905), vol. 3, pp. 171–88. As was typical of that era, Smyth did not identify his sources, one of which was the letter of the orthographically challenged General James Potter to Thomas Wharton, President of the SEC, Dec. 15, 1777, *Pennsylvania Archives*, First Series, 6:97–98, in which Potter described the running engagement with the enemy and roundly criticized General Sullivan (the "Valant Generil Solovan") for not providing him with needed

support. See also McGuire, *The Philadelphia Campaign*, 2 (*Germantown and the Roads to Valley Forge*): 257–64; *Diary of Elizabeth Drinker*, Dec. 12, 1777 ("Some of the Troops are gone over Schuylkill, Fireing heard to day"), 1:263; and Timothy Pickering to his wife, Dec. 13, 1777, in Pickering, *Life of Timothy Pickering*, 1:191–93.

[36] Trial Notes, App. A, p. 142; and for the strategic location of the Black Horse Tavern, see Charles R. Barker, "Colonial Taverns of Lower Merion," *PMHB* 52 (1928): 217–20, 225–27.

[37] *Diary of Elizabeth Drinker*, Apr. 5, 1778, 1:296. Elizabeth and Henry Drinker, reunited, lodged at the Roberts house on the way back to Philadelphia on April 29. John Pemberton was also with them, and taking advantage of a religious opportunity he described "tho' short, yet seasonable," he offered words of comfort to the family before the overnight guests set off the next day. Ibid., Apr. 30, 1778, 1:303; Diary of John Pemberton, 30th 4th mo 1778, Pemberton Papers, HSP (Collection 484A), box 1, p. 113.

[38] Act of Mar. 6, 1778, *Statutes at Large*, 9:201–15; Minutes of SEC, May 8, 1778, *Colonial Records*, 11:482–85; and Young, "Treason and its Punishment in Revolutionary Pennsylvania," 287–313. (Young draws a too rigid distinction between treason trials per se and trials under the conditional attainder statute and proclamations.)

[39] April 23, 1778, *Journals of the Continental Congress*, 34 vols. (Washington, DC: United States Government Printing Office, 1904–1937), 10:381–82; Ambrose Serle, May 23, 1778, *American Journal of Ambrose Serle*, 296.

[40] Message of Livingston to General Assembly, May 29, 1778, published in *Pennsylvania Packet*, June 17, 1778.

[41] *The Examination of Joseph Galloway, Esq; Late Speaker of the House of Assembly of Pennsylvania, Before the House of Commons, in a Committee of the American Papers with Explanatory Notes* (London: J. Wilkie, 1779), 84-85; Roberts, "Memoirs of a Senator," 455.

[42] Order of Zebulon Potts, June 19, 1778, Society Collection, HSP, "Zebulon Potts" folder; Recognizance, June 20, 1778, Pennsylvania State Archives, Harrisburg, PA, RG-33, Records of the Supreme Court of Pennsylvania, Eastern District, Courts of Oyer & Terminer, Court Papers, 1757–1787 (microfilm), reel 4637. Thomas Livezey, a prosperous Quaker miller across the Schuylkill on the Wissahickon, was named as a suspect traitor in the same conditional attainder proclamation that contained the names of Roberts and Carlisle, but Livezey apparently escaped prosecution. He was a member of the American Philosophical Society. For biographical information, see Bell, *Patriot-Improvers*, 1:317–19; and Wayne Bodle, *The Valley Forge Winter: Civilians and Soldiers in War* (University Park, PA: Pennsylvania State University Press, 2002), 84–85. Joseph Mather was also a miller living in Germantown. By Mather's account, Roberts spent the night at Mather's house immediately after the British left Philadelphia, appearing the next day before Potts to comply with the requirements of the attainder proclamation. Affidavit of Joseph Mather and Charles Humphreys, Oct. 15, 1783, in support of a claim of Jane Roberts for compensation submitted after the war. Claims Commission, AO 13/71 pt.2/260–61.

[43] Warrant for the Arrest of John Roberts, July 27, 1778, HSP, Boudinot Papers, vol. 2, p. 44 (also published in "Notes and Queries," *PMHB* 24 (1900): 117). At the same time witnesses were lined up under recognizance of fifty pounds each to give evidence against Roberts in the forthcoming court session. Recognizance, July 27, 1778, Pennsylvania State Archives, RG-33, Records of the Supreme Court of Pennsylvania, Eastern

District, Courts of Oyer & Terminer, Court Papers, 1757–1787 (microfilm), reel 4637. Not all the prospective witnesses identified under recognizance testified at the trial; missing in court were Robert Elliott of Lower Merion, John Jones of Upper Merion, and Matthew Shepherd of the City of Philadelphia, weaver, and his wife, Jane.

[44]Thomas McKean to William A. Atlee, June 5, 1778, *Letters of Delegates to Congress, 1774–1789*, ed. Paul H. Smith et al., 26 vols. (Washington, DC: Library of Congress, 1976-2000), 10:31–33.

[45]*Pennsylvania Evening Post*, July 16 and 18, 1778.

[46]*Pennsylvania Packet*, Aug. 13 (publication of Address of Meeting for Sufferings), 15, and 20, 1778. The address of the Meeting for Sufferings may also be found in Sharpless, *Quaker Experiment in Government*, 2:179–81.

[47]*Pennsylvania Packet*, Aug. 27, 1778. A contemporary diarist recorded that Roberts was sent to the gaol on August 10. Raymond C. Werner , ed., "Diary of Grace Growden Galloway," *PMHB* 55 (1931): 48. At about that same time, Joseph Galloway's wife engaged Elias Boudinot to represent her in resisting confiscation of her property because of her husband's conduct attainted as treason. Ibid., 46–50.

[48]Minutes of SEC, Oct. 23, 1778, *Colonial Records*, 11:600–602 (for the text of the indictment). Roberts and Carlisle were tried before the Court of Oyer and Terminer and General Gaol Delivery for the County of Philadelphia, the tribunal having jurisdiction of homicides and other serious offenses; Supreme Court justices were specially commissioned to sit as trial judges in that court and issue rulings affecting various parties.

[49]Edward Burd, the prothonotary or clerk of the Supreme Court at the time of Roberts's trial, would twice produce in subsequent years a certified copy of the complete docket record of that proceeding, which serves as a reliable source of information concerning the trial. See pp. 125–26, 131–32 herein.

Chapter II—The Prosecution

[1]June 24, 1776, *Journals of the Continental Congress*, 34 vols. (Washington, DC: United States Government Printing Office, 1904–1937), 5:475; Charles Page Smith, *James Wilson: Founding Father, 1742–1798* (Chapel Hill: University of North Carolina Press, 1956), 119.

[2]Act of Sept. 5, 1776 ("An Ordinance of the State of Pennsylvania Declaring What Shall be Treason and for Punishing the Same and Other Crimes & Practices Against the State"), in *Statutes at Large*, 9:18–19. See Bradley Chapin, *The American Law of Treason: Revolutionary and Early National Origins* (Seattle: University of Washington Press, 1964), 36–37; Henry J. Young, "Treason and its Punishment in Revolutionary Pennsylvania," *PMHB* 90 (1966): 289–91, 293–95.

[3]Act of Feb. 11, 1777 ("An Act Declaring What Shall be Treason and What Other Crimes and Practices Against the State Shall Be Misprision of Treason"), in *Statutes at Large*, 9:45–47 (text quoted partially paraphrased). Technically speaking, Roberts and Carlisle were apprehended and arraigned under the SEC's conditional attainder proclamation of May 8, 1778 (see Chap. I, n. 38), but the treason statute passed a year earlier specified the grounds for treason and governed the conduct of their trials.

[4]For duration of Roberts's trial, see *Pennsylvania Evening Post*, Oct. 16, 1778 (postscript of Oct 17); and for duration of Carlisle's trial, see *Pennsylvania Evening*

Post, Sept. 25, 1778 (postscript of Sept. 26). See also *Diary of Elizabeth Drinker*, Sept. 25, 26, and 30, Oct. 1 and 2, 1778, 1:328–29.

[5] The proceedings were originally called for the State House, *Pennsylvania Packet*, Aug. 25, 1778, but the Pennsylvania *Evening Post*, Sept. 21, 1778, announced that the court had opened "at the college" the previous day. G. S. Rowe in *Embattled Bench: The Pennsylvania Supreme Court and the Forging of a Democratic Society* (Newark, DE: University of Delaware Press, 1994), 143, has the first trial session opening at College Hall "before a large and boisterous crowd," the presence of which does not appear independently verifiable. As for the designation of College Hall, see Edward Burd to Jasper Yeates, Sept. 19 (and 20), 1778, Yeates Papers, Jasper Yeates Correspondence (1762–1786), HSP, 1778 folder. "The Minutes of the Trustees of the College, Academy and Charitable Schools," vol. 2 (1768 to 1791), p. 107, is accessible online at http://www.archives.upenn.edu/faids/upa1/upa1/upa1_1online .html. The deplorable condition in which the State House was left may be verified by the substantial expenditures authorized for its repair. Minutes of SEC, July 18 and 21, Aug. 20 and 29, and Sept. 18, 1778, *Colonial Records*, 11:534–35, 558, 564, 581.

[6] For Reed and his appointment, see Minutes of SEC, Aug. 21, 1778, *Colonial Records*, 11:560. The professional qualifications of Wilson, Ross, and Lewis as counsel acting in these treason trials for the defense are touched on in Smith, *James Wilson*, 117–19, whereas Reed's standing is acknowledged in ibid., 23, 121–22, and more extravagantly in Eric Stockdale and Randy J. Holland, *Middle Temple Lawyers and The American Revolution* (Eagan, MN: Thomson West, 2007), 110–32.

[7] In Carlisle's case, which was the first of the Philadelphia cases to be tried, the court made a preliminary determination that the statutes "which regulate the mode of trials in cases of high treason in England" had been repealed by the Pennsylvania Assembly and ruled instead that the indictment and the list of prospective jurors be provided as stated in the text, the defendant "paying reasonable charges therefor." *Pennsylvania Evening Post*, Sept. 23, 1778 (the court's ruling appears to have been made on Sept. 24, as noted in the newspaper postscript); see also *Respublica v. Molder*, 1 Dallas 33 (Oyer & Terminer Court, probably Chester County, 1778), to the same effect. This allowance for receipt of information essential to the preparation of the defense was less generous than that available in treason trials in England, where minimums of five days advance notice for providing the indictment and two days for a list of prospective jurors were the stipulated statutory requirements. John H. Langbein, *The Origins of Adversary Criminal Trial* (New York: Oxford University Press, 2003), 90–92, 95–96.

[8] Carlton F. W. Larson, "The Revolutionary American Jury: A Case Study of the 1778–1779 Philadelphia Treason Trials," *Southern Methodist University Law Review* 61 (2008): 1441–1524.

[9] The right of the accused to challenge peremptorily up to thirty-five jurors (and more with cause) was recognized under English law. J. H. Baker, *An Introduction to English Legal History*, 3d ed. (London: Butterworth, 1990), 581.

[10] Sentencing Statement, App. B, p. 159.

[11] Trial notes, App. A, p. 137; on the Quaker testimony against oaths, see Rufus. M. Jones, *The Later Periods of Quakerism*, 2 vols. (London: Macmillan, 1921), 1:166–68.

[12] Philadelphia Monthly Meeting (Fourth Street Meeting), Minutes, 25th 12th mo 1778, 29th 1st mo 1779, 26th 2nd mo 1779, and 30th 4th mo 1779, Swarthmore (microfilm), MR-Ph 384, pp. 100, 106–7, 116–17, 131. Dickinson's disownment was a foregone

conclusion; the minutes of the January meeting reads that his case "strongly Demands that the Meeting should clear themselves of the Reproach of his Conduct, and leave the Weight of it on himself."

[13] "Journal of Samuel Rowland Fisher," 166–67; "Memorial and Remonstrance of Isaac Howell and White Matlack," submitted to the Pennsylvania General Assembly on 21st of 8th Month, 1782, in Charles Wetherill, *History of the Religious Society of Friends, Called by Some the Free Quakers, in the City of Philadelphia* ([Philadelphia?]: Printed for the Society, 1894), 78. It seems safe to say that disownments for violation of the peace testimony were almost without exception directed against those supporting the patriot cause. See Richard Bauman, *For the Reputation of Truth: Politics, Religion, and Conflict Among the Pennsylvania Quakers, 1750–1800* (Baltimore, MD: Johns Hopkins Press, 1971), 157, 165–67.

[14] Trial Notes, App. A, p. 137; Larson, "Revolutionary American Jury," 1517–24. Both Cadwalader Dickinson and John Campbell traveled the road from comparative prosperity to penury during the Revolution. See Billy G. Smith, *The "Lower Sort": Philadelphia Laboring People, 1750–1800* (Ithaca, NY: Cornell University Press, 1990), 20, 138. (Campbell, the juror, is, however, a problematic identification.)

[15] Larson, "Revolutionary American Jury," 1468; for biographical data on the brothers Henry and John Drinker, see Bell, *Patriot-Improvers*, 2:298–305, 340–44. The proceedings against John Drinker, the bricklayer, are found in Philadelphia Monthly Meeting (Arch Street), Minutes, 1771–1777, 24th 4th mo (adjourned to 7th 5th mo) and 30th 10th mo (adjourned to 5th 11th mo) 1772, Swarthmore (microfilm), MR-Ph 384, pp. 60, 112–13.

[16] For the 1773 annotated jury list, see David W. Maxey, "The Honorable Proprietaries v. Samuel Wallis: 'A Matter of Great Consequence' in the Province of Pennsylvania," *Pennsylvania History* 70 (2003):375. The original jury list is now in the collections of the Muncy Historical Society in Muncy, PA.

[17] Larson, "Revolutionary American Jury," 1474, 1517; Steven Rosswurm, *Arms, Country, and Class: The Philadelphia Militia and "Lower Sort" During the American Revolution, 1775–1783* (New Brunswick, NJ: Rutgers University Press, 1987), 66–72, 260–61; Deborah Mathias Gough, *Christ Church, Philadelphia: The Nation's Church and in Changing City* (Philadelphia: University of Pennsylvania Press, 1995), 137, 188.

[18] Larson, "Revolutionary American Jury," 1475–76, 1521; Bennett S. Pancoast, comp., *The Pancoast Family in America* (Woodbury, NJ: The Gloucester County Historical Society, 1981), 38–40; Minutes of the Council of Safety, Dec. 11, 1776, Jan. 27, Mar. 10 and 13, 1777, *Colonial Records*, 11:44, 104, 142, 145. Pancoast's disownment is recorded in Philadelphia Monthly Meeting (Northern District), Minutes, 1772–1781, 2nd and 30th 4th mo and 4th and 25th 6th mo 1776, Swarthmore (microfilm), MR-Ph 411, pp. 202, 207–08, 213, 215. Pancoast's wife, Sarah, and two daughters, Mary and Elizabeth, were subsequently granted a certificate to relocate to the Monthly Meeting of Hopewell, Virginia. Philadelphia Monthly Meeting (Northern District), Minutes, 1772–1781, 23rd 11th mo 1779, ibid., p. 396.

[19] Rosswurm, *Arms, Country, and Class*, 153–55; *Pennsylvania Packet*, July 25, 1778.

[20] *Pennsylvania Packet*, Sept. 5, 15, 19, 22, 26, and 29, 1778. "Patriotic Association Book, August 18, 1778," Am. 238, HSP, is the roll book recording attendance and the payment of dues. There is no sign of activity of the association after the end of September; the last notice of a meeting appeared in *Pennsylvania Packet*, Oct. 6, 1778.

[21] Trial Notes, App. A, p. 137.

²²Langbein, *Adversary Criminal Trial*, 106–9, 167–77, 291–311; William Blackstone, *Commentaries on the Law of England* (Chicago: University of Chicago Press, 1979, a facsimile of the first edition, 1765–1769), 4:349–50 (Blackstone's *Commentaries* are also accessible at Yale's Avalon site, http://avalon.law.yale.edu/subject_menus/blackstone.asp); Baker, *Introduction to English Legal History* , 582–83; Rowe, *Embattled Bench*, 71–72. James Wilson, appropriating Blackstone's text and analysis almost word for word, congratulates his own state of Pennsylvania and the United States on more enlightened practice in permitting counsel to represent the accused. *Works of James Wilson*, 2:702. The Pennsylvania constitution of 1776, in Article 9 of its declaration of rights, specifically recognized that, "in all prosecutions for criminal offences, a man hath a right to be heard by himself and his council." *Statutes at Large*, 9:588 (also available at http://www.duq.edu/law/pa-constitution/).

²³Langbein, *Adversary Criminal Trial*, 233–51; Allyson N. May, *The Bar and the Old Bailey, 1750–1850* (Chapel Hill: University of North Carolina Press, 2003), 109; Lawrence M. Friedman, *A History of American Law*, 2d ed. (New York: Simon & Schuster, 1985), 152–53; and Matthew P. Harrington, "The Law-Finding Function of the American Jury," 1999 *Wisconsin Law Review*: 377, 387–90.

²⁴Pennsylvania constitution of 1776, *Statutes at Large*, 9:586–89 (Declaration of Rights), 9:590 (broadened franchise in Section 6) (also available at (http://www.duq.edu/law/pa-constitution/); Steven Rosswurm, *Arms, Country, and Class: The Philadelphia Militia and "Lower Sort" During the American Revolution, 1775–1783* (New Brunswick, NJ: Rutgers University Press, 1987), 100–108; Terry Bouton, *Taming Democracy: "The People," the Founders, and the Troubled Ending of the American Revolution* (New York: Oxford University Press, 2007), 52–57.

²⁵Logan Papers, HSP, vol. 38, Dickinson Estate, 1791–1805, folder 44 (survey of Plantation); Becker, *Mill Creek* Valley, 378; Trial Notes, App. A, p. 142. Michael Smith was assessed in a tenant capacity for John Dickinson's estate in 1779, 1782, and 1783, *Pennsylvania Archives*, Third Series, 14:624 and 16:131, 591.

²⁶Trial Notes, App. A, pp. 138–39. The inhabitants of the Welsh Tract received rough treatment during the foraging expedition. An American officer reported of the British marauders, "With a sword they ripped the clothes from the back of one woman, and cut off one of her fingers." Octavius Pickering, *The Life of Timothy Pickering*, 4 vols. (Boston: Little, Brown and Company, 1867–1873), 1:193.

²⁷Trial Notes, App. A, pp. 139–40. Michael Smith claimed losses totaling four hundred fifty-one pounds as a result of the British confiscation of his property. "Assessment of Damages Done by the British Troops During the Occupation of Philadelphia, 1777–1778," *PMHB* 25 (1901): 545. His two sons, Michael and William Smith, veterans of the Revolutionary War, are buried (by best guess) in the cemetery of St. Paul's Evangelical Lutheran Church in Ardmore, PA, the church founded by German immigrants who came to Lower Merion. It was the Smiths' son Bill who was imprisoned in the New Jail and whose release his mother sought. For burial records, see http://www.lowermerionhistory.org/burial/lutheran/.

²⁸Trial Notes, App. A, pp. 140–41. Michael Foster, *A Report of Some Proceedings on the Commission for the Trial of the Rebels in the Year 1746—to which are Added Discourses Upon a Few Branches of the Crown Law* (Oxford: Clarendon Press, 1762), 200–207; *Respublica v. Roberts*, 1 Dallas 39, 39–40.

²⁹The practice in England was to permit objections to be argued in the presence of the jury. J. M. Beattie, *Crime and the Courts in England: 1660–1800* (Princeton: Princeton University Press, 1986), 365.

[30] Mary Emma Boggs and Benjamin Randolph Boggs, "Inns and Taverns of Old Philadelphia" (1917, in typescript at HSP, catalogued Am 3032), 486, 490–92. For the concentration of taverns in and around Strawberry Alley, see Sharon V. Salinger, *Taverns and Drinking in Early America* (Baltimore: Johns Hopkins University Press, 2002), 184–90 and accompanying maps.

[31] Trial Notes, App. A, p. 141. For various property a John Ellis seized as levying officer in 1778, see "the account at present Collected of the Sufferings of Friends Belonging to Haverford Monthly Meeting," 26th 4th mo 1779, Philadelphia Meeting for Sufferings, Miscellaneous Papers, 1779–1780, Haverford, box B5.3, 1779, item 19; and "A State of the Sufferings of divers Friends, Members of the Monthly Meeting of the Northern District of Philadelphia," 23rd 4th mo 1779, ibid., item 18.

[32] Futhey & Cope, *History of Chester County*, 81, 213, 754–55; Trial Notes, App. A, p. 141; Thomas J. McGuire, *The Philadelphia Campaign*, 2 vols. (Mechanicsburg, PA: Stackpole Books, 2006 and 2007), 2 (*Germantown and the Roads to Valley Forge*):136–37, 227, 232; Carlos E. Godfrey, "Muster Rolls of Three Troops of Loyalist Light Dragoons Raised in Pennsylvania 1777–1778," *PMHB* 34 (1910): 5, 8; McGuire, *Philadelphia Campaign*, 1(*Brandywine and the Fall of Philadelphia*):301; Lorenzo Sabine, *Biographical Sketches of Loyalists of the American Revolution With an Historical Essay*, 2 vols. (Boston: Little, Brown, 1864), 1:569, 2:387–88.

[33] Trial Notes, App. A, pp. 141–42.

[34] Trial Notes, App. A, p. 142.

[35] Trial Notes, App. A, p. 143. Some sense of the layout and extent of Blockley may be gained from Scharf & Wescott, *History of Philadelphia*,1:13,15–16, 119. Frederick Vernor, in McKean's identification, was probably Frederick Verner, named in a conditional attainder proclamation of June 15, 1778, and the subject of an advisory opinion McKean gave the SEC in August. Minutes of SEC, *Colonial Records*, June 15 and Aug. 22, 1778, 11:513–18, 561.

[36] Minutes of the Council of Safety, Nov. 22 and Dec. 5, 1776, *Colonial Records*, 11:12, 33. The later occupations of Groves and Stroud appear in Recognizance, July 27, 1778, Pennsylvania State Archives, RG-33, Records of the Supreme Court of Pennsylvania, Eastern District, Courts of Oyer & Terminer, Court Papers, 1757–1787 (microfilm), reel 4637.

[37] Trial Notes, App. A, 143–44. *Respublica v. Roberts*, 1 Dallas 39, 40; Foster, *A Report of Some Proceedings*, 243, and in support of Reed's claim, ibid., 10–11 (*John Berwick's Case*), 240–44. The treason statute of Feb. 11, 1777, provided that "every person so offending and being thereof legally convicted by the evidence of two sufficient witnesses in any court of oyer and terminer shall be adjudged [guilty] of high treason and shall suffer death, and his or her estate shall be and is herby declared to be forfeited to the commonwealth." *Statutes at Large*, 9:46. Whether or not the legislature intended to abolish confessions as a means of establishing treason, Wilson was correct that the statute contained nothing specifically about confessions.

[38] *Respublica v. Roberts*, 1 Dallas 39, 39–40. McKean had similarly admitted evidence otherwise subject to exclusion in the then recently concluded case of *Respublica v. Malin*, 1 Dallas 33, 33–35 (Oyer & Terminer Court, Chester County, 1778), where the defendant joined American forces by mistake, taking them for British troops. In spite of McKean's bending the rules to admit words spoken by Malin showing his intention to join the enemy, the jury acquitted Malin of treason. See *Pennsylvania Packet*, Sept. 22, 1778, for the Chester County location of the trial, which Dallas mistakenly placed in Philadelphia.

[39]Trial Notes, App. A, pp. 144–46. After the Revolution, a Michael Groves, brick-layer, lived with his family in the Northern Liberties, leaving a will dated Jan. 12, 1797, probated five days later in Philadelphia County, No. 357, Will Book X, p. 534

[40]Trial Notes, App. A, pp. 146–47.

[41]Trial Notes, App. A, p. 146. The contrasting shorter periods of acquaintance were: John Ellis, five or six years; Ann Davis, knew him "well"; Michael Smith, "about four years, & that to his sorrow"; Andrew Fisher, for ten years; and Michael Groves, for "many years." The official docket entries for the trial show Stroud as being sworn, and not affirming. Pennsylvania State Archives, Harrisburg, PA, RG-33, Records of the Supreme Court, Courts of Oyer and Terminer General Gaol Delivery Dockets, 1778–1828 (microfilm), roll 1, reel 5008.

[42]An Edward Stroud, Jr., was disowned in 1767 "for not paying his just debts, neglecting to attend Meetings, and repeated breach of promises." Gwynedd Monthly Meeting, Minutes, 1767–1778, 30th 6th mo, 21st 7th mo, and 25th 8th mo 1767, Swarthmore (microfilm), MR-Ph 223, pp. 10, 12, and 14.

[43]See Chapter. I, n. 43, for Recognizance, July 27, 1778; summons dated Sept. 1, 1777, return of service noted on "a true copie" by "Edwd Stroud Constabl," Edward Wanton Smith Collection, Haverford (Collection No. 955), box 3-a. Edward Stroud is repeatedly identified as the distraining constable during the summer of 1778 in the separate accountings of suffering sustained by members of the northern and southern districts of the Philadelphia Monthly Meeting, as itemized in Philadelphia Yearly Meeting for Sufferings, Miscellaneous Papers, 1779–1780, box B5.3 at Haverford, items 18 and 26. An Edward Stroud was also identified as a Philadelphia tavern keeper in 1776 "at the sign of the Lime Kiln, in Fifth street, corner of Spruce street." *Pennsylvania Gazette*, Sept. 4, 1776.

[44]"The Petition of the Subscribers, Inhabitants & Citizens of the [State of Pennsylvania], n. d., *Pennsylvania Archives*, First Series, 7:22–23.

[45]"Notes of C. J. McKean in the Case of Ab'm Carlisle, 1778," Sept. 25, 1778, *Pennsylvania Archives*, First Series, 7:44–52; *Respublica v. Carlisle*, 1 Dallas 35, 38 (Oyer & Terminer Court, Phila. County, 1778).

[46]Trial Notes, App. A, p. 147.

Chapter III—The Defense

[1]Minutes of SEC, Oct. 23, 1778, *Colonial Records*, 11:601.

[2]Wallace Brown, *The King's Friends: The Composition and Motives of the American Loyalist Claimants* (Providence, RI: Brown University Press, 1965), 131.

[3]Sentencing Statement, App. B, p. 161.

[4]"It is familiar knowledge that the old common law rule carefully excluded from the witness stand parties to the record, and those who were interested in the result; and this rule extended to both civil and criminal cases. Fear of perjury was the reason for the rule." *Benson v. United* States, 146 U.S. 325, 335 (1892). See also *Works of James Wilson*, 2:545, 704–705; J. H. Baker, *An Introduction to English Legal History*, 3d ed. (London: Butterworth, 1990), 107–8; George Fisher, "The Jury's Rise as Lie Detector," *Yale Law Journal* 107 (1997): 662–70, esp. 668 and n441 for Pennsylvania legislation. That it was not, however, a hard-and-fast rule uniformly enforced by the Roberts court may be observed in *Respublica v. Keating*, 1 Dallas 110 (Oyer & Terminer Court, Philadelphia County, 1784).

[5] See Morton L. Montgomery, *History of Berks County in Pennsylvania* (Philadelphia: Everts, Peck & Richards, 1886), 558–59; and Roberdeau Buchanan, *Genealogy of the Roberdeau Family, Including a Biography of General Daniel Roberdeau* (Washington, DC: Joseph L. Pearson, 1876), 130–32. For negative Quaker appraisal of him, see Miers Fisher to [Phineas Bond], n.d. [c. 1783], Cadwalader Family Papers, HSP, Correspondence 1783, box 205, folder 10 (Fisher protested about Clymer's treating him "more than once—unlike an old Friend"); and Henry Drinker to Daniel Clymer, 1 mo 14th 1784, Henry Drinker Letter Books (1762–1786), HSP, p. 96 (old debt from Clymer to Drinker remained unpaid).

[6] *Pennsylvania Packet*, Nov. 14, 1778.

[7] Pass dated Jan. 2, 1778, *The Papers of George Washington (Revolutionary War Series)*, ed. Philander D. Chase et al., 18 vols. to date (Charlottesville: University Press of Virginia, 1985), 12:599 n4.

[8] Trial Notes, App. A, pp. 147–48. For treatment of American prisoners of war during the occupation and the role of Henry Hugh Ferguson, see Scharf & Westcott, *History of Philadelphia*, 1:371–72; and Benjamin Rush to Elizabeth Graeme Ferguson, Dec. 24, 1777, *Letters of Benjamin Rush*, ed. L. H. Butterfield, 2 vols. (Princeton, NJ: Princeton University Press, 1951), 1:177–79 and esp. n1 on 179. (Rush expressed the pious hope that Ferguson's office would "enable him to show mercy to our countrymen in captivity, and may prepare the way for his future reconciliation with his country.")

[9] Trial Notes, App. A, p. 148.

[10] James Lovell to George Washington, Dec. 31, 1777, and George Washington to James Lovell, Jan. 9, 1778, *Papers of George Washington (Revolutionary War Series)*, 13:87–88, 192. See also Thomas Fleming, *Washington's Secret War: The Hidden History of Valley Forge* (New York: Harper Collins, 2005), 74–76. For biographical information about Frederick Bicking, a German papermaker, see *The First 300: The Amazing and Rich History of Lower Merion* (Ardmore, PA: The Lower Merion Historical Society, 2000), 61; Charles R. Barker, "Old Mills of Mill Creek, Lower Merion," *PMHB* 50 (1926):15–17; and Gloria O. Becker, *Mill Creek Valley: Architecture, Industry, and Social Change in a Welsh Tract Community, 1682–1800* (Ann Arbor, MI: University Microfilms International, 1984), 327–29.

[11] Trial Notes, App. A, p. 148. *Pennsylvania Gazette*, July 20, 1774, Oct. 16, 1776, and Feb. 5, 1777; *Pennsylvania Archives*, Sixth Series, 1:738 (militia service of David Zell and Michael Smith, Jr., in the fourth company of the Third Battalion of Philadelphia County). The Zells may have become Quakers by convincement. David Zell would appear to have married out of meeting. See Marriage Record of the First Baptist Church of Philadelphia, 1761–1803, *Pennsylvania Archives*, Second Series, 8:766. Joseph Price records the deaths of the two Zells, father and son, the latter being, like Jehu Roberts, Price's "Old School Mate." Price Diary, Oct. 2 and 3, 1796, and Dec. 22, 1826.

[12] Trial Notes, App. A, p. 148. Warner was disowned because he "publicly renounced Peaceable Principles" early in the armed conflict. Radnor Monthly Meeting, Abstract of Minutes, 1773–1782, 10th 5th mo 1776, Swarthmore (microfilm), MR- Ph 540, pp. 455–56. See also Charles R. Barker, "The Haverford-and-Merion Road to Philadelphia: A Walk Over an Old Trail," *PMHB* 58 (1934): 250–51 (Jacob Jones); Thomas Allen Glenn, *Merion in the Welsh Tract with Sketches of the Townships of Haverford and Radnor* (Norristown, PA: Herald Press, 1896), 382–83 (for Warner family). Comparative tax assessment information may be found in *Pennsylvania Archives*, Third Series, 15:435, 436 (1780), and 16:591 (1783).

[13] "The Petition of divers Inhabitants of the Townships of Lower Merrion and Blockley," Aug. 15, 1777, *Pennsylvania Archives*, Second Series, 3:118–19. It would heighten irony to conclude that Michael Smith and John Roberts, Miller, were united in the same petition for relief, but it seems more likely that this petitioner was another John Roberts in the Welsh Tract.

[14] "Journal of Samuel Rowland Fisher," 180–81, 324.

[15] Charles Burr Ogden, *The Quaker Ogdens in America: David Ogden of Ye Good Ship "Welcome" and His Descendants, 1682–1897* (Philadelphia: J. B. Lippincott, 1898), 53–54; *Pennsylvania Gazette*, Apr. 18 and Aug. 8, 1787; and see Scharf & Westcott, *History of Philadelphia*, 3:2139–41.

[16] Trial Notes, App. A, pp. 148–49. It is also possible that, outside the record made in court, McKean knew of Pritchard's service to the British as a watchman at the Middle Ferry. See pp. 56–57, 99 herein.

[17] "Petition of the Jury in the Case of John Roberts," Oct. 18, 1778, *Pennsylvania Archives*, First Series, 7:24.

[18] Trial Notes, App. A, p. 149. Benjamin M. Nead, "A Sketch of General Thomas Procter, With some Account of the First Pennsylvania Artillery in the Revolution," *PMHB* 4 (1880): 454–70; and for the court martial proceeding, including the statement of exoneration from Washington, see *Pennsylvania Gazette*, Nov. 8, 1780.

[19] Trial Notes, App. A, pp. 149–50; *Diary and Autobiography of John Adams*, ed. L. H. Butterfield el al., 4 vols. (Cambridge, MA: The Belknap Press of Harvard University Press, 1961), Sept. 7, 1774, 2:126–27.

[20] Trial Notes, App. A, pp. 150–51 The Republican Society's manifesto, signed by eighty-two anti-constitutionalists, was published in the *Pennsylvania Gazette*, Mar. 24, 1779. Chaloner's demanding army assignment is set forth in Fleming, *Washington's Secret War*, 130–32, 134–36, 306, 348, and his more satisfying career as merchant in Thomas M. Doerflinger, *A Vigorous Spirit of Enterprise: Merchants and Economic Development in Revolutionary Philadelphia* (Chapel Hill, NC: University of North Carolina Press, 1986), 88–89, 228, 235–36.

[21] Trial Notes, App. A, pp. 150–51. For the September crossing of the Schuylkill and the White Horse Tavern destination, see Thomas J. McGuire, *Battle of Paoli* (Mechanicsburg, PA: Stackpole Books, 2000), 17–18, 29.

[22] Trial Notes, App. A, pp. 151–52. The "Bridge" Roberts referred to was the improvised floating bridge the British put in place at the Middle Ferry. Scharf & Westcott, *History of Philadelphia*, 3:2141.

[23] Trial Notes, App. A, p. 152. For biographical detail on Syng, see Bell, *Patriot-Improvers*, 3:31–35.

[24] Trial Notes, App. A, pp. 152–54.

[25] Trial Notes, App. A, p. 154. Murray appears on the tax rolls as a small-time farmer in Lower Merion Township. *Pennsylvania Archives*, Third Series, 14:627 (1779); ibid, 16:590 (1783).

[26] Trial Notes, App. A, p. 154. For Hopkins's service with Moylan, see *Pennsylvania Archives*, Second Series, 11:127–28; and George Washington to David Hopkins, Jan. 2, 1778, *The Writings of George Washington From the Original Manuscript Sources*, ed. John C. Fitzpatrick, 39 vols. (Washington, DC: United States Government Printing Office, 1931–1944), 10:256–57.

[27] Carl Van Doren, *Secret History of the American Revolution* (New York: The Viking Press, 1941), 172–75, 241–51; Richard K. Murdoch, "Benedict Arnold and the Owners

of the *Charming Nancy*," *PMHB* 84 (1960): 22–55. Robert Shewell's niece married Isaac Hunt, a Philadelphia lawyer and a bencher of the Middle Temple, whom a patriot mob drove from his city and country because of his vigorous defense of the Crown and its adherents. In England, where he lived the rest of his life, Hunt took Holy Orders, but not to the complete abandonment of either his former profession or his taste for controversy. He achieved added distinction as the father of the author, poet, and editor Leigh Hunt. See Anthony Holden, *The Wit in the Dungeon: The Remarkable Life of Leigh Hunt: Poet, Revolutionary, and Last of the Romantics* (New York: Little, Brown, 2005), 3–9; and Eric Stockdale and Randy J. Holland, *Middle Temple Lawyers and The American Revolution* (Eagan, MN: Thomson West, 2007), 98.

[28]Trial Notes, App. A, p. 156; "Petition of Wm, Young, &c., In Favor of John Roberts, 1778," Oct. 21, 1778, *Pennsylvania Archives*, First Series, 7:38-39. See p. 25 herein for congressional resolution.

[29]Trial Notes, App. A. p. 156. Sebastian Ale joins Andrew Fisher in the tax records of Blockley Township as a minor property holder, suggesting that McKean had correctly recorded his testimony about Fisher's alleged willingness to trade a cow for silence. *Pennsylvania Archives*, Third Series, 14:569 and 15:7 (1779). A "Boston Ale" also appears as a small property owner in the 1780 tax assessment for Lower Merion Township. Ibid., 15:435. On the assumption that only one person had such a name, Matthew Carey gives us a final glimpse of Sebastian Ale as an old gravedigger at work during the yellow fever epidemic of 1793. In uniting a deceased husband with an earlier buried wife, Ale broke open the wife's coffin and expired as a consequence of inhaling the effluvia emanating from it. Matthew Carey, *A Short Account of the Malignant Fever Which Prevailed in Philadelphia in the Year 1793*, 5th ed. (Philadelphia: Clark & Raser, 1830), 81.

[30]Trial Notes, App. A, p. 156. A Whig Society came into being a year or so earlier made up of staunch defenders of the Pennsylvania constitution of 1776. Its members, positioned on the Radical side of the political spectrum, resisted the repeated Republican calls for revision of the constitution. Walter Shee and Pelatiah Webster were not apt to be members of this group because they are both more plausibly identified as politically conservative in their views. Shee, a merchant on a relatively small scale, was appointed on the eve of Roberts's trial as collector of fees and fines levied on imported negro and mulatto slaves, whereas Pelatiah Webster had a larger reputation as a political theorist who argued for free trade and an open, unregulated economy and who would in due course favor a strong national government. See *Pennsylvania Packet*, Oct. 31, 1778 (for Shee appointment as of Sept. 7); Albrecht Koschnik, "*Let a Common Interest Bind Us Together*," *Associations, Partisanship, and Culture in Philadelphia, 1775–1840* (Charlottesville: University of Virginia Press, 2007), 15–17; Robert H. Brunhouse, *The Counter-Revolution in Pennsylvania, 1776–1790* (Harrisburg, PA: Pennsylvania Historical Commission, 1942), 9–10, 103–4, 204; Steven Rosswurn, *Arms, Country, and Class: The Philadelphia Militia and "Lower Sort" During the American Revolution, 1775–1783* (New Brunswick, NJ: Rutgers University Press, 1987), 196–97, 242, 254–55. The brief Aitken–Paine collaboration is described in John Keane, *Tom Paine: A Political Life* (Boston: Little, Brown and Company, 1995), 92–93, 101–4.

[31]Trial Notes, App. A, p. 157. McGuire, *Battle of Paoli*, 13–16, 29. George Washington to John Hancock, Sept. 15, 1777, and Council of War, Sept, 23, 1777, *The Papers of George Washington (Revolutionary War Series)*, 11:236–37, 295; and for dispatches

of his aides the day before, see *Writings of George Washington*, 9:222–24. Both Mary Miller, Innkeeper, and Jacob Beery (whose surname is variously spelled) appear in tax records for Haverford Township, Chester County, in *Pennsylvania Archives*, Third Series, 12: 36, 37 (1774), 292 (1780), 383, 384, 507, 508 (1781), and 727 (1785). Mary Miller is identified as an innkeeper in 1774, 1780, and 1781.

[32]Trial Notes, App. A, p. 157. For background on Young, see S. Gordon Smyth, "The Land of the Llewellyn and Camp Discharge," *Historical Sketches: A Collection of Papers Prepared for the Historical Society of Montgomery County, Pennsylvania* (Norristown, PA: Herald Printing and Binding Rooms, 1905), vol. 3, p. 209; Charles H. Browning, *Welsh Settlement of Pennsylvania* (1912; repr., Baltimore: Genealogical Publishing Company, 1967), 455. His name appears as a minor property owner in the tax assessments of that period for Lower Merion. See *Pennsylvania Archives*, Third Series, 14:357 (1774), 15:65 (1779), 433 (1780), 16:129 (1782), 592 (1783). Not to neglect entirely the remaining witnesses, Peter Trapler [*Drexler*] was almost certainly Peter Trexler, then or soon afterward the tenant of Charles Thomson's farm located a little over a mile away from Roberts's plantation. Captain Israel Jones, a Lower Merion resident, also belonged to Colonel Warner's Seventh Battalion. See tax assessment lists in *Pennsylvania Archives*, Third Series, 15:67 and 433 (1779) (Israel Jones and Peter Trexler); and "Officers of Seventh Battalion—1777," *Pennsylvania Archives*, Second Series, 13:592. Obadiah Wilday's name (but never spelled the same way twice) consistently appears as a prosperous farmer in the tax assessments for Haverford Township, Chester County, from 1765 to 1785. See e.g., *Pennsylvania Archives*, Third Series, 11:3 (1765) and 698 (1771), 12:37 (1774) and 728 (1785).

[33]Trial Notes, App. A, p. 157. Foster reported in *Alexander M'Growther's* Case a demanding requirement for coercion as excusing otherwise treasonable conduct which Roberts's evidence fell well short of meeting. Michael Foster, *A Report of Some Proceedings on the Commission for the Trial of the Rebels in the Year 1746—to which are Added Discourses Upon a Few Branches of the Crown Law* (Oxford: Clarendon Press, 1762), 13–14.

[34]John H. Langbein, *The Origins of Adversary Criminal Trial* (New York: Oxford University Press, 2003), 321–23; Lawrence M. Friedman, *A History of American Law*, 2d ed. (New York: Simon & Schuster, 1985), 155. One might conclude, as Friedman does, that, given the increasingly circumscribed role of judges, their instructions have tended nowadays to become anodyne and devoid of truly instructive content.

[35]*Respublica v. Chapman*, 1 Dallas 53, 55–60 (Pa. Supreme Ct., 1781). Whether it was possible for someone born in America prior to the Revolution to take the British side and renounce conclusively allegiance to the state of his birth would later be at issue in a decision of the United States Supreme Court in *M'Ilvaine v. Coxe's Lessee*, 8 U.S. (4 Cranch) 209 (1808).

[36]*Respublica v. McCarty*, 2 Dallas 86, 87–88 (Pa. Supreme Ct., 1781). McKean may have ignored English precedent in accepting the confession made on arraignment. See J. M. Beattie, *Crime and the Courts in England: 1660–1800* (Princeton: Princeton University Press, 1986), 364–66.

[37]It did not take much for McKean to be persuaded that criminal intent had been proved, as in *Respublica v. Weidle*, 2 Dallas 88 (Pa. Supreme Ct., 1781), where the defendant was indicted for misprision of treason in having uttered these words: "that he had lived six years in London, and nine years in Ireland; and never lived happier in his life, than he had done under the English government; and that the King of

England is our King, and will be yours." McKean, in charging the jury, found that the words spoken "tended to excite resistance to the Government of this Common-wealth," and this time the jury, so instructed by the court, convicted the defendant.

[38] "Petition of the Jury in the Case of John Roberts," Oct. 18, 1778, *Pennsylvania Archives*, First Series, 7:25; Joseph Reed to [George Bryan], Oct. 23, 1778, Joseph Reed Papers, New York-Historical Society, available on microfilm at David Library, film 266, reel 2.

[39] *Respublica v. McCarty*, 2 Dallas at 88.

[40] *Respublica v. Mulatto Bob*, 4 Dallas 145, 147 (Pa. Supreme Ct., 1795).

[41] *Diary of Elizabeth Drinker*, Oct. 2, 1778, 1:329; and Thomas Franklin to Elias Boudinot, Oct. 4, 1778, Boudinot Papers, HSP, vol. 2, p. 46.

Chapter IV—Inclemency

[1] Sentencing Statement, App. B., p. 159; *Diary of Elizabeth Drinker*, Oct. 17, 1778, 1:332; *Pennsylvania Evening Post*, Oct. 16 (postscript of Oct. 17), 1778. The formal docket record is found in Pennsylvania State Archives, Harrisburg, PA, RG-33, Records of the Supreme Court of Pennsylvania (Eastern District), Courts of Oyer & Terminer & General Gaol Delivery, 1778–1786 (microfilm), reel 787, pp. 2–3.

[2] "Inventory of the Movable Effects Belonging to John Roberts—Lower Merion Township Philada. County Seized in Behalf of the State of Pennsylvania October 3d 1778," Oct. 20, 1778, *Pennsylvania Archives*, Sixth Series, 12:710–16, and the contents of the southwest room, ibid., 710–11.

[3] Ibid., 713–15. Radnor Monthly Meeting, Abstract of Minutes, "An Appendix Con-taining some Minutes and records of the Committee in Suffering Cases during the Revolutionary War," Swarthmore (microfilm), MR-Ph 540, p. 586, in which the loss was rounded out at about five hundred pounds.

[4] Inventory of the Movable Effects," Oct. 20, 1778, 12:714–16; Trial Notes, App. A, p. 155. As to the wartime value of bar iron, see Anne Bezanson, assisted by Blanch Daley, Marjorie Denison, and Miriam Hussey, *Prices and Inflation During the American Revolution: Pennsylvania, 1770–1790* (Philadelphia: University of Penn-sylvania Press, 1951), 165–66; and Thomas M. Doerflinger, *A Vigorous Spirit of Enterprise: Merchants and Economic Development in Revolutionary Philadelphia* (Chapel Hill, NC: University of North Carolina Press, 1986), 50–57.

[5] "Journal of Samuel Rowland Fisher," 179, 276. The Pennsylvania Assembly, recog-nizing that the old gaol had been put to use in that period for the confinement of "felons, criminals and other prisoners" contrary to the 1773 statute authorizing construction of the new prison to house them there as soon as construction was completed, found it necessary to indemnify the two successive sheriffs responsible for holding such prisoners in the old gaol "against any and all suits and actions which may lie or be brought by reason of the keeping and imprisoning of any person or persons in the said old gaol who ought to have been holden in the proper gaol of the said city and county." The assembly specifically acknowledged that the Walnut Street prison was being used as a military prison, "and may be needed for that purpose for some time to come." Act of Aug. 27, 1778, *Statutes at Large*, 9:255–57. Fisher's pardon, when finally granted, was premised in part on the crowded and unhealthy conditions prevailing in the old gaol ("contagious disorders arising from . . . the narrow

limits of that place of confinement"). Minutes of SEC, July 23, 1781, *Colonial Records*, 13:13.

[6] James Boswell, *The Life of Samuel Johnson*, ed. R. W. Chapman (Oxford: Oxford University Press, 2008), Friday, Sept. 17, 1777, 849.

[7] *Main Line Times*, Apr. 7, 1955 (on microfilm at Ludington Library, Bryn Mawr, PA). The letter to Clymer is now in the Quaker Collection at Haverford (in Collection 851).

[8] Clymer's name appears inscribed in the "Patriotic Association Book, August 18, 1778," Am. 238, HSP, as of Sept. 29, 1778.

[9] Minutes of SEC, Nov. 2, 1778, *Colonial Records*, 11:613. That no petition from Roberts could be found after diligent search in the State Archives in Harrisburg was confirmed to the author in a letter dated Mar. 26, 2008, from Aaron McWilliams, Assistant Archivist, Bureau of Archives and History, Pennsylvania Historical and Museum Commission.

[10] Futhey & Cope, *History of Chester County*, 714.

[11] Ibid., 115; Thomas Franklin to Elias Boudinot, May 28, 1778, and Thomas Franklin to Thomas Bradford, June 15, 1778, Bradford Family Correspondence, HSP (Collection 1676), Series 3, Thomas Bradford, box 21, folder 4. This version of events favorable to Roberts, as published in Futhey and Cope's history, has been uncritically accepted as true in all respects by Thomas J. McGuire in his *The Philadelphia Campaign*, 2 vols. (Mechanicsburg, PA: Stackpole Books, 2006 and 2007), 2 (*Germantown and the Roads to Valley Forge*):258.

[12] Jasper Yeates to Colonel James Burd, Oct. 10, 1778, Shippen Family Papers, HSP, vol. 8, p. 39. The estimate of as many as seven thousand petitioners in Robert H. Brunhouse, *The Counter-Revolution in Pennsylvania, 1776–1790* (Harrisburg, PA: Pennsylvania Historical Commission, 1942), 164, and again in Peter C. Messer, "'A Species of Treason & Not the Least Dangerous Kind': The Treason Trials of Abraham Carlisle and John Roberts," *PMHB* 123 (1999): 304, is without any reliable record count to support it. A more defensible estimate of four hundred petitioners for Carlisle and one thousand for Roberts is found in Isaac Sharpless, *A Quaker Experiment in Government*, 2 vols. in one (Philadelphia: Ferris & Leach, 1902), 2:194.

[13] "The petition of the Wife, Children & other, the Relatives of John Roberts, Miller of Lower Merion Township," n. d., *Pennsylvania Archives*, First Series, 7:25–27. The several petitions and other submissions for Roberts are found in ibid., 7:21–44. For Thomas McKean, Sr., see G. S. Rowe, *Thomas McKean: The Shaping of an American Republicanism* (Boulder, CO: Colorado Associated University Press, 1978), 118. Chief Justice McKean spent his youth in Chester County. Ibid., 2–3.

[14] The appeal of the Meeting for Sufferings dated Aug. 5, 1778, was published in the *Pennsylvania Packet* on Aug. 13, 1778, and these two outbursts followed in the Aug. 15 and 20 editions of that newspaper.

[15] Undated memorandum, Philadelphia Yearly Meeting for Sufferings, Miscellaneous Papers, 1779–1780, Haverford, box B5.3, item 73. The member of council consulted that morning was Joseph Hart. See text at Chap. V, n.46, for more information about the response from the member of the council.

[16] "The Memorial of the Subscribers," Oct. 29, 1778, *Pennsylvania Archives*, First Series, 7:21–22. Clymer's name also appears as a signatory to the more generously framed "Memorial of Phila & Chester Co's, in Behalf of Jno. Roberts, 1778," n. d., ibid., 29–36 (third column on p. 33).

[17] Minutes of SEC, Nov. 2, 1778, *Colonial Records*, 11:613; "Deposition of Sam'l Wallis in Favor of J. Roberts, 1778," Nov. 3, 1778, *Pennsylvania Archives*, 7:41.

[18] Carl Van Doren, *Secret History of the American Revolution* (New York: Viking Press, 1941), 272–80, 411–13.

[19] Ibid., 217–20; and for Wallis's career as agent and land speculator, see David W. Maxey, "The Honorable Proprietaries v. Samuel Wallis: 'A Matter of Great Consequence' in the Province of Pennsylvania," *Pennsylvania History* 70 (2003): 361–95. With respect to the dangerous conditions in and around Muncy that would have caused Wallis and his family to leave, see Wallis's letters from Muncy to Timothy Matlack, July 24 and Aug. 8, 1778, *Pennsylvania Archives*, First Series, 6:664–65 and 687–88. It appears that his wife took refuge with her mother in Elkton, Maryland, where her daughter Sarah was born on Aug. 19, 1778. John F. Meginness, *History of Lycoming County, Pennsylvania* (Chicago, IL: Brown, Runk & Co., 1892), 74.

[20] "Deposition of Sam'l Wallis," Nov. 3, 1778, *Pennsylvania Archives*, First Series, 7:41; and as to the Galloway–Wallis connection, see Maxey, "Honorable Proprietaries v. Samuel Wallis," 364, 372–73. After Galloway was forced to leave Philadelphia with the evacuating British forces, Wallis frequently consoled Galloway's abandoned wife in tea and sympathy sessions—Grace Growden Galloway recognizing him "as a friend of JG." "Diary of Grace Growden Galloway," *PMHB* 55 (1931): 86, and *PMHB* 58 (1934): 156, 160, 166, 181.

[21] Wallis and Abraham Carlisle may have known each other. They were both members of the Carpenters' Company of Philadelphia, Carlisle legitimately so as a carpenter by trade. See Charles E. Peterson, "Carpenters' Hall," in *Historic Philadelphia: From the Founding Until the Early Nineteenth Century* (Philadelphia: American Philosophical Society, 1953), 126 (list of names of members, past and present, recorded in 1786).

[22] For warrant and survey information of land taken up by Roberts and his two sons, see *Pennsylvania Archives*, Third Series, 25:280 (Roberts on May 25 and all three on June 15, 1774) and Epilogue, n.8.

[23] See *Pennsylvania Archives*, First Series, 7:21–44.

[24] "Memorial of Phil. & Chester Co's., in Behalf of Jno. Roberts, 1778," n. d., *Pennsylvania Archives*, First Series, 7:29–30; in a note appearing ibid., 7:36, Samuel Hazard, as editor, states that he has consolidated the signatures in twelve separate petitions, "all similar to the one now printed," in this single petition. Isabella Batchelder James, *Memorial of Thomas Potts, Junior, who Settled in Pennsylvania; with an Historic-Genealogical Account of his Descendants to the Eighth Generation* (Cambridge, MA: n. p., 1874), 157–59. As for Galloway's opportunity to prepare the petition, it appears that he left New York for England on October 17 or 18, giving him time to do so. "Diary of Grace Growden Galloway," *PMHB* 55 (1931): 55. Galloway may also have had a hand in preparing a petition to the peace commission appointed by Lord North and headed by the Earl of Carlisle, urging the commissioners, then in New York, to intervene on behalf of Roberts, Carlisle, and James Stevens, "respectable Inhabitants of the City of Philadelphia and faithful Subjects of His Majesty's [who] now lie confined in a dungeon under sentence of death." There is no evidence, however, that the commissioners sought to intervene, and any attempt on their part to have done so would have been decidedly counterproductive. Petition (duplicate copy, unsigned), New York, Oct. 2, 1778, Great Britain, Colonial Office, American & West Indies Correspondence, on microfilm at David Library (film 590), CO 5/181/9-10 (1778–1779).

[25] *Pennsylvania Archives*, First Series, 7:22, 25.

[26] *Pennsylvania Packet*, Oct. 31, 1778. It would be interesting to know who Rectifier was. Someone certainly well versed in legal and political theory, like Joseph Reed, undertook pseudonymously to advise the newspaper publisher John Dunlap on the impropriety of signing a petition requesting clemency for Carlisle that was directed to the legislature.

[27] Pennsylvania constitution of 1776, Section 20 of the "Plan or Frame of Government," in *Statutes at Large*, 9:596 (also available at http://www.duq.edu/law/pa-constitution/. Doubt as to where the power to grant pardons lay in certain treason cases was partially eliminated by a 1780 amendment to the treason statute providing that the president or vice president of the SEC might grant such pardons "on condition that such person or persons [convicted of treason and applying for pardon] shall, within a limited time, depart from this state to foreign parts beyond the sea, and that he or they shall not return to this state or any of the United States of America." Act of March 8, 1780, *Statutes at Large*, 10:111. Remaining constitutional doubt was disposed of in Article 2, Section 9, of the Pennsylvania constitution of 1790, which provided that the "Governor has the right to grant reprieves and pardons, except in cases of impeachment." The *Federal and State Constitutions Colonial Charters, and Other Organic Laws of the States, Territories, and Colonies Now or Hereafter Forming the United States of America* , comp. and ed. Francis Newton Thorpe, 7 vols. (Washington, DC: Government Printing Office, 1909), 5:3096 (also available at http://www.duq.edu/law/pa-constitution/.

[28] *Works of James Wilson*, 2:442–45.

[29] Joseph Reed to [George Bryan], Oct. 23, 1778, in Joseph Reed Papers at New-York Historical Society, but consulted on microfilm at David Library (film 266), reel 2. For the court's session in Newtown, see *Pennsylvania Packet*, Oct. 29 and Nov. 3, 1778.

[30] William B. Reed, *Life and Correspondence of Joseph Reed*, 2 vols. (Philadelphia: Lindsay and Blakiston, 1847), 2:35

[31] John F. Roche, *Joseph Reed: A Moderate in the American Revolution* (New York: Columbia University Press, 1957), 147–49.

[32] Reed to Bryan, Oct. 23, 1778.

[33] Ibid., and see Sentencing Statement, App. B, p. 159.

[34] Minutes of SEC, Oct. 23, 1778, *Colonial Records*, 11:606.

[35] Brunhouse, *Counter-Revolution in Pennsylvania*, 53–56.

[36] Bradley Chapin, *The American Law of Treason: Revolutionary and Early National Origins* (Seattle: University of Washington Press, 1964), 57–58. Chapin dealt imaginatively with the record he purported to consult, stating that "Roberts had given the army direct aid by recruiting men and furnishing supplies" and that he went "to the Head of the Elk to give information to Robert [sic] Galloway, who he knew had joined the British." Ibid., 57, 68. For the exemplary value of the executions on future juries in treason cases, see Carlton F. W. Larson, "The Revolutionary American Jury: A Case Study of the 1778–1779 Philadelphia Treason Trials," *Southern Methodist University Law Review* 61 (2008):1446, 1499–1500, 1509.

[37] *Pennsylvania Evening Post*, Sept. 2 and Nov. 6, 1778,

[38] James Humphreys, Jun., to Joseph Galloway, Nov. 23, [1778], quoted in Catherine S. Crary, comp. and ed., *The Price of Loyalty: Tory Writings from the Revolutionary Era* (New York: McGraw-Hill, 1973), 237.

[39] Isaac Ogden to Joseph Galloway, Nov. 22, 1778, quoted in ibid.

[40] *Diary of Elizabeth Drinker*, Nov. 4 and 5, 1778, 1:333–334; Diary of John Pemberton, 6th 11th mo 1778, Pemberton Papers, HSP (Collection 484A), box 1, p. 125; Francis R. Taylor, *Life of William Savery of Philadelphia, 1750–1804* (New York: Macmillan, 1925), 23. "The Execution of Abraham Carlisle and John Roberts," *Bulletin of Friends' Historical Association* 15 (No. 1, Spring, 1926):28–29, appears to be a reliable contemporary account of the final hours of the two men, including a visit paid them on the morning of their execution by their wives and children accompanied by George Dillwyn.

Chapter V—Doubt

[1] Albert Post, "Early Efforts to Abolish Capital Punishment in Pennsylvania," *PMHB* 68 (1944): 38–53.

[2] Pennsylvania constitution of 1776, Sections 38 and 39 of the "Plan or Frame of Government," in *Statutes at Large*, 9:600 (also available at http://www.duq.edu/law/pa-constitution/). See also Robert H. Brunhouse, *The Counter-Revolution in Pennsylvania, 1776–1790* (Harrisburg, PA: Pennsylvania Historical Commission, 1942), 184, 219–20; and Louis P. Masur, *Rites of Execution: Capital Punishment and the Transformation of American Culture, 1776–1865* (New York: Oxford University Press, 1989), 73–92.

[3] Benjamin Rush, *An Enquiry Into the Effects of Public Punishments Upon Criminals and Upon Society* (Philadelphia: Joseph James, 1787) (the title page discloses the meeting at Franklin's house on March 9, 1787), 4, 15–16; and Rush, *Considerations of the Injustice and Impolicy of Punishing Murder by Death, Extracted From the American Museum* (Philadelphia: Mathew Carey, 1792); Cesare Beccaria, *On Crimes and Punishments*, trans. David Young (1764; repr. Indianapolis, IN: Hackett Publishing Company, 1986), 9–17 (chap. 3–7), 23 (chap. 12), 48–53 (chap. 28), and 74–75 (chap. 41).

[4] Act of Apr. 22, 1794, *Statutes at Large*, 15:174; William H. Loyd, *The Early Courts of Pennsylvania* (Boston: Boston Book Company, 1910), 131.

[5] Act of Apr 22, 1794, *Statues at Large of Pennsylvania*, 15:175; Section 33, Act of April 30, 1790 ("An Act for the Punishment of Certain Crimes Against the United States"), *Public Statutes at Large of the United States of America*, ed. Richard Peters (Boston: Charles C. Little and James Brown, 1845), vol. 1, p. 119. As for the framers' debate on the states' concurrent ability to punish treason, see Bradley Chapin, *The American Law of Treason: Revolutionary and Early National Origins* (Seattle: University of Washington Press, 1964), 81–82.

[6] Joseph Reed to Nathanael Greene, Nov. 5, 1778, in The *Papers of General Nathanael Greene*, ed. Richard K. Showman et al., 13 vols. (Chapel Hill: University of North Carolina Press, 1976–2005), 3:40–46, together with notes on 3:47. For the similarity of the Astrea de Coelis attack, see *Pennsylvania Evening Post*, July 18, 1778.

[7] For the battle at Fort Wilson, Wilson's house, see text at Chap. VI, n. 21. Wilson's self-defense appears in *Pennsylvania Gazette*, Oct. 18, 1780.

[8] *Pennsylvania Evening Post*, Oct. 16, 1778 (postscript Oct. 17); John H. Langbein, *The Origins of Adversary Criminal Trial* (New York: Oxford University Press, 2003), 21–25.

[9] "Journal of Samuel Rowland Fisher," 164–66.

[10] The United States Supreme Court has ruled that the reasonable-doubt standard is an essential part of due process to which a defendant charged with committing a crime is entitled under the constitution notwithstanding the fact that the words "reasonable doubt" are nowhere found in the constitution. See *In re Winship*, 397 U.S. 358 (1970). As to the historical development of the standard, see Langbein, *Adversary Criminal Trial*, 261–66; and John Henry Wigmore, rev. ed. Peter Tillers, *Evidence in Trials at Common Law*, 10 vols. (Boston: Little, Brown, 1983), 9:404–19.

[11] *Patterson v. Colorado*, 205 U.S. 454, 462 (1907); J. H. Baker, *An Introduction to English Legal History*, 3d ed. (London: Butterworth, 1990), 88; John H. Langbein, "Historical Foundations of the Law of Evidence: A View From the Ryder Sources," *Columbia Law Review* 96 (1996): 1169–71.

[12] See pp. 20–24, 44–48, and 65 herein.

[13] Langbein, *Adversary Criminal Trial*, 190–99; Wigmore, *Evidence*, 1A:1180–1217.

[14] "Journal of Samuel Rowland Fisher," 180; Minutes of SEC, Oct. 24, 1781, *Colonial Records*, 13:94.

[15] Minutes of SEC, May 5, 1779, *Colonial Records*, 11:768.

[16] For Jones as a neighbor and friend of Joseph Galloway's distraught wife, see "Diary of Grace Growden Galloway," *PMHB* 55 (1931): 41–43, 46–47, 57–59, 84–87, and *PMHB* 58 (1934): 152, 158, 188. Neither Roberts's presence as their guest in residence nor Owen Jones's Tory sympathies protected the Joneses from rough treatment by the British occupying forces. Elizabeth Drinker made the following entry in her diary a week after Roberts went on the foraging expedition: "we are told this evening, that Owen Joness Family have been very ill used indeed, by an Officer who wanted to quarter himself, with many others on them, he drew his Sword, us'd very abusive language, and had the Front Door split in pieces &c." *Diary of Elizabeth Drinker*, Dec. 19, 1777, 1:267.

[17] See p. 58 herein; Proctor would later have a run-in with Thomas McKean, who fined Proctor eighty pounds for assaulting a local election official and delivered a tongue-lashing as only McKean could. G. S. Rowe, *Thomas McKean: The Shaping of an American Republicanism* (Boulder, CO: Colorado Associated University Press, 1978), 183–84.

[18] Steven Rosswurn, *Arms, Country, and Class: The Philadelphia Militia and "Lower Sort" During the American Revolution, 1775–1783* (New Brunswick, NJ: Rutgers University Press, 1987), 155–56; "Minutes of Session of the Scots Congregation in Philadelphia," Sept 7, 1778, Presbyterian Historical Society, Philadelphia, PA. See also Alexander Mackie, "The Presbyterian Churches of Old Philadelphia," in *Historic Philadelphia: From the Founding Until the Early Nineteenth Century* (Philadelphia: American Philosophical Society, 1953), 222–24.

[19] Act of Feb. 26, 1773, *Statutes at Large*, 8:327–30, and Act of Mar. 9, 1771, ibid., 12–14. The inventory taken of his personal effects immediately following his conviction confirms Roberts as a fisherman. In the southwest room on the first floor which we have assumed was his (see pp. 71–72 herein), the appraisers located "29 fish hooks and sneads [fishing poles], fishing tackle, . . . fishing Angleing." Inventory, *Pennsylvania Archives*, Sixth Series, 12:710–11.

[20] McKean's sentencing statement for Wright was published in *Pennsylvania Packet*, Dec. 8, 1778. See "Journal of Samuel Rowland Fisher," 170 (but another Abijah Wright is mentioned by Fisher, ibid., 332).

[21] Minutes of SEC, May 21, 1778, *Colonial Records*, 11:493–95; *Pennsylvania Gazette*, Apr. 14, 1779 (Stevens acquitted week before); "Journal of Samuel Rowland Fisher," 152; and Futhey & Cope, *History of Chester County*, 94.

[22] Fisher was accused of passing along intelligence to the enemy in two intercepted and seemingly innocuous letters to his brother in New York. "Journal of Samuel Rowland Fisher," 155–58. The United States Supreme Court has held that, when a legislature by statute conditions the imposition of capital punishment on particular factual findings, the jury, and not the trial judge, must make that separate determination, as established beyond a reasonable doubt. *Ring v. Arizona*, 536 U.S. 584 (2002); see also *Apprendi v. New Jersey*, 530 U.S. 466 (2000), where the same rule had earlier been held to apply in a noncapital case.

[23] For the Pennsylvania experience with clemency in the colonial and postcolonial periods, see Jack D. Marietta and G. S. Rowe, *Troubled Experiment: Crime and Justice in Pennsylvania, 1682–1800* (Philadelphia: University of Pennsylvania Press, 2006), 75–79. As for the experience in England, "By the late seventeenth century pardons had become a fundamental element in the administration of the criminal law." J. M. Beattie, *Crime and the Courts in England: 1660–1800* (Princeton, NJ: Princeton University Press, 1986), 431; see also Langbein, *Adversary Criminal Trial*. 60–61, 324–25.

[24] "Journal of Samuel Rowland Fisher," 152, 167, 176; G. S. Rowe in *Embattled Bench: The Pennsylvania Supreme Court and the Forging of a Democratic Society* (Newark, DE: University of Delaware Press, 1994), 146; *Pennsylvania Gazette*, May 5, 1779.

[25] J-P. Brissot de Warville, *New Travels in the United States of America, 1788*, trans. Mara Soceanu Vamos and Durant Echeverria and ed. Durant Echeverria (Cambridge, MA: The Belknap Press of Harvard University Press, 1964), ix–xi, xiv–xvi.

[26] François-Jean, Marquis de Chastellux, *Travels in North America in the Years 1780, 1781 and 1782*, revised trans. and ed. Howard C. Rice, Jr., 2 vols. (Chapel Hill: University of North Carolina Press, 1963), 1:166–67, 320–21 n 90. George Grieve was the English translator who caused Brissot particular outrage.

[27] Brissot de Warville, *New Travels*, xi.

[28] Ibid., 331–32. Joseph Reed to [George Bryan], Oct. 23, 1778, quoted on p. 87 herein.

[29] Trial Notes, App. A, p. 137. Carlton F. W. Larson, "The Revolutionary American Jury: A Case Study of the 1778–1779 Philadelphia Treason Trials," *Southern Methodist University Law Review* 61 (2008): 1517, 1520.

[30] Rufus M. Jones, *The Quakers in the American Colonies* (London: Macmillan, 1911), 554–55.

[31] Radnor Monthly Meeting, Abstract of Minutes, "An Appendix Containing some Minutes and records of the Committee in Suffering Cases during the Revolutionary War," adjourned meeting held at Merion, 19th of 10th mo 1778, Swarthmore (microfilm), MR-Ph 540, p. 579.

[32] Undated memorandum (two parts), Philadelphia Yearly Meeting for Sufferings, Miscellaneous Papers, 1779–1780, Haverford, box B5.3, item 73. This one-page memorandum, relating two separate conversations, was evidently prepared for record purposes some time after Roberts and Carlisle died, for the first part (perhaps in Henry Drinker's hand) begins, "On the 2d day of the week on which our Quarterly Meeting in the 11th month Last was held..."

[33] Philadelphia Meeting for Sufferings, Minutes, 1756–1834, 19th 11th mo 1778, Swarthmore (microfilm), MR-Ph 501, pp. 186–87.

[34] Ibid., 17th 12th mo 1778, pp. 190–91; 12th 8th mo 1779, p. 209 (report, dated 4th 8th mo 1779, "produced and further consideration deferred to next meeting"); and 16th 9th mo 1779, p. 211 ("concurrence with General Tenor expressed").

[35] Committee Report, App. C, p. 164.

[36] Philadelphia Meeting for Sufferings, Minutes 1756–1834, 15th of 12th mo 1785, pp. 3–6; John Gough, *A History of the People Called Quakers: From Their First Rise to the Present Time: Compiled From Authentic Records and From the Writings of That People*, 4 vols. (Dublin: Robert Jackson, 1789–1790).

[37] See Introduction, n.16; the Carlisle trial notes is item 71 in the identified Swarthmore and Haverford sources.

[38] For consideration of the charge that Quaker plainness in speech, or caution in the use of words, may amount to evasiveness, see Francis Clarkson, *A Portraiture of Quakerism, Taken From a View of the Moral Education, Discipline, Peculiar Customs of the Society of Friends*, 3 vols. (London: R. Taylor, 1807), 3:276–78.

[39] Committee Report, App. C, pp. 164–65.

[40] Committee Report, App. C, p. 165.

[41] Undated memorandum (two parts), Philadelphia Yearly Meeting for Sufferings, Miscellaneous Papers, 1779–1780, Haverford, box B5.3, item 73.

[42] *Diary of Elizabeth Drinker*, Nov. 24, 1777, 1:257; see text at Chap. I, n.41 regarding Galloway's advice to Carlisle.

[43] Committee Report, App. C, p. 165; see Radnor Monthly Meeting, Abstract of Minutes, 1773–1778, 25th 12th mo 1777 (disownment of William Burns, Jr., and James Lawrence), and "An Appendix Containing some Minutes and records of the Committee in Suffering Cases during the Revolutionary War," Monthly Meeting held at Merion, 8th of 8th mo 1777, Swarthmore (microfilm), MR-Ph 540, pp. 480 and 576. On the other hand, it seems rather less convincing that a year later, in answer to the customary inquiry about adherence to Quaker principles, the Radnor meeting certified to the quarterly meeting that "We have bore a Testimony against such who Deviated from our Christian Testimony by bearing arms." Radnor Monthly Meeting, Abstract of Minutes, 1773–1778, 14th 7th mo 1778, p. 486.

[44] Committee Report, App. C, pp. 165–66; Trial Notes, App. A, pp. 149–50.

[45] Committee Report, App. C, pp. 166–67.

[46] Diary of John Pemberton, 1st and 2nd 11th mo 1778, Pemberton Papers, HSP (Collection 484A), box 1, pp. 124–25. It appears from these entries that the first visit with Bryan occurred on Sunday, Nov. 1, and with Hart, on Monday, Nov. 2. John Pemberton was the youngest of the three Pemberton brothers; all three of whom (Israel, James, and John) were among the Virginia exiles.

[47] See text at n.6 above.

Chapter VI—Toward Forgetting

[1] Paul Ricoeur, *Memory, History, Forgetting*, trans. Kathleen Blamey and David Pellauer (Chicago: University of Chicago Press, 2004), 452–54. Beccaria, whose influence was far-reaching among many of the founding fathers, reasons that the sovereign's recourse to clemency is symptomatic of an ill-designed criminal code: "One should

consider that clemency is the virtue of the lawgiver and not of the executor of the law, that it ought to shine forth through the law code, not in particular judgments." Cesare Beccaria, *On Crimes and Punishments*, trans. David Young (1764; repr. Indianapolis, IN: Hackett Publishing Company, 1986), 80 (chap. 46).

[2] See pp. 84–86 herein.

[3] Ricoeur, *Memory, History, Forgetting*, 454. Presidents Clinton and George W. Bush both caused controversy about their use of the pardoning power—Clinton by pardoning Marc Rich and Bush by not pardoning Scooter Libby.

[4] Sarah J. Purcell, *War, Sacrifice, and Memory in Revolutionary America* (Philadelphia: University of Pennsylvania Press, 2002), 67–71, 159; Gordon S. Wood, *The Radicalism of the American Revolution* (New York: Alfred A. Knopf, 1992), 176–77. Admittedly, the data on loyalist restoration must be regarded as somewhat mixed. The Allen and Penn families never recovered their former status, but the Willings, the Tilghmans, the Shippens, the Chews, and, among the Virginia exiles, Henry Drinker and the Fisher brothers (Thomas, Miers, and Samuel Rowland) did substantially. See Bell, *Patriot-Improvers*, 3:193–99 (William Allen); 3:176–85, 226–33 (John Penn, Richard Penn); 3:117–23 (Thomas Willing); 3:95–101 (James Tilghman); 3:59–66, 107–14 (Edward Shippen, Jr., Joseph Shippen); 3:123–29 (Benjamin Chew); 2:298–305 (Henry Drinker); 2:48–53 (Fisher brothers). See also Randolph Shipley Klein, *Portrait of an Early American Family: The Shippens of Pennsylvania Across Five Generations* (Philadelphia: University of Pennsylvania Press, 1975), 207–9; Thomas M. Doerflinger, *A Vigorous Spirit of Enterprise: Merchants and Economic Development in Revolutionary Pennsylvania* (Chapel Hill, NC: University of North Carolina Press, 1986), 218–23; and, for a parallel process of reconciliation in New York, Judith L. Van Buskirk, *Generous Enemies: Patriots and Loyalists in Revolutionary New York* (Philadelphia: University of Pennsylvania Press, 2002), 183–95.

[5] Minutes of the SEC, May 18, 1790, *Colonial Records*, 16:363; Joseph Galloway to Thomas McKean, Mar. 7, 1793, Thomas McKean Papers, HSP, vol. 2, p. 108.

[6] Jacob E. Cooke, *Tench Coxe and the Early Republic* (Chapel Hill: University of North Carolina Press, 1978), 25–43.

[7] Act of March 6, 1778, *Statutes at Large*, 9:201–15.

[8] Act of Oct. 6, 1779, ibid., 9:409–10; *Pennsylvania Archives*, Sixth Series, 12:226, 230, 231, 233, 235 (net sum realized from the sale of cattle and sheep jointly owned by Vernon and Roberts).

[9] George Washington to John Hancock, Oct. 16, 1777, *The Writings of George Washington From the Original Manuscript Sources*, ed. John C. Fitzpatrick, 39 vols. (Washington, DC: United States Government Printing Office, 1931–1944), 9:382–83; John F. Roche, *Joseph Reed: A Moderate in the American Revolution* (New York: Columbia University Press, 1957), 137–43; and Anne M. Ousterhout, *The Most Learned Woman in America: A Life of Elizabeth Graeme Ferguson* (University Park, PA: Pennsylvania State University Press, 2004), 201–7, 216–24.

[10] Act of April 2, 1781, *Statutes at Large*, 10:381–82. See also Ousterhout, *Most Learned Woman*, 253–58; and Benjamin Rush to Elizabeth Graeme Ferguson, Dec. 24, 1777, *Letters of Benjamin Rush*, ed. L. H. Butterfield, 2 vols. (Princeton, NJ: Princeton University Press, 1951), 1:177–79.

[11] See *Pennsylvania Packet*, Nov. 19, 1778, for advertised notice of sale of various items of personal property, including livestock, and other household goods "too tedious to mention"; and "An Inventory of Sundry Goods Necessary for the Support of Jane

Roberts, Relict of John Roberts (Deceas'd) and Family," *Pennsylvania Archives*, Sixth Series, 13:278–81. The restraining order or stay was granted on Nov. 27, 1778, and the final decree on Apr. 23, 1779, ibid., 281.

[12] "Sundries Belonging to Given [*sic*] Lloyd," ibid., 281. Gwen Lloyd's will dated Apr. 7, 1782, was probated in Philadelphia on Nov. 29, 1783, No. 302, and recorded in Will Book S, p. 409.

[13] "List of the Goods & Chattels Late the Property of John Roberts Sold this First Day of December 1778" (George Smith, agent for sale), *Pennsylvania Archives*, Sixth Series, 12:716–19. It is possible that others bid at the sale as friends of the family and that Joseph Mather provided some interim funds for that purpose. See a suggestion to that effect in the inventory of seized property submitted to the Claims Commission, AO 12/42/78.

[14] Nov. 27, 1778, *Pennsylvania Archives*, Sixth Series, 13:280. Thomas Roberts testified in 1786 about the extended holdover occupancy permitted his mother. See Claims Commission, AO 12/42/82. The Supreme Court evidently issued a supplemental decree confirming this extension on May 4, 1779, as certified to by Edward Burd in "A List of Claims and Decrees against the Estates of Persons attainted of Treason," dated July 7, 1787, and in Claims Commission AO 12/95/63.

[15] "Memorial of Widow, &c. of John Roberts, 1778," *Pennsylvania Archives*, First Series, 7:122–23; Petition of Jehu Roberts, June 3, 1780, ibid., 8:296; and Minutes of SEC, June 3, 1780, *Colonial Records*, 12:374.

[16] *Pennsylvania Gazette*, Apr. 14 and Aug. 4, 1779.

[17] See "Return of Sundry forfeited Estates in the County of Philadelphia—not yet Sold," Dec. 16, 1779, *Pennsylvania Archives*, Sixth Series (as to this 300-acre parcel, the agent noted "we have not yet been fully informed"), 12:792–93; and *Pennsylvania Gazette*, Nov. 24, 1779, and May 17, 1780. In disposing of this property in 1792, Thomas Roberts described three contiguous parcels near the Schuylkill and along Mill Creek that had an aggregate content of about 162 acres. Deed of Thomas Roberts to Rees Price and Richard Tunis dated Sept. 11, 1792, and recorded in the Office of the Montgomery County Recorder of Deeds on Apr. 23, 1793, in vol. 7, p. 399.

[18] Notice to creditors of attainted traitors to submit claims prior to sale in *Pennsylvania Gazette*, Apr. 14, 1779; sale advertised in *Pennsylvania Gazette*, Aug. 4, 1779; sale on Aug 25, 1779, of 100 acres owned by Roberts to Daniel Climer and Company, confirmed in *Pennsylvania Archives*, Sixth Series, 12:569, 792. For deed to Clymer dated Apr. 19, 1780, see Minutes of SEC, Apr. 19, 1780, *Colonial Records*, 12:323–24.

[19] For deed to Clymer dated May 10, 1780, see Minutes of the SEC, May 12, 1780, *Colonial Records*, 12:348.

[20] Payment by Eckhardt on Oct. 6, 1779, in *Pennsylvania Archives*, Sixth Series, 12:919; see also ibid., 12:720. Upon taking title, Clymer immediately turned around and conveyed the property to Eckhardt by deed dated April 20, 1780, and recorded in Philadelphia County on Sept. 23, 1791, in Deed Book D-29, p. 444.

[21] On the Fort Wilson battle, see Charles Page Smith, *James Wilson: Founding Father, 1742–1798* (Chapel Hill: University of North Carolina Press, 1956), 129–39; Scharf & Westcott, *History of Philadelphia*, 1:401–3. Samuel Rowland Fisher had a ringside seat in the Old Gaol located a mere two blocks to the north of Fort Wilson. "Journal of Samuel Rowland Fisher," 169–74. For the bond Clymer was required to post, see Minutes of SEC, Oct. 13, 1779, *Colonial Records*, 12:128.

[22] Act of March 13, 1780, *Statutes at Large*, 10:117–19.

[23] Petition of Jehu Roberts, June 3, 1780, *Pennsylvania Archives*, First Series, 8:296; and see note 17 above. One is left to speculate what "proofs," in the language of the 1792 deed, Thomas Roberts exhibited to the Supreme Court that persuaded Chief Justice McKean and Justice William Augustus Atlee that his father had given him "but not actually conveyed," prior to the Declaration of Independence, these three parcels that John Roberts had separately acquired in his own name. The recital all but negates the possibility that the gift was evidenced by an unrecorded deed.

[24] Minutes of SEC, Dec. 16, 1780, *Colonial Records*, 12:571–72, and deed from SEC to Edward Milner bearing same date, recorded in Philadelphia County on Sept. 15, 1781, in Deed Book D-3, p. 72. The original deeds of transfer into Milner and subsequent grantees through George McClenachan in 1797 may be found in Collections of GSP, Gen ZC1 at HSP, Miscellaneous Records, 1671–1959, vol. 1 [Bk. 38], at pages 91 through 99. The property was offered for sale as early as 1792. See notice in *Pennsylvania Gazette*, Feb. 29, 1792 (interested parties were directed to Edward Milner, "on the premises"). Ground rent due the University of Pennsylvania is recorded in the Book of Rent, 1782–1787 (Guide 1523 and 1524), University of Pennsylvania Archives, as paid on occasion by "John Donaldson, son in law to Edward Milner."

[25] For Thomas Roberts's holdover rental arrangement, see his testimony before the Claims Commission, AO 12/42/82 and his memorial, dated May 9, 1786, at AO 13/71 pt.2/267–68.

[26] Michael Smith died without a will in early 1786. Letters of administration were granted his wife and son William, and an inventory of his personal property was made under date of Feb. 20, 1786, in the aggregate amount of a little over three hundred ninety pounds, showing household goods, a silver watch, farm animals and equipment, and wheat and rye then planted in thirty-two acres. Estate of Michael Smith, Dec'd, Register of Wills of Montgomery County, PA (microfilm), Will Folders 16337 to 16638, Adm. File No. 16443, reel 69, frames 911–16.

[27] Minutes of SEC, *Colonial Records*, Aug. 23, 1783, 13:671.

[28] Minutes of SEC, May 6, 1786, *Colonial Records*, 15:17, and Forfeited Estates, *Pennsylvania Archives*, Sixth Series, 13:281–82. For a sampling of subsequent years, see Minutes of SEC, *Colonial Records*, 15:225 (1787), 15:467 (1788), 16:65 (1789), and 16:350 (1790).

[29] The texts of the preliminary treaty signed in Paris on Nov. 30, 1782, and the definitive treaty signed there on Sept. 3, 1783, may be found in *Treaties and Other International Acts of the United States of America*, ed. Hunter Miller, 8 vols. (Washington, DC: Government Printing Office, 1931–1948), 2:96-101 (Art. 5 at 99), and 2:151–56 (Art. 5 at 154).

[30] In 1783 Galloway published on his own a brief critique of Article 5 in its provisional form, expressing doubt that as a practical matter any of the loyalists might reasonably expect to receive adequate restitution of their former estates, especially those "who have borne arms against the United States." *Observations on the Fifth Article of the Treaty with America: And on the Necessity of Appointing a Judicial Enquiry Into the Merits and Losses of the American Loyalists* (London: printed by author, [1783]), 11. Five years later he published a much more closely reasoned and extensive work arguing for full compensation to the loyalist claimants whose interests had been sacrificed when His Majesty's minister negotiating the treaty, under instructions to end a costly war, "unconditionally confirmed the independent sovereignties of the usurpation, and with them the sanguinary laws by which the persons of the Loyalists were attainted

and their property confiscated." *The Claim of the American Loyalists Reviewed and Maintained Upon Incontrovertible Principles of Law and Justice* (London: G. and T. Wilkie, 1788), 14.

[31]Francis Maseres to Benjamin Franklin, June 20, 1785, and Benjamin Franklin to Francis Maseres, June 26, 1785, *The Works of Benjamin Franklin*, ed. Jared Sparks, 10 vols. (Boston: Tappan, Whittemore, and Mason, 1840), 10:187–90, 190–94.

[32]Wallace Brown, *The King's Friends: The Composition and Motives of the American Loyalist Claimants* (Providence, RI: Brown University Press, 1965), 127–53, 257, 317–21; and *Mary Beth Norton, The British-Americans: The Loyalist Exiles in England, 1774–1789* (Boston: Little, Brown, 1972), 185–222. Variation exists in the estimated number of claims submitted, but the total was about five thousand, of which close to twenty percent were either withdrawn or not pursued. Although there is a considerable literature on the work of the loyalist claims commission, the just-cited chapter in Norton's book provides the best overall view of the claims process, particularly for the loyalists in exile in England. See also Maya Jasanoff, *Liberty Exiles: American Loyalists in the Revolutionary World* (New York: Alfred A. Knopf, 2011), 113–45. The records of the Commission Appointed for Enquiring into the Losses and Services of the American Loyalists (herein sometimes Claims Commission) have been preserved in the Audit Office records in the National Archives of Great Britain at Kew and are available on microfilm at various repositories in the United States, including the Library of Congress, the New York Public Library, and the David Library at Washington Crossing, PA. The principal source of material that the author has consulted at the David Library on microfilm (film 263) is the collection of volumes identified as AO 12, and specific reference will herein be made first to the volume and then to page number or numbers, as in the case of the Roberts claim, which is found in volume 42 at pages 73 through 85, or cited as AO 12/42/73–85; additional supporting documents submitted to the Claims Commission may be found on microfilm (film 264) at AO 13 /71 pt.2/260–72.

[33]Doerflinger, *A Vigorous Spirit of Enterprise*, 167.

[34]Abel James to Benjamin Franklin, n.d. [but before Dec. 8, 1782], *The Papers of Benjamin Franklin*, ed. Ellen R. Cohn et al., 39 vols. to date (New Haven, CT: Yale University Press, 1959–), 38:426–29, together with explanatory note at 38:425 and n.8 at 427.

[35]Petition of Abel James, Feb. 25, 1786, Records of Pennsylvania's Revolutionary Governments, 1775–1790, Pennsylvania State Archives, Harrisburg, PA, RG 27 (microfilm), roll 43, frames 299–301.

[36]Committee Report, App. C, p. 167. See Arthur J. Mekeel, *The Quakers and the American Revolution* (York, Eng: Sessions Book Trust, 1996), 385.

[37]Claims Commission, AO 13/71 pt.2/262, 265; *Diary of Elizabeth Drinker*, 1:444. Captain Robinson also had a connection with the Drinkers, his brother having married Elizabeth Drinker's cousin. Ibid., Oct. 23, 1785, 1:441. Thomas Roberts complied with Quaker requirements in obtaining a certificate from the Radnor meeting authorizing his trip, and an endorsement from the Devonshire House meeting when leaving England. Radnor Monthly Meeting, Abstract of Minutes, 1782-1803, 9th 3rd mo 1786, and 9th 1st mo 1787, Swarthmore (microfilm), MR-Ph 540, pp. 44–45, 57.

[38]Memorial of Thomas Roberts, London, May 9, 1786, Claims Commission, AO 13/71 pt.2/267–68.

[39]Memorial and Petition of Jane Roberts, Claims Commission, AO 12/42/73–75.

[40] Claims Commission, AO 12/42/ 77–83. See Chap. IV, n. 3 and related text.

[41] Claims Commission, AO 12/42/76–77, 83–84. Potts and Bond were pardoned by the SEC on Oct. 3, 1786, *Colonial Records*, 15:93, and Shoemaker by Governor Mifflin on Dec. 27, 1793, *Pennsylvania Archives*, Ninth Series, 1:699.

[42] Claims Commission, AO 12/42/83. For Rankin and his double role, see Carl Van Doren, *Secret History of the American Revolution* (New York: Viking Press, 1941), 130–34, 221–24, 404–5, 415–17. On April 27, 1781, following his prison break, the SEC proclaimed Rankin attainted of treason and offered a reward of fifty pounds for his apprehension. Minutes of SEC, *Colonial Records*, 12:710–11

[43] Thomas Roberts to "The Hon'ble Commissioners for American Claims, &c &c &c," Aug. 10, 1786, and William Dillwyn to Philip Hunter Esq, "Office of the Commission on the Claims of American Loyalists, Lincolns Inn Fields," Oct. 30, 1787, Claims Commission, AO 13/71 pt.2/269–70, 271–72.

[44] Claims Commission, AO 12/109/ 260-61 (for award to Jane Roberts). The claim of Ann Carlisle with supporting documents is found at Claims Commission, AO 12/ 43/1–13 and AO 12/ 95/3,1–15, and the award at AO 12/109/108–9.

[45] For biographical detail on Price, see http://www.lowermerionhistory.org/texts/price/. On his relationship with Thomas Roberts as referred to in the text, see Price Diary, Mar 4, 14, and 18, 1796; Oct. 27 and 30, 1798; and May 24, 25, and 26, 1799. Thomas Roberts would be disowned by the Radnor meeting for his irregular marriage. Radnor Monthly Meeting, Abstract of Minutes, 1782–1803, 8th 6th mo, 13th 7th mo, 10th 8th mo 1797, Swarthmore (microfilm), MR-Ph 540, pp. 204, 206, 208.

[46] Ibid., 13th 5th mo 1791, p. 120; and Uwchlan Monthly Meeting, Minutes, 1776-1795, 6th mo 9th 1791, Swarthmore (microfilm), MR-Ph 626, p. 306. Jehu married Elizabeth Jones on 23rd 11th mo 1792 at the Haverford meeting. Uwchlan Monthly Meeting, Minutes, 1776–1795, 4th 10th mo 1792, p. 324. Jehu was appointed an overseer of the Uwchlan meeting as early as 1793 (ibid., 4th 4th mo 1793, p. 330), and for a brief appreciative portrait of him in Chester County, see Francis G. Brown, *Downingtown Friends Meeting: An Early History of Quakerism in the Great Valley* (Glenmore, PA: Glenmore Corporation, 1999), 13–14, 20–22. He and his wife had two children: a daughter, Ann, and a son, John. Jehu died on Jan. 3, 1818; his will and codicil dated 12th 6th mo 1815 and 23rd 12th mo 1817 were probated in Chester County on Feb. 27, 1818, and recorded in Will Book 12, p. 26. See also Price Diary, Nov. 22 and Dec. 2, 1792; Jan. 14, 1818; and Futhey & Cope, *History of Chester County*, 714–15.

[47] Price Diary, Nov. 1, 1795; Will of Jane Roberts, dated 23rd 10th mo 1795, and probated in Chester County, on Nov. 21, 1795, Will Book vol. 9, p. 378.

[48] See George Johnston, *History of Cecil County, Maryland* (1881; reprint ed., Baltimore: Genealogical Publishing Co., 1989), 347–48.

Epilogue

[1] See Chap. VI, n. 26; and for the distinction between public and private memory, see Alfred F. Young, *Liberty Tree: Ordinary People and the American Revolution* (New York: New York University Press, 2006), 5–6.

[2] Bell, *Patriot-Improvers*, 3:518; 2:270–80; Charles Page Smith, *James Wilson: Founding Father, 1742–1798* (Chapel Hill, NC: University of North Carolina Press, 1956), 376–90.

— Notes —

³ Bell, *Patriot-Improvers*, 3:63–66, 397–409; Randolph Shipley Klein, *Portrait of an Early American Family: The Shippens of Pennsylvania Across Five Generations* (Philadelphia: University of Pennsylvania Press, 1975), 183–90, 207–9.

⁴ Edward Burd to Jasper Yeates, Sept. 2, 1778, Jasper Yeates Correspondence, 1762–1786, HSP, 1778 folder; Klein, *Portrait of an Early American Family*, 186–87. The basis for the imposition and collection of fees by civil officers was the Act of August 22, 1752, in *Statutes at Large*, 5:164–78, as amended by the Act of March 26, 1778, ibid., 9:229–30, which latter statute doubled the fees set forth in the former for a period of one year "by reason of the high and extravagant prices of the necessaries of life." The flow of fees actually paid Burd and others in the treason trials may be partially traced in the Dorothy Merriman Schall Papers, "Edward Burd court accounts, 1778–1810," Haverford (Collection No 1182), boxes 4 and 14.

⁵ Burd to Jasper Yeates, Sept. 30, 1778, Yeates Correspondence, HSP, 1778 folder.

⁶ The committee's report was published in *Pennsylvania Gazette*, Feb. 8, 1792. Act of Mar. 8, 1792, *Statutes at Large*, 14:204–5, contained a parallel provision revesting any remnant property in Abraham Carlisle's son, as his then sole survivor.

⁷ By deed dated May 27, 1794, Jane Roberts conveyed to Benjamin Brooke title to this 36-acre tract for the sum of five hundred pounds Pennsylvania currency. Deed recorded in the Office of the Recorder of Deeds of Montgomery County on July 22, 1794, in vol. 7, page 860. The other remaining property in Lower Merion owned by John Roberts was an island in the Schuylkill River, "opposite land belonging to Hugh Roberts," coming to a little over an acre, together with a nearby sandbar, which Jane Roberts conveyed to William Hagey, a papermaker, for the sum of twenty pounds. Deed from Jane Roberts to William Hagey dated Apr. 20, 1794, and recorded in Montgomery County on Aug. 11, 1794, in vol. 7, p. 905. "Hagey" was a variant spelling of "Hagy." See Charles R. Barker, "The Stony Part of the Schuylkill: Its Navigation, Fisheries, Fords and Ferries," *PMHB* 50 (1926): 356.

⁸ Copy of survey dated July 29, 1774, pursuant to a warrant of John Roberts dated May 25, 1774, and returned in the Land Office on Nov. 22, 1774, in Society Collections, HSP, box Robb-Robe ("Roberts").

⁹ The record of this proceeding initiated in the Lycoming County Court of Common Pleas in 1799, as thereafter certified for trial before two justices of the Supreme Court sitting on circuit is found in Society Collections, HSP, box Robb-Robe ("Roberts"); for background on ejectment suits as a means of disposing of title claims and the legal fictions resorted to, see David W. Maxey, "The Honorable Proprietaries v. Samuel Wallis: 'A Matter of Great Consequence' in the Province of Pennsylvania," *Pennsylvania History* 70 (2003):373–74.

¹⁰ See David Hackett Fischer, *Washington's Crossing* (New York: Oxford University Press, 2004), 205, 426.

¹¹ About Stacy Potts and his varied career, see A *History of Trenton, 1679–1929* (Princeton, NJ: Princeton University Press, 1929), 126–27, 135, 139–40, 165–66, 323, 611; William Henry Egle, comp., *Pennsylvania Genealogies; Scotch-Irish and German* (Harrisburg, PA: Lane S. Hart, 1886), 99–100; and *Pennsylvania Gazette*, Apr. 20, 1785 (advertised sale, as Potts is about to leave for points westward, of his several valuable properties in Trenton, which he promotes as "the Federal Town intended for the future residence of Congress").

¹² Burd's certified record of the Roberts treason trial bearing date of Sept. 28, 1803, is found in Society Collections, HSP, box Robb-Robe ("Roberts").

[13] Docket entries and judgment in circuit court as of Oct. 24, 1804, following trial before the "Honorable Edward Shippen Esqr. Doctor of Laws, Chief Justice of the said Supreme Court, and the Honorable H. H. Brackenridge Esqr, his associate," and a duly empanelled jury, all as in a copy thereof certified by John Kidd, the clerk of the Lycoming County court under date of Oct. 7, 1805, in Society Collections, HSP, box Robb-Robe ("Roberts"). Fictions multiplied in the proceeding because John Roberts was mistakenly identified in the original suit as one of the fictional plaintiff's lessors, it being thereafter necessary to substitute his son Jehu; by the time the suit came to trial, Thomas Roberts, who was originally a party in interest, had died.

[14] Petition of Stacy Roberts to the Senate and House of Representatives of the Commonwealth of Pennsylvania, Lancaster, Jan. 30, 1806, as found in Society Collections, HSP, box Robb-Robe ("Roberts").

Index